I'll Be Seeing You

Tonie and Valmai Holt

I'll Be Seeing You

WORLD WAR II THROUGH ITS PICTURE POSTCARDS

Tonie and Valmai Holt

MPC

British Library Cataloguing in Publication Data

Holt, Tonie
    I'll be seeing you: picture postcards of
    World War II.
    1. Postcards — History 2. World War,
    1939-1945 — History — Pictorial works
    I. Title II.Holt Valmai
    769'.4994053   D734.27

ISBN 0 86190 201 7

Published by:
Moorland Publishing Co. Ltd.,
Moor Farm Road, Airfield Estate,
Ashbourne, Derbyshire
DE6 1HD, England

Printed in the UK

Acknowledgements

Firstly our thanks go to the postcard publishers: Messrs. Bamforth & Co. Ltd., J. Salmon Ltd., Raphael Tuck and Valentines of Dundee for their kind permission to reproduce postcards published by them during World War II. Secondly, to accumulate the unique collection of World War II postcards illustrated here we travelled to Belgium, France, Germany, Holland, Italy, North Africa, the United States of America and to most parts of the British Isles. We would like to thank the many fellow collectors and dealers who we met on our travels or with whom we corresponded and who helped us to find some very special, rare or previously unrecognised World War II cards. They include Michael Clarke, of 'Desiderata', for a superb selection of German items; Gordon Rosen for many comic American cards; the extraordinarily generous Klaus Gruner for much of the Portuguese propaganda material; R. G. Auckland, Drene Brennan, Marshall Collins, Jack and Thelma Duke, John Hall, Ken Lawson, Ron Mead, Joan Venman, Clive Smith, Gordon and Honor Webb and a host of others in Berlin, Hamburg, Brussels, Liege, Lille, Metz, Rouen, Verdun, Paris, Washington, New York, Naples, Rome, Tunis and most areas in the UK!

We would also like to thank the ever helpful staff of the North London Public Libraries of Harrow, Hendon and Edgware and the equally resourceful staff of the South East Kent Libraries of Canterbury, Deal and Sandwich to whose area we have moved.

Finally, we would like to thank our Dutch, German, Iranian, Israeli, Italian, Polish and Portuguese friends and associates who have helped us to translate some of the more abstruse captions and messages on the postcards.

Contents

Introduction

I t is now more than 40 years since the end of World War II.

To those of us who lived through that grim, yet often exhilarating time, it seems unbelievable that half of our present population has been born since 1945 and so has no first hand experience or knowledge of the war at all.

Historians present their versions of this conflict to the young at school and university – together with the First World War. But the conventional historian exercises retrospective judgment on the events of the past. Actions are analysed, results codified, battles judged as victories or losses. The historian uses his knowledge of wider issues to reflect upon the thoughts and deeds of those who lived in the past and his words are isolated from what actually took place, not from lack of understanding, but simply by the passage of time.

It need not be that way.

In the past decade there has been a widespread interest in things past — the label is 'nostalgia.' At first this was merely an extension of an interest in antiques. Soon, however, with the falling value of money, everyone wanted to collect something old in the hope that it would retain its value, and with the fast increasing demand, the range of collectable items expanded. Victoriana became popular, then Edwardiana, and now even the *Kitsch* style of the 'Twenties and 'Thirties is an accepted collecting area.

The nostalgia theme was picked up by the entertainment media and some fine and successful films (like *Yanks*) and television series (like *Upstairs Downstairs*) were made, each one awakening an ever-increasing public interest in the near past.

One Edwardian phenomenon which was revived was the collecting of old picture postcards. At the turn of the century the picture postcard was the newspaper, radio, television and picture magazine of the period. It recorded absolutely everything. It had its own artists, its own terminology, its own

postal rate, and, above all, it carried messages. So many cards were produced that contemporary writers voiced the fear that 'Europe will be drowned in a sea of postcards.' Everyone, Royalty included, not only sent postcards but also collected them.

The modern nostalgic hunt for these old cards grew apace, following an exhibition put on by the Victoria and Albert Museum in 1971. By the mid 1970's, international postcard dealing was established in its own right and major auction houses such as Sotheby's, Christies and Phillips, listed picture postcards in their catalogues. Another accolade was bestowed on the hobby with the publication of the biennial Stanley Gibbons Postcard Catalogue. Yet despite these developments, postcards are still collected essentially for their picture appeal or philatelic value.

But they have much more to offer. They are unwitting contemporary observations of the life and times in which they were used — written and drawn at the time by the people involved. They are living folk history.

Slowly the social significance of these old cards is being recognised, although, at present, awareness is mostly confined to photographic cards detailing the life and times of Victorian and Edwardian Britain (with a parallel situation in France, America and all the countries throughout the world in which postcard collecting was once a national mania). Photographers like Francis Frith and Louis Levy produced series after series of excellent scenes which are enthusiastically collected, but the interest of present day collectors drops exponentially in anything produced after 1918. It is popularly supposed that with the advent of radio, illustrated newspapers and magazines for mass consumption, coupled with the doubling of postcard postage to 1d at the end of the First World War, the postcard dropped dead.

Well it almost did.

It recovered, however, during World War II. The shortage of newsprint, the need to be

economical in all things, the requirement for cheap, readily disseminated propaganda, revived the postcard in all the involved nations. The cards are not easy to find because they were not collected and prized in albums as the Edwardian cards had been, but they can be found. And, like their predecessors, they provide a vivid record of the past, a record of World War II that, for the first time, is assembled here in a series of cameos grouped under a variety of subject headings.

The postcards in this book illustrate every facet of the war, the men and the machines, the politicians and the generals, the warfare in all three elements — air, land and sea. They show the propaganda and the humour, the devastation and the bravery, the fear and the hopes, the ordinary, everyday struggle to survive on the Home Front and in the Front Line. Their variety is astonishing — in terms of styles, subject matter and quality. They range from the frankly old fashioned type of patriotism which was a hangover from the First World War to designs with biting satire that seem as modern as anything published today. In occupied Europe cards were printed in secret, under almost impossibly adverse conditions, as acts of defiance against the invaders. There are sad and funny cards, exciting and banal cards. There are cards from most of the countries who were engaged in the war, in which their national characteristics can easily be recognised.

The Germans excelled in dramatic but restrained presentation, using uniforms and insignia to full effect. The strong Nazi symbols retain a hint of hidden menace that made men take them seriously. The Americans opted for brash humorous designs that stress the irritations and pleasures of service life and its comradeship, but which seem to betray the nervousness of a nation joining a foreign war. The Italian temperament showed itself in the pomp of rich colours and flamboyant patriotic statements, while the British cards are mostly comic, concerned in that odd, under-stated Anglo-Saxon manner with poking fun at adversity.

An attractive genre emerges in the designs of Mabel Lucie Attwell, Dinah and other exponents of the 'cute kiddie' which, on closer examination of the caption, are revealed as comments on all manner of wartime phenomena — from gas masks to queuing to rationing to air raids. These apparently amusing and frivolous drawings performed an important function in familiarising people in a homely, gentle fashion with frightening or disagreeable aspects of life during the war, which has been hitherto unrecognised.

The postcards produced in France during the war fall into three distinct groups. Firstly there are the cards of 1939-40 — of the *Drôle de Guerre* (Phoney War). They resemble the French postcards of the First World War in their stilted, posed style and in the fact that they were produced both for French and British consumption. Then, from 1941, and particularly in 1944 and 1945 the spirit of the Resistance Movement inspired some powerful, vibrant designs that transcend the poor quality board which was all that was available to print them on. Finally, there are cards produced for the Occupiers and the Occupied. Whatever the country of origin, the postcards of World War II form a comprehensive patchwork that records life at all levels during the six years that changed the world.

A rudimentary valuation is included in the description of each card captioned:

Value A	:	worth between	£1 & £3
Value B	:	worth between	£3 & £5
Value C	:	worth between	£5 & £15
Value D	:	worth over	£15

The values apply to cards in good condition.

CHAPTER ONE

The Nazis

CHAPTER ONE

1 *'Torch Relay from Olympia to Berlin.'* The card shows an artist's impression of one of the German relay runners bringing the Olympic flame from Olympia to Berlin. The route is marked on the map behind. It was Hitler's intention that the 1936 Olympic Games should demonstrate to the world the superiority of German blood and the wonders of the Nazi State. This political exploitation of the Games produced a considerable reaction in America where a movement was established to boycott the event – an oddly parallel situation to that of the Olympic Games held in Moscow in 1980. However, the movement did not succeed. Hitler's objective was not realized, despite world appreciation of the magnificence of the spectacle, the stadium and the organization, for in direct rebuff of the Nazi theory of the superiority of the fair-haired blue-eyed Teuton type, seven American negro athletes won gold medals. J.C. (Jesse) Owens won four golds, set two Olympic records and, with the 400m relay team, broke the world record. The card has a printed title in German on the reverse: *'Propaganda card number 6 for the 1936 Olympic Games . . . proceeds to the Fund for German Sport.'*
German: (Pub. Reichssportverlag GmbH, Berlin) 1936.
The card was cancelled on 16 August 1936 with the official Berlin Stadium mark.
Value D

It is said that World War II was a continuation of the First World War. Extrapolation back to the Franco-Prussian War could probably be justified and some authorities go even further back and half joking lay the blame on Napoleon's defeat of the Austrians at Marengo in 1800! Hitler was Austrian after all.

Adolf Hitler was born in 1889 and it seems very likely that without him World War II would not have been fought or, if it had, would have been fought very differently. In the absence of Hitler, a resurgent Germany might have joined with France and Britain to oppose the spread of Russian Communism, a scenario much like that which exists in the 1980's.

Whether World War II 'began' in 1800, 1870, 1889, 1914 or 1939, it is certain that the economic and social collapse of Germany following the Armistice of 1918, and the punitive terms of the surrender document, were major contributing factors to the gathering of the momentum which led to the conflict.

At the beginning of 1918, the last year of the First World War, socialist inspired workers' strikes were spreading throughout Germany, and by the end of January 1½ million men were refusing to work. They demanded an honourable end to the war and the democratisation of the Hohenzollern regime. Although the Kaiser and the Chief of Army Staff, Eric Ludendorff, were concerned by the strikes, the peace treaty signed in March with Russia meant that Germany now had to wage war on only one front, and the military opportunity this offered for an all-out offensive in France, took priority in their minds.

On 21 March 1918 the *Kaiserschlacht* (the 'Kaiser's Battle') began. Ludendorff launched his concentrated forces towards Amiens and Paris, and for a while Germany rejoiced in what seemed to be inevitable victory. But it was not to be, and the Allied counterattacks beginning in July recovered all the recently lost territory and continued to advance. Germany sued for peace. The Kaiser abdicated and

on the same day the German High Seas Fleet at Kiel refused to sail against the British. The mutinous sailors formed themselves into Russian style soviets (councils) and their action was quickly imitated across Germany in reaction to the anti-climax of defeat and the departure of the Kaiser.

Socialist organisations manoeuvred for power and the dozen or so different German States which had made up Imperial Germany struggled to maintain control of law and order by using locally raised armed forces to discipline mutineers and strikers. Moderate Socialists fought for survival against extreme left-wing Bolsheviks, and, fearing the repetition of the Revolution which had taken place in Russia, they enlisted the help of the Army. But insurrections continued to spring up even after the Armistice and it was only by enlisting the help of the paramilitary forces like the ultra right-wing Freikorps that the German Communist Party was defeated in both the political and the military sense, with hundreds of people being killed.

In February 1919, following elections in which the Socialists emerged as the largest party in Germany, a democratic republican government was established, with its headquarters at Weimar, the capital of Saxe-Weimar. It was from about this time that the story of the *'Dolchstosslegende'* began to be told, encouraged by the harsh Peace Terms announced by the Allies in May. According to this story, the German Army had not been defeated in the field, but the war had been lost because of internal unrest stirred up by the Socialists at home. The new Weimar Republic took over a country in turmoil, with ultra left-wing and right-wing factions frequently meeting in armed conflict. The Army set out to restore order, and as part of that function set up a political department to keep an eye on the myriad of revolutionary parties that had proliferated since the cessation of hostilities. One of the spies employed by that department was Adolf Hitler.

In September 1919, Hitler was sent to Munich to observe the activities of a small political group called the German Workers' Party. He went to a meeting in the Sterneckerbrau beer cellar and became so involved with what went on that instead of denouncing the party as subversive, he joined it.

Less than a year later he changed its name to the National Socialist German Workers' Party (the NAZI Party) and announced a 25 point Party Programme. Point Number Four was to lead to the deaths of millions of people. It read, 'None but members of the Nation may be citizens of the State. None but those of German blood, whatever their creed, may be members of the Nation. No Jew, therefore, may be a member of the Nation.'

In the turbulent years that followed, Hitler used overt and covert violence to achieve his aims. For a while he was imprisoned and there began his book, *Mein Kampf* (My Struggle), using the time to reflect upon his future tactics, determining that he would cloak all his actions with a veneer of legality. He perfected his philosophy of mass persuasion, the core of which demanded that a great leader should offer his people just one enemy in order to concentrate their allegiance. Hitler's chosen enemy was the Jewish race, but his own fear of Bolshevism fell only a pace behind his hatred of the Jews, and when he finally became Chancellor in 1933 he systematically began to replace all government officials of Jewish descent, or of Socialist belief, with Nazis.

In Hitler's view, the Nation, the 'Reich,' was omnipotent. Everything was to be subservient to it. Art and sport had to reflect its virtues, while armed strength was to promote its aims. Not all the German Generals were sympathetic to the Nazi cause, but Hitler won their co-operation by subscribing to the Dolchstosslegende, by developing the strength of the armed forces, and by progressively seeking to recover the lands lost by Germany in the Treaty of Versailles. Perhaps without the punitive Allied

measures of 1919, Hitler would have found it more difficult to carry the Army with him, but such was the power of the Nazi propaganda machine that Germany en masse became 'Ein Volk, Ein Reich, Ein Führer.'

Much of the splendid pageantry and spectacle that the Nazis used to sway their massive audiences was copied from Mussolini's Fascists, but Hitler, unlike Mussolini, gathered around him a team of competent aides who extended and improved upon Il Duce's innovations. Great use was made of 'Special Days,' such as 'Reich Party Day,' or 'Workers' and Farmers' Day' in order to encourage community marching and singing with an inevitable Nazi speech at the end. It was superb showmanship with the Führer travelling frenetically from one event to another.

The momentum built upon the oppression of the Jews, a fanatic belief in the purity of German blood, resentment against the Treaty of Versailles and the oratory of a charismatic leader, drove Germany forward. Employment surged upwards, industry boomed and the Nation felt ready to flex its muscles. The first exercise took place in the Saar.

In the four years from 1935 to 1939 Hitler climbed the ladder to war. Each rung on the ladder was the recovery of land taken from Germany by the Treaty of 1919. Hitler didn't even have to fight for his acquisitions — the Saar in 1935, the Rhineland in 1936, Austria in 1938 and the Sudetenland in 1939. At each step Europe backed down, led by Neville Chamberlain of England, the 'Pilgrim of Peace.'

It was at Munich that Czechoslovakia was dismembered in her absence, and Hitler gained his last bloodless territory. Next on the Führer's agenda were the elimination of the Polish corridor and the reclamation of the port of Danzig.

For those aims he had finally to go to war.

2

2 *'Reich Chancellor Adolf Hitler greets the Reich President von Hindenburg.'* Following the July elections in 1932 the Nazis held more seats in the Reichstag than any other party, although power still remained with Chancellor von Papen. When the Nazis contrived to outvote Papen, the latter dissolved the chamber and called for new elections in November. However, Papen did not gain any advantage from his action and was forced to resign. On 17 November 1932, Hindenburg offered the Chancellorship to Hitler who turned it down because the President would not grant him full powers. Reichswehr General Kurt von Schleicher took office as Chancellor in December but was unable to obtain co-operation from the Nazis and the Communists to form a government, and so he too asked the President if elections could again be held. Former Chancellor von Papen, meanwhile, had obtained behind the scenes guarantees of co-operation from the Nazis and the Nationalists and he persuaded Hindenburg to refuse Schleicher's request and to offer the Chancellorship once more to Hitler. This time, aware of a decline in the popularity of his Nazi Party, Hitler accepted, and on 30 January 1933 became Chancellor of a coalition government. It was the beginning of the end for democratic government in Germany. Hindenburg had only another year to live and during that time Hitler took great pains to see that his public attitude towards the ageing President was deferential.
German: (Pub. Hoffmann, Munich) 1933. Value C

3 *'Germany Awake.'* After the failure of his Munich putsch in November 1923, Hitler was jailed. During his confinement he wrote *Mein Kampf* and reflected upon how he could gain power in Germany. He resolved that everything he did would always have the cloak of legality and part of that plan was to fight elections both for regional and national representation. The Nazi Party had 150,000 members by 1928, two years after Hitler's release from prison, and two years after that polled 6.5 million votes in the national elections for seats in the Reichstag. Early in 1932 Hitler contested the Presidential elections against Hindenburg and lost narrowly, but on 31 July 1932 the Nazi Party became the largest group in the Reichstag by winning 230 seats in the national election and polling over 13,700,000 votes. This card shows a Brownshirt S.A. team electioneering on behalf of Hitler and the Nazis. The place is Bad Oeynhausen but the year is uncertain. It is certainly 1932 or earlier because once the Nazis had gained control there was no further need for elections. The large swastika on wheels reads *'Germany Awake. Vote.'* The word 'swastika', of Sanskrit origin, means 'all is all,' and had been used by Teutonic Knights. The origins of the sign are certainly pre-Christian and, until the Nazis adopted it in 1920, it had been universally regarded as a good luck symbol.
German: (Pub. N. Rybak, Bad Oeynhausen) Circa 1930. Value C

4 *'The Saar is Free! Saarbrucken, 13 January 1935.'* After Germany's defeat in the First World War, the Saar mining area was ceded to France as part of the war reparations that Germany was required to pay under the Treaty of Versailles, and from January 1920 was placed under a governing commission of the League of Nations. At the end of 15 years, on 13 January 1935, a plebiscite was held in which the population of the Saar were able to choose between remaining under the control of the League of Nations, becoming part of France, or becoming part of Germany. Following much Nazi propaganda and alleged intimidation at the polls, the area cast over 90% of its votes for a return to Germany. The picture shows the scene of celebrations shortly after the poll result had been made known. The mass of flags carrying swastikas is clear evidence of the Nazi fever.
German: (Pub. T. Klem, Saarbrucken) January 1935. Value B

5, 5A *'The Olympic Games.'* Hitler is here seen leading a column of dignitaries across the field within the Berlin Olympic Stadium in 1936. Oddly, the terraces behind the column are empty so this may have been a rehearsal for the event which was intended to demonstrate to the world the superiority of the Master Race. The Nazis had learned very early on that detailed state management was essential if the desired results were to be obtained from rallies and parades, and by 1936 they were masters of the art. The Olympic Stadium, now Headquarters of the British Forces in Berlin, was designed to seat 100,000 people and a radio station was built in order to broadcast German victories to the world.
German: (Pub. Atlantic – Photo, Berlin) Official Olympic card number 19. Value B

3

4

5A

5

6 *'National Holiday 1934.'* On 23 March 1933 Adolf Hitler was given total power by the Reichstag to destroy 'the red peril.' He wasted no time in intensifying a process which had already begun and which was called *Gleichschaltung* (Streamlining). Local officials at all levels of government and state administration were dismissed and replaced by Nazis. Soon attention turned to the Trades Union, whose officials were attacked and beaten, prompting a formal complaint to the Chancellor from the Chairman of the Trades Union Congress. The traditional May Day celebrations took place under the title National Labour Day with apparent Nazi approval but 24 hours later the S.A. broke into left-wing Trades Union offices, arrested the officials and sent most of them to concentration camps. In June the Trades Union movement was dissolved and replaced by the German Labour Front. This official card celebrates May Day 1934, the first Labour Day of the Nazi regime.
German: (Official card) May 1934. Value B

7 *'Party Day. Nuremberg 1934.'* The standard bearer is probably a member of the S.S. and the flag carries the slogan *'Germany Awake'*, beneath the letters NSDAP – the Nationalsozialistische Deutsche Arbeitspartei, the Nazis. Beginning in 1929 the highlight of the NSDAP calendar was the Nuremberg Rally or *Reichsparteitag*, held annually in September. In 1934, with Hitler in total control of the Reichstag and with Nazis moving into all levels of state administration, the rally was the biggest so far held. The rally, on 4 September, followed the bloody purge of the S.A. earlier in the year and was a six day spectacle aimed at reassuring the party faithful and the Nation. The site for the event was the Nuremberg Zeppelin field where Goering stationed 130 Luftwaffe searchlights for

floodlighting and where on the second evening 200,000 people, with a flag between every ten of them, gathered to hear their Führer. The whole rally was filmed by Leni Riefenstahl.
German: (Official card) September 1934. Value B

8 *'23.9.1933. The first spadeful. 23.9.1936. 1000 km of* autobahn *ready.'*
Hitler's Germany was a one-party state and part of his solution to the massive problem of unemployment was to direct State funds into national projects. One such project was the building of wide, dual carriageway roads, between major population centres. The Italian Fascists had introduced their *autostrada* in the 1920's and now Hitler, shown on the postcard digging the first spadeful, began the *autobahns*. By 1938 over 3000 km had been built, and an examination of the routes then covered by the *autobahns* makes it clear that they had another object besides providing employment–they were able to supplement the role of the German railways in providing quick lines of internal communications for Hitler's armed forces. As always Hitler's opening ceremony was timed to achieve maximum effect. September was the Party Month and 1936 the year of the Berlin Olympic Games. In the background are Julius Streicher, publisher of the anti-Semitic newspaper *Der* Stürmer, and Dr. Todt, whose organization super-vised construction.
German: (Official card) September 1936. Value B

9 *'Everlasting vigil for South Tirol.'* South Tirol was a province of Austria lying with the Alps between Bavaria and Italy. Both Hitler and Mussolini had designs on it. When Hitler was in prison in 1924, following the failure of the Munich putsch, Goering attempted to borrow two million lire from Mussolini to help Hitler's cause. In return, Goering offered the public support of the Nazi Party for Mussolini's claim on the Tirol. The pressure from greedy neighbours led to the formation of private Tirolese political armies for self-defence, of which the major

ones were the *Schutzbund*, organized by the Social Democrats, and the *Heimwehr* of the Christian Socialists. This card, issued by the Friends of the *Heimwehr*, was probably sold as a fund raiser.
Tirolean: (Pub. Tirolean Homeland League, Innsbruck) Early 1930. Value D

10 *'The Eternal Jew.'* Hitler professed in *Mein Kampf* that the way in which great leaders inspired their followers was to focus their attentions against one enemy. Hitler's choice was Judaism and it was an extremely flexible one. Whenever the Nazis wished to attack a section of the community or to make accusations against another country, they were able to claim that the Jews were always behind the scenes causing the trouble. The very internationality of the Jewish race made such Nazi propaganda plausible to those who wished to believe it. Eventually the venomous hate of the Nazis for the Jews would lead to the mass deportations and the horrors of the concentration camps. Only marginally behind the

Nazis' oppression of the Jews came their dislike of communists, stemming from the days in 1919 when Red Brigades took control in many areas and not only threatened to overthrow the emerging Republic but also to prevent Hitler's rise to power. Here the Jew is depicted as the grasping Shylock out for his pound of flesh, and under his arm complete with hammer and sickle is tucked Germany. The card is an official government issue advertising a political exhibition in the Munich Museum Library and carries a printed stamp on the reverse showing the head of Hindenburg. The cancellation includes the words *'Der Ewige Jude.'*
German: (Official card) Anti-Semitic Exhibition,' Munich, November 1937. Value D

11 *'In the Spring of Life.'* Hitler saw all forms of art as representing the ideology of the State. He had tried his hand at painting pictures, and had considerable ability as an amateur architect. The professional architect he most admired was Professor Paul Ludwig Troost, and

10

11

12

Reichskanzler Adolf Hitler vor seinem

Wohnhaus in Berchtesgaden

13

13A

the hammer broke. The invited audience fell silent remembering an old superstition that if such a hammer broke, the architect would soon die. Even Goebbels, who was present with his leader, was unable to restore the spirit of the assembly. Oddly, within a few months Troost died. The *Haus* opened on 18 July 1937 with a grand exhibition of German art and Hitler's photographer, Hoffmann, was given the task of selecting the best works. This card is one of a large series which probably records Hoffmann's choices.
German: (Pub. Hoffmann) HDK 411 (Haus der Deutschen Kunst). Artist Johann Schult. Value C

12 'Berlin. View of the Brandenburg Gate.' The Brandenburg Gate was built between 1788 and 1791 on the site of a customs barrier on the western boundary of the old 18th century capital. On top of the gate, clearly seen in this card, is a chariot drawn by four horses carrying the Goddess of Peace and known as The Quadriga. When Napoleon entered Berlin in 1807, the Quadriga was taken to Paris but returned seven years later. Here the gate and the Goddess form part of an impressive display of draped flags and skilful lighting, evidence of the sense of drama that Hitler instilled into the hundreds of carefully staged rallies and Party Days that he attended. The *Brandenburger Tor* was Berlin's most widely known architectural landmark and was frequently used as a background and ceremonial entrance for visiting Royalty and Heads of State. In 1933 a four hour long torchlit procession passed through it celebrating Hitler's appointment as Chancellor, in 1936 Olympic athletes paraded through it and in July 1940 German soldiers goosestepped through it to rejoice in the collapse of France.
German: Circa 1935. Value B

13, 13A *'Reich Chancellor Adolf Hitler in front of his house at Berchtesgaden.'* Berchtesgaden is a town lying on the northern side of the Alps in South East Bavaria close to Salzburg and the Austro-German border. It had been used as a resort by the Bavarian monarchy and Hitler chose it

Troost's major work on the Führer's behalf was to design and construct a modern art museum in Munich to replace the Bauhaus institution dismantled by the Nazis. The museum was called the *Haus der Deutschen Kunst* (the House of German Art), and work began on it in 1933. The stone laying ceremony was performed by Adolf Hitler himself, and when he struck the corner stone with the silver ceremonial hammer,

as a retreat in the early 1920's. At first he stayed in the Pension Moritz using the assumed name of Herr Wolf but in 1928 found a place to himself—the Haus Wachenfeld (later renamed 'the Berghof'), at Obersalzburg, 1500ft above Berchtesgaden. The house was a simple, typically Bavarian structure with a wooden verandah, which Hitler used as his headquarters, frequently inviting top Nazis to visit him there. He was fond of walking over the mountain slopes and often wore *lederhosen*. At the mountain top over Obersalzburg Bormann built him a private retreat which he named the 'Eagle's Nest,' and many propaganda pictures show Hitler in his leather shorts gazing thoughtfully out across the mountains.
German: (Pub. Photo-Pringstl, Berchtesgaden) Posted 13 September 1933. Value D

14 'The Führer and the Duce. The Guarantors of Peace.' Benito Mussolini founded the Italian Fascist Movement in 1919 with a violent programme of nationalism, anti-capitalist propaganda and anti-socialist terrorism. By 1926 he was complete dictator of Italy and Hitler saw him as Germany's natural ally against communism. The outbreak of the Spanish Civil War in 1936 gave them the opportunity to co-operate in supporting the fascist regime of General Franco, although they were to have their difficulties shortly after this card was posted. The date stamp shows the slogan *'München. Hauptstadt der NSDAP Bewegung,'* (Munich. Capital of the NSDAP) and the date, 9 November 1937. Four months later Hitler annexed the Tirol between Italy and Bavaria, which Mussolini had himself coveted. On hearing the news Mussolini is reported to have said, 'That damned German!' and it was two days before he could bring himself to congratulate the German leader.
German: (Pub. Hoffmann) M.10. 9 November 1937. Value C

15 'International Exhibition Paris 1937.' This is a view of the entrance to the German pavilion at the 1937 Paris

Exhibition. France had taken a lead in the presentation of exhibitions almost 150 years earlier and it was in Paris in 1855 that the first truly universal exposition was held. In 1889 the Paris Exhibition featured the especially constructed Eiffel Tower, and it was at this **time that the picture postcard** became firmly established as a major method of communication. Hundreds of thousands of visitors bought picture cards of the *Tour Eiffel* and posted them at the summit. It was the beginning of a flood of cards that threatened to submerge Europe in paper. The international exhibitions were competitive showplaces and of all the venues Paris was the most prestigious. Following the 1936 Olympic Games in Berlin where Nazi Germany won 33 gold medals, the highest of any nation, Leni Riefenstahl was awarded a gold medal in Paris for her film of the 1934 Nuremberg Rally, 'Triumph of the Will.' The Nazi cup was running over.
French: (Pub. H. Chipault) No. 107. Value B

16 *'The S.A. National Competition.'* The *Sturm Abteilung* (Storm Troopers), were the uniformed officials of the Nazi Party and the direct descendants of the armed anti-communist *Freikorps* of 1919. Both in and out of their brown uniforms they provided their own brand of discipline based upon physical violence. It was through their strong-arm tactics, in combination with his own hypnotic powers as an orator, that Hitler gathered the massive following that lifted him to power in 1933. However the founder and leader of the S.A. movement, Ernst Röhm, had, like many of the S.A. hierarchy, seen Adolf Hitler only as a tool to be used in order to create a socialist revolution in Germany. Once Hitler became Chancellor in January 1933 he no longer had need of the brutish tactics of the S.A., yet the organization and its leader began to clamour for reward. Not only were they looking to socialize the German Government but they sought to supplant the *Reichswehr*,

Der FÜHRER und der DUCE
„Die Garanten des Friedens"

14

EXPOSITION INTERNATIONALE
PARIS 1937

15

16

17

JEUX DE PRINCES

18

THE PRIME MINISTER
THE RT. HON. NEVILLE CHAMBERLAIN, M.P

20

the professional '100,000 Army' set up under the Treaty of Versailles, as the armed forces of the State. Hitler could not accept these aims. It was a considerable problem. The S.A. numbered some 3.5 million members and the *Reichswehr* was becoming uneasy. Hitler's solution was 'The Great Blood Purge' or 'The Night of the Long Knives' of 30 June 1934, when Röhm and over 100 other Nazi S.A. leaders were murdered. The card shows Germany with a jigsaw gap on its right side (Sudetenland and Czechoslovakia) and with an isolated East Prussia in the top right hand corner. The gap between East Prussia and Germany is the Polish Corridor at the coastal end of which lay Danzig. The artist, Axel-Heudtlass, is named as an S.A. *Sturmhauptführer*. Axel-Heudtlass drew many official cards during the war. This card probably commemorates an S.A. sporting competition.
German: (Official card) Artist Axel-Heudtlass. Printed stamp. Value B

17   *Left to right in the foreground are Goering, Mussolini, Hess, Hitler and Ciano. The occasion is unknown but Hitler sought close ties with Italy and in the early days of the Nazis rise to power, based many of his tactics upon the activities of Mussolini's blackshirts. Count Galeazzo Ciano was both Italy's Foreign Minister and Mussolini's son-in-law, and it was he who visited Hitler in Berchtesgaden in October 1936 in order to initiate greater liaison between the two dictatorships. 'Mussolini is the first statesman of the world,' said Hitler to Ciano. The Foreign Minister's visit resulted in a secret agreement which Mussolini referred to in a speech in Milan a few days later. 'This Berlin–Rome line is . . . an axis, around which can revolve all those European states with a will to collaboration and peace.' German: (Pub. J. E. Huber) No. 125 'Manner der Zeit' ('Men of the World'), equivalent to the First World War 'Men of the Moment' series. Circa 1937. Value C*

19

18 *'Sport of Princes.'* Left to right are seated Hitler, the German Führer, Edouard Daladier, the French Premier, Neville Chamberlain, the British Prime Minister and Benito Mussolini, the Italian Duce. The picture has been cleverly composed by placing the heads of the leaders onto a real photograph of four card players. The game is poker and the stake in the centre is *'Paix'* (Peace). Apparently Daladier has been 'called' and his declared hand can be seen to be a full house. Chamberlain has just laid his hand down and obviously believes that his Queen high straight flush is a winner. Mussolini is about to go one better with his still hidden hand of four Kings while Hitler sits back in complete mastery of the result holding four aces. The reference is clearly to the machinations preceding Munich
Swiss: (Pub. Lilian, Lausanne) Circa 1938. Value C

19 *One People, One State, One Leader. 10 April 1938.* When Hitler and his forces marched into Austria in 'Operation Otto' they were welcomed by the mass of the population. Almost one million people were un-employed and the prospect of uniting with a thriving Germany seemed a solution to that problem. Hitler too was excited by the event. Austria was his homeland and now he had brought it back into a Greater Germany. A nationwide Nazi controlled plebiscite was held on 10 April 1938. Germans approved of the annexation because it was a step towards obtaining the *Lebensraum* (Living Space) that Hitler had led them to anticipate. Austrians saw Hitler as a saviour. This picture shows Greater Germany with East Prussia at the top separated by the Polish Corridor. Super-imposed upon the map is a golden German eagle with the word *Ja!* (Yes!). The card was presumably a propa-ganda issue to encourage Germans to vote in Hitler's favour. 99% did.
German: Adhesive stamps. Cancelled 10 April 1938. Value C

20 *'The Prime Minister. The Rt. Hon. Neville Chamberlain MP.'* Chamberlain believed that France was safe behind her Maginot Line and Britain secured by the strength of the Royal Navy and the friendship of America. Germany had fortified her own Western Frontier, so to Chamberlain the situation appeared to be one in which no nation had aggressive designs or needs in Western Europe. Eastern Europe was a different matter, and provided that the Nazis implemented their *Lebensraum* policy in an orderly manner, the British Prime Minister's view was that Hitler's Germany would provide a buffer against Soviet Communism. He made known his feelings to the Führer in November 1937, giving Hitler the encouragement he needed to carry out his plans to recover, step by step, Austria, the Sudetenland, Western Czechoslovakia, Memel and Danzig. It was this policy of appeasement, many historians maintain, which led directly to World War II. Hitler came to believe that the European nations would not fight. *Caption on reverse reads, 'The World acknowledges and will remember with gratitude, the successful efforts Mr Chamberlain has made with such decision and courage to maintain the peace of the world.'*
British: (Pub. Tuck) Real Photograph No. 3844. Circa 1938. Value B

21 *'13 March 1938. One People, One State, One Leader.'* After the First World War, Austria formed itself into an independent republic with nine states: Vienna, Tirol, Lower Austria, Upper Austria, Burgenland, Styria, Salzburg, Carinthia and Vorarlberg. The mix of political aspirations within the new republic, although frequently violent, did not shake the structure of the constitution until the situation was exacerbated by the swift rise of Nazism in the early 1930's. The increasing tensions between the major ideologies of Marxism, Christian Socialism and National Socialism led to economic difficulties and the Nazis became increas-ingly vociferous about seizing power. In 1938 Kurt von Schuschnigg, the Chancellor of Austria, held an ill-fated plebiscite to decide upon Austrian independence from Germany.

13·MÄRZ 1938
EIN VOLK EIN REICH
EIN FÜHRER

21

22

THE PILGRIM OF PEACE
BRAVO! MR. CHAMBERLAIN

23   24

Der Führer Adolf Hitler

Der Duce Benito Mussolini

25

German: (Official card)
Printed stamp. 10 April 1938.
Value B

22 *'The Nuremberg Stadium.'* The top picture shows the Rostrum of Honour, a stone structure 1,300ft long and 80ft high built by Albert Speer for the 1934 party rally and from which Hitler spoke. The lower view is towards the *Totenehrung*, the Memorial to the Dead, and the stadium, when completed in 1934, was the largest in the world.
German: (Pub. Riffelmacher)
Value C

23 *'The Pilgrim of Peace. Bravo! Mr. Chamberlain.'* Neville Chamberlain was determined to avoid war and in his intent he echoed the wishes of not just the British nation but the French and Americans too. His weakness lay in the price he was prepared to ask others to pay to maintain that peace. This card depicts the period between Hitler's annexation of Austria in March, and the signing of the Munich Agreement on 29 September 1938, in which Britain and France forced Czechoslovakia to give in to Nazi demands to hand over the Sudetenland. During the summer of 1938 Chamberlain shuttled back and forth to Germany by air, like an early Kissinger, seeking a way in which Hitler's threatened use of force could be avoided. In England he was seen as the 'Pilgrim of Peace,' the Poet Laureate, John Masefield, wrote a poem about him and when he returned to Heston Airport waving the agreement signed in Munich he was given a hero's welcome. From the window of 10 Downing Street he later told a cheering crowd, 'I believe it is peace in our time.'
British: (Pub. Tuck) Real Photograph No. 3845. Circa 1938. Value B

24 *'Kufstein. 29 September 1938. The Meeting.'* When Hitler threatened to invade Czechoslovakia in order to save the oppressed Sudeten Germans, he threw Britain and France into a panic. Chamberlain appealed to Mussolini to use his good offices with Hitler so that a way could be found to avoid war. But Hitler needed the Duce's support even more, because it seemed quite possible that if Britain and France believed that Germany stood alone, they might find the courage to meet force with force. Chamberlain put forward a plan that essentially handed over the Sudetenland to Hitler, and Mussolini sent a message saying, 'Whatever you decide Führer, Fascist Italy stands behind you.' The Italian leader suggested that Chamberlain's proposed conference to discuss the plan should be held at Munich, and so the meeting between Chamberlain, Daladier, Mussolini and Hitler was set for 29 September. Il Duce left Rome in his luxurious train, despatched by cheering crowds, and Hitler met him at the small town of Kufstein, near the Austrian border, early on the 29th so that they could travel to Munich together and compare notes. This picture shows the joyous excitement shared by both leaders as Mussolini stepped from his train to greet the Führer. It was to be an exhilarating day for them. *Italian: (Pub. Fotorapida Milan) No. A.XVI. Value D*

25 *Twin Card. The Führer Adolf Hitler. The Duce Benito Mussolini.* Following the 'Axis' agreement negotiated in September/October 1936 by Count Ciano on behalf of Mussolini, Hitler tried his utmost to persuade the Italian leader to come to Germany. Eventually Mussolini agreed provided that he was not required to wear civilian clothes at dinner and that he could address a large crowd. Il Duce arrived in Munich on 25 September 1937 attired in a new Fascist uniform which had been designed for the occasion, to be met by Hitler in a plain Nazi Party uniform. These are probably the uniforms shown on this twin card. The card was issued in Berlin when the leaders went on to the capital two days later, each travelling on his own train. The event was superbly stage-managed with almost one million spectators and over 50,000 S.S. to control the crowds. On 29 September Mussolini had his wish to address a crowd fulfilled and Hitler introduced him to a packed Olympic Stadium. *German: (Pub. Alfred Oemler, Berlin) No. I.113 and No. I.114 (Mussolini).*

Adhesive stamp on each card cancelled (translated) 'Mussolini—Hitler Rally Berlin 29 September 1937.' Value C

26 *Centre, Prime Minister Edouard Daladier of France signing the Munich Agreement.* Czechoslovakia's first reaction to Germany's threat of invasion had been to mobilize. Chamberlain persuaded President Benes to stand down his forces and accept a solution based on a plebiscite that the British had constructed in concert with the French. When Chamberlain put his ideas to Hitler a day or so later the Führer turned them down and announced his intention of occupying the Sudetenland by 28 September. The French began to mobilize their forces and rejected Hitler's intent, but when the Nazi leader baldly stated that if Germany could not have peaceful ownership of the Sudetenland then she would go to war with Britain and France to get it, the appeasers panicked and gave in. However, in less than twelve months, Premier Daladier was to declare war on Germany. Adolf Hitler can be seen over Daladier's right shoulder. *Caption on reverse (translated) reads: 'Minister—President Daladier signing the Munich Agreement.' German: (Pub. Hoffmann) 51014. Value D*

27 *'We Thank Our Leader.'* The territory of Czechoslovakia thrust into the eastern flank of Germany as a thumb pushes into putty, and glove-like between the thumb and the putty lay a narrow strip known as the Sudetenland. In that strip, also Czech territory, lived over three million German speaking people with a vociferous indigenous Nazi Party supported by German funds. Hitler had frequently maintained that the Sudeten Germans were being 'severely persecuted' by the Czechs, and following the successful annexation of Austria in March 1938, he was encouraged to turn his eyes to Czechoslovakia. Goebbels conducted an intensive propaganda campaign intended to vilify the Czech's treatment of the Sudeten Germans and also to encourage the latter to support a union with Greater

26

WIR DANKEN UNSERM FÜHRER

27

28

29

30

Germany. On 12 September 1938, the last day of the annual party rally at Nuremberg, Hitler spoke of his support for the Sudetenlanders, who reacted enthusiastically and violently, egged on by their own Nazi Party, parading through the streets shouting and waving Nazi flags. It was at Munich on 29 September that the Sudeten strip was handed over to Hitler and, on the card, the inhabitants are thanking their Führer. *German: (Official card) Printed stamp dated 4 December 1938. Value B*

28   *Left to right Chamberlain, Daladier, Hitler, Mussolini, Ciano.* These are the men who decided the fate of Czechoslovakia and hence of Europe. The Czechs were not represented at Munich and this study of the faces of the signatories to the Agreement, presumably photographed while the ink was still wet on the document, suggests that Chamberlain and Daladier were not as pleased with themselves as they later appeared to be to their peoples back home. The caption on the reverse (translated) reads: '*Historic Four Power World Conference in Munich 29 September 1938*' but it also carries an adhesive Czech stamp, both cancelled and bearing the Nazi eagle and swastika with the slogan, '*We have borne the yoke. Now we are free and remain free.*' The slogan and cancel are back-dated 21 September 1938, the day that Eduard Benes President of Czechoslovakia, gave in to Chamberlain. *German: (Pub. Hoffmann) 54. Value D*

29   '*Danzig is German.*' Under the Treaty of Versailles, German-inhabited Danzig had become a Free City, and a corridor of land belonging to Poland and leading to Danzig, separated the Reich from East Prussia. By 1939 Hitler had achieved all his territorial aims by threats without having to go to war, but the significance of Danzig and East Prussia was far greater than that of anything he had annexed to date. It was his belief that Poland would willingly become a German satellite in order to gain protection from communist Russia, and, oddly, Britain and France felt that Germany had justifiable claims on the Corridor and upon Danzig. But the Poles disagreed. Hitler once again threatened war and waited for a repeat of Munich. It did not happen. Britain guaranteed Poland's integrity and Hitler was too far committed to draw back. On 1 September 1939, at dawn, German troops crossed the Polish frontier. Danzig was about to return to Germany

31

32

but World War II had begun.
German: (Official NSDAP card) Artist Gottfried Klein. Printed stamp. Fund raiser for the War W.H.W. (the Winter Relief Campaign). Cancelled 7 January 1940. Value C

30 *'2–11 September 1939. Party Day. Nuremberg.'.* In 1938, the year that Adolf Hitler gained Austria and the Sudetenland to build his Greater Germany, the annual NSDAP Nuremberg Rally was named 'Party Day of Peace,' doubtless reflecting Hitler's confidence that he could take Danzig and solve the Polish problem merely by threats rather than by war. The day before the rally began, German forces invaded Poland and bombed Warsaw. The day after the rally, Britain and France declared war on Germany.
German: (Official NSDAP Rally card) Printed stamp. 2–11 September 1939. Value C

31 *'70 Years of Postcards. 1 Oct. 1869–1 Oct. 1939.'* The postcard had been born in Austria and within its first year of life had been used to carry messages by balloon from the besieged city of Paris. Now, exactly 70 years later at the end of a month in which Poland had been over-run by the German *Blitzkrieg*, the Nazis commemorated the birth.
German: (Official card) 1 October 1939. Value D

32 *German: (Official Nuremberg NSDAP Rally card) 1938. Value B*

33, 34, 35, 36, 37 *'The Prepared Neutral.'* Switzerland had prepared herself for the outbreak of a general war and mobilized her army early in September 1939. Frontiers were guarded, reservists called to the colours and conscription of labour brought in. The adhesive stamps on these Military Postcards (to be used only on Military Service) represent the country's preparedness for battle: her infantry, her artillery, her anti-aircraft defences and the sophistication of her radio communication links.
Swiss: (Official cards) 1939. Each card value B

38 *Party Rally card showing S.A. marchers. A percentage of the sale price went to the party 'Culture Fund.'*
German: (Official card) Value B

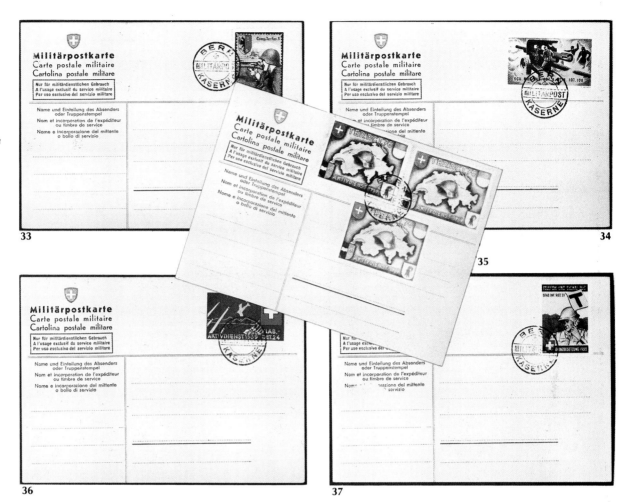

39

CHAPTER TWO

The Personalities

40

39 *Adolf Hitler. The card border is linked by swastikas. No publisher or photographer is named but the picture was probably taken by Hoffman.*
German: (Official card) Printed stamp on reverse. Designed as part of a reply-paid card. Value C

40 *Adolf Hitler. This card was issued for the 1938 'Party Day of Greater Germany,' which celebrated the acquisition of Austria. It carries a hand stamp (translated): 'Historic Meeting, Chamberlain—Hitler.' The card has been posted twice. The first time at Nuremberg on the last day of the rally, 12 September, when Hitler threatened to use force against Czechoslovakia, and the second time at Berchtesgaden on 15 September, the day that Chamberlain flew there to meet Hitler for the first time. German: (Pub. J. E. Huber) No. 91. 'Manner der Zeit' series September 1938. Value D*

World War II, despite being a war of machine versus machine on the battlefield, became a war of personality against personality in the struggle for the hearts and minds of the competing nations. The supreme leader in each country was singled out by his fellows to represent everything that was worth fighting for, and by his enemies as everything that was worth fighting against.

In Germany, Adolf Hitler had stage-managed and perfected the image of his Nazi Party and his personality from the early 1930's by the use of massed rallies, pomp, circumstance, merit badges, dramatic uniforms and a bewildering array of impressive insignia.

One of the most striking uniforms, effective in its simplicity, was the black dress of the S.S., Hitler's own force, who, up to and including Obersturmbahnführer (Lieutenant Colonel), wore their rank symbol on the left collar and the silver S.S. runes on the right collar. After that rank no S.S. collar runes were worn. Hitler himself favoured simple dress, including the traditional Bavarian *lederhosen*, which he wore when walking on the hills around his beloved Berchtesgarten.

Although simplistic in his personal affectations, (he neither smoked nor drank alcohol), Hitler's personality was exceedingly complex. Many historians believe that he was balanced upon the knife edge which borders genius and insanity, and there is no denying that he exhibited the first during his early days in power and the latter towards the end.

As Führer (Leader), Hitler dragged his country from defeat in 1918 to the position of the most powerful nation in Europe by 1938. He built major roads (the *autobahns*) inspired the people's car (the Volkswagen) and gave the German population a sense of purpose (*Lebensraum* — living space). Yet the means he employed to achieve his ends were oppressive in the extreme, particularly towards the Jews and other 'non-Aryan' minority groups.

Ultimately his methods were entirely unacceptable to the rest of Europe.

Initially the German Army General Staff believed that they could make use of the 'little Corporal' for their own ends, but Hitler outmanoeuvred them. He obtained their co-operation by a mixture of successful acts, such as the re-occupation of the Rhineland, his own assumption of the role of Commander-in-Chief and the conciliatory policy to keep the army free from Nazification. Accustomed to rigid codes of discipline and conduct, most German servicemen, traditionally bound to obey without question, did exactly that. They found in 'orders from above' the excuse to carry out any task that was required of them – even to acts of extreme inhumanity and cruelty.

In the early part of his career Hitler, like Henry Ford, was skilled at choosing the right man for the right job. But as his health deteriorated with German defeats from 1942 onward, his choices became increasingly illogical. Initially, however, the Nazi team of figurehead Führer, popular war hero Goering and master propagandist Goebbels, was a winning one. The Wehrmacht Generals were never fond of Goering and his Luftwaffe, but despite their own inner conflicts and established loyalties to the old Imperial Germany, which would finally lead to the unsuccessful assassination attempts on Hitler, they went along with the successful combination.

In the last 12 months of his life, when his health was rapidly deteriorating, Hitler frequently hoped that some supernatural event or miracle would occur to save the Reich and he sought men through whom the miracle might be worked. One such man was Otto Skorzeny, the S.S. officer who rescued Mussolini and who became known as 'the most dangerous man in Europe.' Although Hitler and his nominated successor, Goering, both became ineffectual fighting commanders as the war passed its mid-point, the Wehrmacht continued to fight bravely and well despite difficulties. In North Africa a 'clean' war was fought, where soldiers of both sides respected each other and observed such rules as are possible to observe in war. There were no S.S. formations present and the German General, Erwin Rommel, was regarded almost with affection by the men of the British 8th Army, who had their own charismatic leader — Bernard Law Montgomery.

General Montgomery, aside from General Wavell, was the first British Field commander able to stand up to the Prime Minister, Winston Churchill. In 1942, Churchill was anxious for a victory and immediately Montgomery was appointed to command the 8th Army, he pressed him to attack Rommel. Montgomery refused to do so until he was ready, but when he finally took the offensive he gained a victory at El Alamein. From then onwards the Germans went backwards until they were driven out of North Africa.

Allied co-operation was symbolised by the 'Big Three' — Churchill, Roosevelt and Stalin — and while things were going Germany's way, adversity kept the Three in harmony. However, once the Nazis were driven out of Africa in 1943, only Russia remained in direct fighting contact with the Axis, and Stalin insisted that Britain and America should get back into the war. The Americans wanted to assault mainland Europe, while Churchill, fearing the spread of communism from the East, insisted that Britain and America should land in Italy and drive north into the Balkans, thus meeting the Russians in Eastern, rather than in Western Europe. In the end Italy was invaded in 1943 and mainland Europe in 1944.

The Big Three managed to hide their differences, but not all of their subordinates could. Montgomery and Patton harboured an open feud, which had begun in 1943, when the Englishman had criticised the behaviour of the American troops at the Battle of the Kasserine Pass. As the Allied armies pushed across Europe from the invasion beaches, Patton and Montgomery competed for the attention of their Supreme Commander, Dwight D. Eisenhower, and for the lion's share of petrol and ammunition. General de Gaulle, who had insisted that as each part of France was liberated it should be put under his control as the only true leader of his country, agitated for equal status with the Big Three. His campaign was eventually successful when, after the war, Britain gave up part of its Berlin sector to form the French sector. The Russians, however, refused to give up any of their allocation, despite their support of de Gaulle's Resistance forces during the war.

America, following Pearl Harbour, enlisted the help of the Chinese Nationalist leader, Chiang Kai-Shek. Chiang had suppressed the Chinese Communists in the 1920's and there was no affection for him in Russia, while Britain, occupied more with Europe rather than the Far East, attached little importance to him.

Official policy and Allied solidarity demanded that a united front should be presented to the populations and armies engaged in the war. The picture postcard reflected that attitude, simply and effectively. There was no room on it for hyperbole.

The postcard did not show, nor was it intended to, the inner tensions in the war of personalities. Today it records what people saw and felt at the time and it is that record, uncluttered by learned analysis, that makes the contemporary postcard collection a unique passport to the years of World War II.

In the 1940's European Royal Families still commanded strong feelings of respect and allegiance from their subjects. Soldiers still fought 'For King and Country.' During the war the British Royal Family earned the love and affection of their people by their obvious unreserved sharing of the people's hardships and adversities, for their genuine sympathy and caring, for remaining in areas of danger to prove that they too could 'take it.' They formed a simple, close, unsophisticated family group, with whom many middle class citizens could identify.

To the many European Monarchs, whose countries were occupied by the invading Germans, the task of acting as effective morale-raising figureheads was an extremely difficult one. The majority took refuge in Britain and attempted to perform their duties from London. Communication was almost impossible as stiff penalties were imposed by the Germans on anyone caught listening to the BBC — the only practicable link. Without the reassuring presence of a figurehead to rally round, a number of citizens throughout occupied Europe found collaboration the better part of valour. Local Nazi groups were formed, notably in Holland and in Norway — both of whose monarchs were in exile in London — with outwardly strong and enthusiastic membership. Sometimes party membership was a cloak for Resistance work, as it gave access to vital information for sabotage work.

World War II saw the end of many long lines of Royalty. In Italy, for instance, King Victor Emmanuel maintained an uneasy collaboration with Mussolini, but lost his throne just after the war. He had lost his place as Italy's figurehead even before the war, however, usurped by the flamboyant Mussolini. Yugoslavia and Rumania both changed from monarchies to communist states. King Peter of Yugoslavia, another of Britain's Royal exiles, ceded his throne to Josip Broz, better known to the world as Tito, in January 1945, and King Carol of Rumania was forced to abdicate in favour of his 19 year old son, Michael in 1940. Michael in turn lost his throne in 1947. But the young Princess Elizabeth, only 13 when the war broke out, is now on the Throne of England and continues to be the subject of a variety of picture postcards.

41, 41A *Adolf Hitler. Hitler's uniform, including the Sam Browne belt, bears an extraordinary similarity to the British officer's Service Dress. While Hitler's entourage sported expensive plumage, he himself would often dress very simply. The cancellation on the reverse commemorates the Führer's visit to Vienna and has a written message: 'Dear Zenzl, I send you this card for your collection. Yours sincerely, Helen. Heil Hitler!' German: (Pub. Keystone, Berlin) No. 168. 16 March 1938. Value C*

42 *'Chancellor Adolf Hitler.' The Führer is wearing lederhosen, the leather shorts popular in Bavaria and Austria. He also has a black shirt, a uniform he styled upon Mussolini's Fascists and which was adopted by the S.S. in contrast to the brown shirts of the S.A. The reverse carries an adhesive stamp showing Hitler's head and shoulders and is cancelled 'Geburtstag des Führer. 20 April 1938.' The Führer's birthday. He was 49. German: (Pub. Hoffman) 20 April 1938. Value C*

43 *'A strange encounter.' The three cyclists are chimney sweeps and the one on the right is holding the traditional top hat which is still worn on the continent today. In the mid 1920's, following his release from prison, Hitler drove around the countryside with a small group of associates, planning his return to public life. One of the group was the photographer Hoffman. It is quite possible that the Führer's car met these sweeps on one such drive and Hoffman arranged the picture as an omen of good luck. Such sweeps with bicycles can still be seen in Germany today. German: (Pub. Hoffman) No. 314. Value D*

44 *'The Führer having a quiet break in the mountains.' The Führer probably needed a break. The card was posted on 15 August 1943, by which point in the war the Germans had been driven out of North Africa, the Allies were in control of Sicily and poised to invade the Italian mainland, and the Russian summer offensive was in full swing. German: (Pub. Hoffman) No. 676. Value D*

41

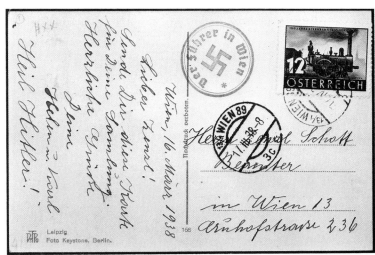

41A

42

43

44

45

46

47

48

49

50

45 'Field Marshal Rommel.' The Desert Fox, Erwin Rommel, is the German general most British people commonly associate with World War II. Rommel served with distinction in the First World War, winning Imperial Germany's highest award for bravery, *Pour La Mérite*, which can be seen in the picture beneath his Knight's Cross. Between the wars Rommel had several appointments, including a period at the Wiener Neustadt Military Academy where the inventor of the postcard, Dr. Emanuel Hermann, had taught half a century earlier.
Like Guderian and Patton, Rommel led from the front and was often out of touch with his headquarters staff. Oddly, exactly that situation arose at Army Group B when the Allies landed in Normandy on 6 June 1944. Rommel had spent seven months strengthening the coastal defences but was away celebrating his wife's birthday the day the invasion began. He was implicated in the 20 July 1944 bomb plot and was forced to commit suicide on 1 October 1944. *German: (Pub. Hoffman) No. 1520. Circa 1943. Value D*

46 'General Jordan.' By the beginning of 1944 Soviet Russia had 13 times more men under arms than Nazi Germany and her forces were pushing westwards from the Baltic to the Black Sea. Hitler's interference with his generals' conduct of their campaigns became increasingly irrational, he made his decisions intuitively, believing that he possessed some mystical military insight. Frequently his attitude was one of 'no withdrawal' and in the vastness of the isolated Eastern Front the lack of freedom for the German generals to organize strategic withdrawals resulted in the loss of whole armies. Some commanders overcame their fear of the Führer and acted upon their own military appreciations of the situation. Perhaps General Hans Jordan did that. He was dismissed from the command of the 9th Army for 'irresolute leadership' during the Russian spring offensive in 1944. *German: (Pub. Hoffman) No. R250. Circa 1943. Value C*

47 'R. Hess The Führer's Deputy.' Rudolf Hess, like Hitler, served in the 16th Bavarian Reserve Regiment during the First World War and joined the National Socialist Party at the end of 1919. He, Rosenberg and Hitler, formed the nucleus of the NSDAP, and his contributions ranged from formidable pugilistics in the beer hall days, to typing *Mein Kampf* while he and Hitler were in prison at Landsberg following the failure of the 1923 Munich putsch. He became the Führer's Deputy and major fund raiser, tapping the fortunes of Fritz Thyssen, the steel magnate, and Carl Bechstein, the piano maker. To his Leader's surprise, he flew to Scotland on 10 May 1941 hoping to negotiate a peace with Britain. He was jailed for the duration of the war and then given life imprisonment at the Nuremberg Trials. In 1979 it was suggested that the 'Hess' in the Spandau Prison in Berlin was an imposter. *German: (Pub. Hoffman) No. 306. Circa 1937. Value D*

48 'Colonel-General Heinrici.' Heinrici was a professional soldier, originally an infantryman, who commanded his forces without resorting to the brutality which many generals showed both towards their own men and the enemy. For some time he served under Guderian at the beginning of 'Operation Barbarossa,' then commanded XL Panzer Corps on the Dnieper Front, the German 4th Army, and, in March 1945, took over Army Group Vistula from Himmler who had been trying his hand at being an Army general. *German: (Pub. Hoffman) No. R208. Value C*

49 'Colonel-General Model.' Walther Model is ranked by some military historians alongside Manstein and Kesselring. He was the youngest next to Rommel to hold the rank of Field Marshal. His rapid rise (he was a Colonel in 1939) is sometimes attributed to his strong allegiance to the Nazi Party and to his good relationship with Hitler, but he became known to some as the 'Führer's Fireman' because of his success in rebuilding broken fronts—particularly following 'Operation Citadel,' the

Kursk-Orel offensive in the summer of 1943. His most dramatic, if to him small scale operation, was his improvised defence at Arnhem, which was a major factor in the failure of 'Operation Market Garden' in September 1944. After the Allies crossed the Rhine in April 1945, he found his forces surrounded and, in a quiet wood near the Ruhr town of Duisberg, he shot himself.
German: (Pub. Hoffman) No. R82. Circa 1942. Value C

50 *'Fieldmarshal von Kleist.'* Paul Ludwig Ewald Baron von Kleist was a German Cavalry General of the old school who was retired by the Nazis in 1938. He was not a Party member, but was brought back to service in 1939. In Poland he commanded XXII Panzer Corps and in France in 1940 his Panzer Group included Guderian's XIX Corps, and although the latter later criticized his Commander, Kleist gained formidable victories in both campaigns. He was appointed Field-marshal on 1 February 1943. In Russia he again did well, although he was re-primanded by Hitler when Rostov had to be given up. When, in March 1944, Kleist recommended withdrawal behind the line of the Dniester River, the Führer relieved him of his command.
German: (Pub. Hoffman) Value C

51 *'Reich Chief Forester Hermann Goering.'* Goering held an extraordinary range of jobs, or at least titles, at one time. While he was Chief Forester he was also head of the Luftwaffe, Minister-President of Prussia, a Cabinet Minister and overseer of Hitler's 'Four Year Economic Plan.' He loved to dress in fancy uniforms and to wear gold and jewels, and luxuriated in the opulent living that his position gave him access to. He was perhaps the best-liked personality of the Nazi hierarchy, apparently bluff and jovial. In reality he was brutally jealous of anyone that might cast a shadow upon his own importance, and his concern with self-gratification led to his loss of favour with Hitler as early as 1942.
German: (Pub. Hoffman) Circa 1937. Value D

Reichsjägermeister Hermann Göring

Familie Dr. Goebbels

52

HAUPTMANN GÖRING

53

54

55

56

57

52 *'Dr. Goebbels and Family.'* Paul Josef Goebbels, pictured with his wife Magda and three of their children, joined the Nazi Party in 1922. Immediately the Nazi Party came to power in 1933, Goebbels was appointed Minister of Reich Propaganda and with total control of all communications media—including postcards—employed his energies in the Führer's cause. When the tide of victory ebbed, he assumed responsibility for maintaining the Reich's morale, and alone of all Hitler's close associates remained in the Berlin bunker until his Leader was dead. His wife then poisoned the six children they had with them, and she and her husband were shot by the S.S. Their bodies were burned.
German: (Pub. Hoffman) No. 711. Circa 1937. Value C

53 *'Commander Goering.'* Hermann Wilhelm Goering was a leading air ace of the First World War with 22 victories to his credit, and, after Baron von Richthofen's death, followed the Red Baron's immediate replacement as leader of the famous Richthofen Circus. He met Hitler in 1922 and joined the Nazi Party later that year, becoming the first commander of the S.A. He went on to be Hitler's right hand man and, in September 1939, the Führer designated Goering as his successor. Goering's drive and panache built the Luftwaffe from small beginnings into a superbly efficient tactical air force. However, he was unable to fulfil his boast that the Luftwaffe, which he commanded as Field Marshal, would prevent enemy planes reaching German soil and he fell from favour. In the picture Goering is wearing at his throat the insignia of *'Pour La Mérite'*, the coveted 'Blue Max' of Imperial Germany.
German: (Pub. Hoffman) No. 140. Value C

54 *'Colonel-General Guderian.'* Heinz Guderian served in the First World War, after which he specialized in the study and development of armoured warfare. In 1938 he published his book, *Achtung! Panzer,* in which he set out the principles of future tank combat including tactics such as rapid movement, supported by airpower, on a narrow front. Commanding a Panzer Group in 1940 he was the first to cross the Meuse (at Sedan) and the first to reach the Channel. In 1941 he argued with Hitler about the direction of the German effort in Russia and was dismissed. A tough, burly man who led from the front and was popular with his troops, Guderian was the Nazis' Patton. When the war ended he surrendered to the Americans and no proceedings were taken against him. He wrote his memoirs, *Panzer Leader,* in 1952 and died aged 66 in 1954.
German: (Pub. Hoffman) Value C

55 *'Colonel-General Ernst Udet.'* Oberleutenant Udet was second only to the Red Baron von Richthofen in his total of 62 victories as a fighter pilot in the First World War and spent many years in America between the wars as a stunt flyer. Goering, Colonel General and Commander-in-Chief of the Luftwaffe, gave the job of aircraft production to his old friend Udet in 1937. He is said to have had a major role in conceiving and developing the Stuka dive bomber but became the scapegoat for the failure of the Luftwaffe to control the sky over Europe. He fell out of favour with Goering and committed suicide in November 1941. The Nazi propaganda machine announced that he had died testing a new plane.
German: (Pub. Hoffman) Value D

56 *'General of Tank Troops Hube'.* Hans-Valentin Hube led the 16th Panzer Division under Runstedt in the invasion of Russia, later rising to command the 1st Panzer Army. In March 1944 his 22 divisions were trapped in a pocket north of Odessa between the rivers Bug and Dnestr. Hube and Army Group Commander von Manstein struggled with Hitler to obtain permission for the 1st Army to break out. Manstein was summoned to the Berghof where, after a furious argument, he obtained the Führer's consent to a compromise withdrawal. Much equipment was lost but the Army was saved and the line closed. Hitler rewarded Manstein by dismissing him.

German: (Pub. Hoffman) No. R249. Circa 1943. Value B

57 *Lieutenant Benzin.* Benzin was a 'full' lieutenant, who in the British Army would wear two pips in contrast to the Second Lieutenant's one. The reason for his appearance on a postcard may have been his winning of the Knight's Cross with oak leaves, which can be seen at his throat. Over his left breast there is just visible a metal badge with outstretched oak leaves. Such emblems were awarded to those who took part in specific actions and raids. Perhaps Hoffman recorded all those who won the Knight's Cross. *German: (Pub. Hoffman) Value B*

58 *'Colonel-General von Brauchitsch.'* It was part of Hitler's policy to keep the Army independent of the Nazi Party. In this way he hoped to retain the continuing co-operation of the Senior Officer Corps of the *Wehrmacht*. In 1938, Brauchitsch was chosen as head of OKH and Commander-in-Chief of the Army in preference to the openly pro-Nazi Reichenau. But Brauchitsch was unable to stand up to the Führer and wielded no influence with him. He was blamed for the failure to capture Moscow in 1941 and dismissed. Hitler took over as Chief of the Army. In 1944 Hitler ordered the destruction of Paris. Walter von Brauchitsch is credited with saving the city. *German: (Pub. Hoffman) Value C*

59 *'Julius Streicher.'* Streicher was one of the most important men in Hitler's immediate circle, particularly in the early years. He was obsessively anti-Semitic and propagated a violent anti-Jewish campaign through his weekly newspaper, *Der Stürmer*, which had been founded in 1922. On 1 April 1933, just days after Hitler gained effective control over Germany and dissolved the Weimar Republic, Streicher, through *Der Stürmer*, proclaimed a nationwide boycott of Jewish shops. Gangs of S.A. thugs enforced what was essentially an official edict. *German: (Pub. Hoffman) No. 680. Circa 1937. Value C*

60 *'S.S. Major Skorzeny.'* On 12 September 1943 a detachment of S.D. (*Sicherheitsdienst*, the Security Service) men, plus members of the Luftwaffe Parachute Demonstration Battalion, rescued Mussolini from a small hotel in the Gran Sasso, in the Abruzzi mountains, where the new Badoglio government had held him for two months. The leader of the *coup de main* force was Skorzeny. Hitler rewarded him with promotion and the Knight's Cross. Mussolini gave him a gold watch. In 1944 Skorzeny kidnapped the pro-Soviet Nicholas Horthy from Budapest and was rumoured to be leading bands of Germans, dressed as Americans, on sabotage missions between Allied lines in Normandy. When the Americans captured the vital Rhine bridge at Remagen, Skorzeny tried to blow it up but failed. *German: (Pub. Hoffman) No. R174. Circa 1943. Value C*

61 *'Fieldmarshal von Runstedt.'* On 1 October 1920, Karl Rudolf Gerd von Runstedt, having just left the old Germany army, joined the *Reichswehr* as a Lieutenant-Colonel. By 1932 he was a full general. In 1936 he represented the *Wehrmacht* at the funeral of King George V in London and in 1938 commanded the Second Army with the task of marching into Silesia if the Munich talks failed. He retired on 31 October 1938 but was recalled to lead Army Group South when war began in 1939. He was 64. His ideas were largely responsible for the German breakthrough in France in 1940 but he was defeated on the Ukranian Front in 1942. In the German preparations for the Allied Channel assault he clashed with Rommel who believed that the enemy should be stopped on the beaches and not inland as Runstedt maintained. He was captured by the Americans and served three years in prison, partly in Britain where he was extensively interviewed by Liddell Hart. He was probably Germany's oldest senior soldier and certainly one of the most respected. *German: (Pub. Film Foto, Berlin) No. C2233. Posted 8 February 1943. Value C*

58

59

60

R 128　　Generalfeldmarschall v. Rundstedt

61

The Spirit of Britain

WE SHALL GO ON TO THE END....WE SHALL FIGHT IN FRANCE, WE SHALL FIGHT ON THE SEAS AND IN THE OCEANS, SHALL FIGHT WITH GROWING CONFIDENCE AND GROWING STRENGTH IN THE AIR.. WE SHALL DEFEND OUR ISLAND,WHATEVER THE COST MAY BE. WE SHALL FIGHT ON THE BEACHES,WE SHALL FIGHT ON THE LANDING GROUNDS, WE SHALL FIGHT IN THE FIELDS AND STREETS AND IN THE HILLS.... WE SHALL NEVER SURRENDER,AND EVEN IF, WHICH I DO NOT FOR A MOMENT BELIEVE,THIS ISLAND, OR EVEN PART OF IT,IS SUBJUGATED AND STARVING,THEN OUR EMPIRE ACROSS THE SEAS, ARMED AND GUARDED BY THE BRITISH FLEET, WILL CARRY ON THE STRUGGLE,UNTIL, IN GOD'S GOOD TIME, THE NEW WORLD, IN ALL ITS STRENGTH AND MIGHT, SETS FORTH TO THE RESCUE AND LIBERATION OF THE OLD. BRITAIN WILL FIGHT THE MENACE OF TYRANNY FOR YEARS, AND, IF NECESSARY, ALONE.
— WINSTON CHURCHILL

62 'The Spirit of Britain.' Winston Leonard Spencer Churchill has been called the 'Greatest Englishman.' Certainly during World War II he came to symbolize the dogged determination of the British people. He inspired the Nation not just by his presence or by his pugnacious resemblance to the British Bulldog, but by his fighting words delivered in his gruff voice. On this card is included one of Churchill's most mis-quoted phrases, *'We shall fight on the beaches . . . ,'* a part of the speech he made on 4 June 1940 to the House of Commons and hence the Nation.
British: (Pub. Valentine's) 'Helpful Thoughts' series. No. 583. Value B

63 *Le Très Honorable Winston S. Churchill.* On 10 May 1940 Chamberlain resigned as Prime Minister and Churchill took over—and 'take over' is exactly what he did. His policy for the country's war effort was very simple— *'Victory at all costs.'* He did, however, cause considerable consternation in higher military circles by his insistence upon playing a major role in service affairs, not just at a strategic level but also tactically. Nevertheless he impressed Fieldmarshal Alan Brooke, the Prime Minister's wartime adviser, who said of him, *'He is quite the most wonderful man I have ever met.'*
British: (Pub. Tuck) Photo by Cecil Beaton. French and British versions were produced. Value B

64 *Mr Winston Churchill wearing his steel helmet.* Winnie did inspire confidence. His smile, his cigar, his famous V sign, all sustained the British through their darkest hours and for occupied Europe he became a symbol of hope. Churchill's mother Jennie was American and he sought to develop a special relationship with President Roosevelt of the United States. One of the many fruits of the concord between the two leaders was the Lend-Lease Act passed on 11 March 1941, by which Britain, and later other Allied nations, received massive dollar and material aid.
British: (Pub. Photochrom) Value B

65 'Mr Winston Churchill.'
Churchill was born at
Blenheim Palace on
30 November 1874. He
reported the Boer War as a
young newspaper man,
carrying a gun which was
officially forbidden and
being captured by, and
escaping from, the Boers. In
the First World War he
inspired the Dardanelles
operation and when it failed
he left his post as First Lord
of the Admiralty and served
on the Western front
commanding the 6th
Battalion of the Royal Scots
Fusiliers. Between the wars
he called for the Nation to
re-arm in order to counter
the growing strength of Nazi
Germany and when
Chamberlain signed the
Munich Agreement he
roundly denounced it. On
3 September 1939 Britain
declared war on Germany
and the Admiralty radioed
the Fleet, 'Winston is back.'
He was First Lord of the
Admiralty again. At
Churchill's feet in the
picture can be seen his gas
mask holder. The card was
used as an advertising item
by The Sunday Dispatch.
On the reverse is a printed
message from the Editor: 'I
am proud to tell you that Mr
Winston Churchill's brilliant
articles, written before the
war, will be published every
week in The Sunday
Dispatch . . .'
British: Posted 27 February
1940. Value B

66 'Our Skipper.' The
handwritten message on the
reverse reads: 'Was on fire
guard last Monday night and
got to go on again tonight.
Short staffed, sick and on
holidays. I'm having that ray
treatment twice a week.
7/6d a time. Bit expensive
but cheap if I benefit in
health by it. Two lamps are
used, one for 3½ minutes
and the other for 7½ . . .
Cheerio. Mother XXXXX.'
British: (Pub. Photochrom)
Posted 8 September 1943,
(the day before the Salerno
landings, an enterprise
inspired by Churchill).
Value B

67 'The Allied Leaders.'
King Leopold of Belgium,
President Roosevelt of the
U.S.A., King George VI and
Queen Elizabeth of Great
Britain, Prime Minister
Winston Churchill of Great
Britain, General de Gaulle of
Free France, Prince Bernhard
and Princess Juliana of the
Netherlands and Chairman

Le Très Honorable Winston S. Churchill
Premier Ministre de Grande Bretagne

63

64

MR. WINSTON CHURCHILL
WEARING HIS STEEL HELMET &
THE SMILE OF CONFIDENCE.

MR. WINSTON CHURCHILL

65

OUR SKIPPER

66

of the People's Commissars Stalin of the U.S.S.R. The inclusion of de Gaulle dates this unposted card as after the Fall of France.
Belgian: Circa 1940. Value C

68 *'Prime Minister Winston Churchill.'* It is often forgotten that in the 1930's Winston Churchill was considered by many to be a failure in politics. When war broke out he was 65 years old. However, it was his image which came to represent the hope of a return to freedom for those occupied by the Nazis.
Belgian: Circa 1940. Value C

69 *'King Leopold III of Belgium.'* In February 1934, Leopold succeeded his well-loved father, Albert I, who died in a mountaineering accident in the Ardennes. A year afterwards his beautiful and popular wife, Astrid, was killed in a motor accident. When Germany invaded Belgium in 1940, Leopold commanded his army, as his father had done in 1914–1918, until forced to surrender. He was interned by the Germans at Laeken, moved to Germany and then Austria until he was liberated by the U.S. Army in 1945.

Leopold came under much criticism for not leaving to set up Government in London. The communist campaign mounted against him during the war and in July 1945 his brother, Prince Charles, again took over the Regency he had undertaken while Leopold was still interned.
Belgian: Circa 1940. Value C

70 *'General Charles André Joseph Marie de Gaulle.'* De Gaulle had shown himself to possess greater intellectual powers than the usual soldier in his inter-war writings, *'Le Fil de L'Epée,' 'Vers l'armée de métier'* and *'La France et son armée,'* in which he urged a defence based on mobility with tanks and aircraft, declaring the static fortifications that had served the French so well at Verdun during the First World War, obsolete. His published views brought him into conflict with the orthodox military powers. Always self-willed and self-opinionated, he had the strength and charisma required to rally the Free French under his symbol of the Cross of Lorraine.
Belgian: Circa 1940. Value C

71 *'Princess Juliana and Prince Bernhard of Holland.'* Although Bernhard was a German Prince (of Lippe-Biesterfeld) he led the defence of the Royal Palace at the Hague when the Germans attacked in 1940. Escaping to England, he acted as liaison officer for the Dutch and British forces and helped to organise the Resistance in Holland.

Juliana spent most of the war years in Canada with her children, while her mother, Queen Wilhelmina, took her Cabinet to London. She returned with the Allied armies in 1945. Other 'Royals', who set up home and Government in Britain, were King George of the Hellenes, Prince Paul (the Regent) and King Peter of Yugoslavia, King Haakon of Norway and the Grand Duchess Charlotte of Luxembourg.
Belgian: Circa 1940. Value C

Field-Marshal Sir Bernard Montgomery, K.C.B., D.S.O.
("Monty")

73

Le Très Honorable Anthony Eden
Ministre des Affaires Etrangères de Grande Bretagne

74

72 'King George VI and Queen Elizabeth.' This quiet, home- and family-loving couple started their married life with no idea of ever being King and Queen of Great Britain and her Empire. On the abdication of his brother, Edward VIII, in 1937 George took up his royal duties as Monarch and, with Elizabeth to support him, unassumingly built up the respect and affection of his people. It was a supreme effort to conquer his natural shyness, even reserve, and the slight stammer that made public speaking an ordeal.

When war was declared on 3 September 1939, George was visited by an unceasing flow of callers at Buckingham Palace, led by the Prime Minister, Chamberlain, and Lord Gort, commander of the B.E.F. The Queen joined him from Balmoral and from then on, the Royal couple remained in London, at Buckingham Palace, resisting all efforts to move them to safety. Their children were not 'evacuated' as many other London children were. 'The children can't go without me. I can't leave the King, and the King won't go,' said the Queen.
Belgian: Circa 1940. Value C

73 'Monty.' Bernard Law Montgomery became the most successful and well-known British general of World War II. His experiences in the trenches during the First World War greatly influenced his conduct of battles in World War II. While accepting that men under his command would be killed, he determined that there should not be needless loss of life and would not proceed with an action until he felt himself to be totally prepared. He commanded the 3rd Division at Dunkirk and then at the head of the 8th Army won what many believed to be the most important battle of the war—El Alamein. Later he came into conflict with American general, George Patton, when he said that the 8th Army should be given the Americans' equipment and then they could finish the war swiftly.
Printed message from the Prime Minister on reverse reads: 'We shall continue steadfast in faith and duty till our task is done.'
British: (Pub. Tuck) Value B

74 'The Most Honourable Anthony Eden.' In 1915 Robert Anthony Eden was an infantry officer in France, where he won the Military Cross. He entered Parliament in 1923 as member for Warwick and Leamington and sided with Churchill against Chamberlain's appeasement policy. In December 1940 he became Foreign Secretary in Churchill's wartime government, and proved himself a valuable emissary to the Allied conferences in Washington, the Middle East, Algiers and Moscow.
British: (Pub. Tuck) Value B

75 'General Eisenhower and Fieldmarshal Montgomery.' Dwight David Eisenhower was Supreme Allied Commander in Europe and Montgomery commanded the Allied ground troops. The Fieldmarshal did not agree with his commander's broad front policy and relationships were further strained by the struggle between Montgomery and Patton for both supplies and public acclaim. Monty could never fully accept his loss of the Allied ground force command and during the Battle of the Bulge in December 1944 he agitated again for American units to be returned to his permanent control. Eisenhower had to threaten to take him to the **Chiefs of Staff before he** would drop his demands.
British: (Pub. Tuck) Dutch edition. Circa 1945. Value B

76 'President Roosevelt and Mr Molotoff.' When Hitler invaded Poland in September 1939, Russia followed suit a few days later from the East. In Moscow, on the 28th, the day after Warsaw capitulated, Ribbentrop and Vyacheslav Molotov, the Russian Foreign Minister, signed an agreement which divided the spoils between their countries. By mid-1941 Germany and Russia were at war. This card commemorates a meeting in May 1942 in Washington between Molotov and Roosevelt, who welcomed the visit for he believed that world peace depended upon rapprochement with the U.S.S.R. In London, Molotov had already concluded a 20 year Anglo-Russian Alliance.
British: (Pub. Tuck) 1942. Value B

77 'President Roosevelt in the role of grandfather.' In March 1905 at the age of 23, Franklin D. Roosevelt married his sixth cousin, Anna Eleanor Roosevelt, a strong woman who furthered her husband's political career and sustained his morale through a debilitating attack of infantile paralysis. Her uncle, President Theodore Roosevelt attended the wedding ceremony.

Their eldest son, James, served during World War II and was awarded the Navy Cross for exemplary courage in the assault of Makin Atoll in August 1942.
British (Pub. Tuck) Photo Associated Press. Value B

78 'The Allied General Staff.' Front row, left, *Air Chief Marshal Arthur William Tedder,* who became Eisenhower's Deputy Supreme Commander in December 1943. Behind, left to right: *Lieutenant General Omar Nelson Bradley,* who ranked equal to Montgomery as an Army Group Commander, handling 1¼ million men; *Admiral Sir Bertram Home Ramsay,* who was knighted by the King for his handling of the Dunkirk evacuation and appointed Naval Commander-in-Chief for D-Day (Operation Neptune); *Air Vice-Marshal Trafford Leigh-Mallory,* who commanded No. 12 Group Fighter Command during the Battle of Britain and was appointed Chief of the Allied Expeditionary Air Force for Overlord in 1943; *Lieutenant General Walter Bedell Smith,* known by his contemporaries as 'Beetle,' was Eisenhower's Chief of Staff during the Torch and Overlord operations until the German surrender in May 1945. He and Fieldmarshal Jodl signed the surrender document.
British: (Pub. Tuck) French captions probably done overseas judging by 'Biddle Smith.' Posted in Holland. Circa 1944. Value B

79 'General ("Blood and Guts") Patton.' George Smith Patton believed himself to be a warrior more akin to the days of individual combat than to the 20th Century, and destined for greatness. He fought against Pancho Villa in Mexico, led the first American tank attack at Saint Mihiel in 1918 and took command of the

American troops in North Africa after the Kasserine Pass fiasco, turning them into a formidable fighting unit. He was probably the most effective American field commander of World War II, waging 'simple, direct and ruthless' war and moving his armoured forces with great dash and boldness.

Prime Minister's message on reverse reads: 'This is a time for everyone to stand together and hold firm.'
British: (Pub. Tuck) Value B

80 *'Queen Wilhelmina of Holland and Fieldmarshal Montgomery.'* Wilhelmina Helena Pauline Maria of Orange-Nassau, had been Queen of the Netherlands for over 40 years when the Germans invaded her country. She set up a government in exile in London and broadcast regular messages to her people via the B.B.C. -operated Radio Orange.

When the Allied invasion forces spread out from the Normandy beaches, Montgomery's armies progressively liberated the Low Countries, and on 4 May 1945 he accepted the surrender by Admiral Friedeburg of all German forces in North-West Germany, Holland and Denmark. This card is dated 12 May 1945 and is doubtless one of a large celebratory series.
Dutch: (Pub. J. Chr. Olsen) Value C

78

Lt. Gl. Bradley   Amiral Ramsay   Vice Maréchal de l'Air Leigh Mallory   Lt. Gl. Biddle Smith

Maréchal de l'Air Tedder   Général Eisenhower   Maréchal d'Armée Montgomery
L'État-Major des Armées Alliées

Generaal Eisenhower en Maarschalk Montgomery
75

Le Président Roosevelt et Mr. Molotoff
76

Le Président Roosevelt dans le rôle de grandpère
77

General ("Blood and Guts") Patton
79

80

MARSHAL STALIN

For Freedom

81

PRESIDENT ROOSEVELT

For Freedom

82

GENERALISSIMO CHIANG KAI-SHEK

For Freedom

83

GENERAL DE GAULLE

For Freedom

84

FOUR LEADERS. These coloured cards are part of the 'For Freedom' series published by G.P.D., which may well have been the Government Publicity Department. All four are numbered G.P.D 445/2/5 on the reverse while the black and white 'For Victory' card of Princess Elizabeth (illustrated in 'Propaganda') is numbered GPD365/63. These cards were probably issued in late 1942 or early 1943.

81   *'Marshal Stalin.'* Before Lenin died in 1924 he warned, 'Remove Stalin.' His followers did not, and by 1929 Joseph Vissarionovich Dzhugashvili was dictator of Russia, a position he had secured by mass murder and terrorism. Of course these aspects were 'overlooked' when Stalin became an Ally following Nazi Germany's assault on Russia in June 1941. He successfully out-manoeuvred Roosevelt at the Big Three conferences, and, as the Red Armies swept westward, established puppet regimes in the 'liberated' territories—much to Churchill's chagrin. *British: (Pub. G.P.D.) Value B*

82   *'President Roosevelt.'* In 1921 Roosevelt suffered a severe attack of polio-myelitis, which interrupted his political career for seven years, and left him paralysed from the waist down, reliant on leg braces, crutches and a wheelchair. It speaks plainly for his strength of character that despite this he rose to be President four years after his return to active politics in 1928. He believed the Presidency was, '. . . pre-eminently a place of moral leadership,' and was often accused of being dictatorial. But between his form of dictatorship and that of Joseph Stalin lay a huge gap bridged only by the expediency of war. *British: (Pub. G.P.D.) Value B*

83   *'Generalissimo Chiang Kai-Shek.'* Chiang Chung Cheng trained as an officer in Tokyo and became the first commandant of the Chinese Republic's Whampoa Military Academy. In 1926 he was head of the Army and set out to quash the new born communist party and the power of the regional war-lords, forcing them into the

85

86

87

88

89

90

91

Long March north. In 1932 the Japanese annexed Manchuria, an escalation of territorial avarice which, in 1937, ended in open conflict. When the Japanese attacked Pearl Harbour in December 1941 he gained America as a firm Ally. In 1943 Chiang was President of China and, as Allied Supreme Commander of the China Theatre of Operations, he attended the Cairo Conference with Roosevelt and Churchill. Despite American enthusiasm, Chiang's relations with his Allies were frequently strained and the British (perhaps because their major interests lay in Europe) never became convinced of his potential value to the war effort.
British: (Pub. G.P.D.) Value B

84   *'General de Gaulle.'* 'I am France,' declared Charles de Gaulle. And he was. During the First World **War he fought under Pétain** at Verdun, was captured and imprisoned for almost three years until the war ended. His first major book, *The Edge of the Sword*, was published in 1932. In his second work he recommended that French military policy should be based on an offensive stance with armoured divisions. He was ignored. When the Germans invaded France he was 49 and the youngest general in the French Army. almost alone he insisted upon continuing the war, from North Africa if need be, but **just before Pétain, his old** commander, negotiated a peace with the Reich which led to Vichy France, de Gaulle was spirited to London. There he began a personal struggle to keep France in the battle, including regular radio broadcasts to his home land. He created a fighting force called 'The Free French' (changed later to 'Fighting French') but it was not until May 1944 that he was able to generate sufficient impetus with his British and American Allies to form a provisional government in exile. In a private agreement, Eisenhower agreed to recognize him as the French political power and on 26 August 1944 de Gaulle triumphantly entered liberated Paris.
British: (Pub. G.P.D.) Value B

85   *'Guderian.'* Heinz Guderian was Germany's greatest tank expert. By 1934 with the help of the War Minister, Blomberg, he had succeeded in persuading Hitler to form a tank battalion at Ohrdruf. In 1938 he was appointed General of Armoured Troops and gained tactical experience during the invasions of Austria and Czechoslovakia. By the time Poland was invaded, in September 1939, Guderian had seven Panzer divisions under his command. They took part in the swift invasion of France in May 1940 and the invasion of Russia in June 1941. Falling from favour he was dismissed from his command on Christmas Day 1941, but in March 1943 was created Inspector of Armoured Troops and in July 1944 attained the position of Army Chief of Staff. He was again dismissed by Hitler in March 1945.

Caption on reverse (translated) reads: *Our Tank Forces. Colonel General Guderian, Panzerwaffe. Creator and Chief of our Victorious Tank Forces. German: (Pub. for the National League for Germans Abroad) Artist W. Willrich. 1940. Value C*

SIX FUND RAISERS During the First World War the picture postcard played a major role in raising funds to sustain the fighting effort, and it was used in large quantities by every combatant nation. A typical card is that shown at Number 89. On every card sold 'ONE HALFPENNY' went to the National Relief Fund. During World War II the British made less use of the postcard than most other nations. However, one fund raising series of similar style was that published in 1939–40 by Academy. The price of war had doubled. By 1939 'ONE PENNY' went to the War Relief Fund.

86   *'Neville Chamberlain.'* Chamberlain remained Prime Minister during the 'phoney war' period, following the failure of his appeasement policy. On the day the Nazis invaded Holland and Belgium he resigned and died five months later on 9 November 1940.
British: (Pub. Academy Patriotic Publications) Value B

87 *'The Right Hon. L. Hore Belisha.'* Isaac Leslie Hore Belisha was an energetic and aggressive Secretary of State for War, who, in the years immediately before hostilities, introduced considerable improvements into Army equipment and organization. His strong personality led him into conflict with the Prime Minister, Neville Chamberlain, and he resigned in 1940. He is mainly remembered for his introduction, in the 1930's, while Minister of Transport, of the belisha beacon at pedestrian crossings.
British: (Pub. Academy Patriotic Publications) Value B

88 *'General Gamelin.'* Maurice Gustave Gamelin was Commander-in-Chief of the Allied forces on the Western Front in 1939—the B.E.F., through Lord Gort, was directly under his control. Gamelin rose rapidly to high command. Since the Marne battles of 1914, he had developed a rigid yet philosophical approach to warfare in which he neither maintained an effective mobile reserve nor gave explicit orders to his subordinate com-manders, relying upon a codified policy. He was severely criticized for his conduct of operations during the May 1940 battles and was replaced by Weygand. In September, the Vichy Government arrested and interned him. Despite being a prisoner in Buchenwald and Itter, Gamelin survived the war and was liberated by the Americans in May 1945.
British: (Pub. Academy Patriotic Publications) Value B

89 *'National Relief Fund.'* H.R.H. The Prince of Wales, looking suitably appealing in Naval uniform, also featured in khaki.
British: (Patriotic Post Card) Series 1. Posted 6 October 1914. Value A

90 *'General Lord Gort.'* John Standish Surtees Prendergast Vereker Gort won the V.C., D.S.O. with two bars and the M.C. in the First World War. In 1939 he commanded the B.E.F. in France, and while his decision to disengage from the enemy and fall back to the coast upset the French, it probably saved the B.E.F. After Dunkirk he was

relieved by Sir John Dill. Later he became Com-mander-in-Chief in Malta, and helped the island to withstand the German onslaught during 1942.
British: (Pub. Academy Patriotic Publications) Value B

91 *'Sir Cyril Newall.'* During the years 1937 to 1940 Cyril Newall was Chief of Air Staff. It was a critical period in which the R.A.F. was re-equipping to meet a better armed enemy and within the higher echelons of the Air Force there was considerable friction as to both strategic and tactical policies. Newall had originally been an Army Officer and had transferred to the Royal Flying Corps in the First World War.
British: (Pub. Academy Patriotic Publications) Value B

92 *'General Sir W. E. Ironside.'* William Edmund Ironside, 6ft 4in tall and known as 'Tiny,' was an international rugby player and a linguist. John Buchan is said to have based the adventures of Richard Hannay of *The Thirty-Nine Steps* upon Ironside's activities as an intelligence officer during the Boer War. In 1939, Hore-Belisha, Minister for War, sent Gort, who he found difficult to work with, to France with the B.E.F., replacing him with Ironside. Ironside did not do well as C.I.G.S. and was relieved of his command in 1940 with much of the poor British performance being laid at his door.
British: (Pub. H. B. Limited) Value A

93 *'President Roosevelt.'* Franklin Delano Roosevelt became President of the United States in 1932 and led his country out of the Depression. He used all his great persuasive powers to convince America that she had to forget her isolationist policies, and that the war in Europe was of major importance to her. In March 1941, at the beginning of an unprecedented third term of office, he signed the Lend-Lease Act, a courageous commitment in which he was encouraged by Winston Churchill. He put great energy into the planning of the United Nations and soon after being elected for a record fourth term, died of cerebral haemorrhage on

General
Sir W. E. Ironside
Chief of the
Imperial General Staff

92

PRESIDENT ROOSEVELT SIGNS THE LEASE-AND-LEND BILL
MARCH 11TH, 1941

93

General Eisenhower
Supreme Allied Commander

94

Army General FEDOR TOLBUKHIN was given the rank of Marshal of the Soviet Union on September 12, 1944.

95

The Presidium of the Supreme Soviet of the U.S.S.R. awarded Marshal of the Soviet Union GEORGI ZHUKOV the Order of Victory on April 10, 1944, and a second Gold Star Medal on August 29, 1944.

96

Army General RODION MALINOVSKY was given the rank of Marshal of the Soviet Union on September 10, 1944.

97

98

99

12 April 1945. Hitler heard the news in his bunker and thought the President's death might be the miracle needed to save the Reich. It was not. *British: (Pub. Tuck) 1941. Value B*

94 *'General Eisenhower, Supreme Allied Commander.'* During the First World War Eisenhower was in charge of training for the infant American tank corps and saw no combat. While he was based in America, a young George Patton served in France as A.D.C. to General 'Black Jack' Pershing and later the two men became friends. Eisenhower was a protege of General George C. Marshall, the U.S. Army Chief of Staff, and rose rapidly from being American liaison officer in London, to commanding the North African Torch landings. He went from Lieut.-Colonel to Lieut.-General in two years. 'Torch' was in effect a rehearsal for D-Day and Eisenhower was the Supreme Allied Commander upon whose shoulders the whole of the latter operation rested. He was a superb staff officer, negotiator and committee man, and skilfully maintained the balance between the Allies, whose fractious opposites were represented by Montgomery and Patton. His political talents became more evident after the war when he was twice elected President of the United States. *Printed message on reverse from the Prime Minister reads: 'This is a time for everyone to stand together and hold firm!' British: (Pub. Tuck) Value B*

95 *'Army General Fedor Tolbukhin.'* In 1942, Walter Ulbricht, who was later to lead East Germany after the war, visited Tolbukhin's 57th Army with a group of German communists from their 'Party in Exile' in Moscow with a view to sending selected German captives back to their units as spies. Tolbukhin, fearing that the returnees would give away the location of his headquarters, over-ruled the plans. Later his army played a principal role in the boxing-in of the German 6th Army at Stalingrad and were in the vanguard of the drive to Bulgaria and Hungary, where they captured Budapest. Tolbukhin, like Malinovsky, with whom he

had worked closely, was made a Marshal of the Soviet Union in September 1944. *Prime Minister's message on the reverse reads: 'We have to gain victory. That is our task.' British: (Pub. Tuck) Value B*

96 *'Marshal of the Soviet Union George Zhukov.'* Zhukov was a conscript in the Tzarist army who joined the Bolshevik Revolution of 1917 and enlisted in the Red Army in 1919. By 1941 he had risen to Chief of the General Staff and was one of Stalin's most trusted and able military leaders. He worked with Voroshilov in the defence of Leningrad and planned the Soviet counter-attack from Moscow in late 1941, although the Germans never reached Moscow. Zhukov went on to lead the forces that took Warsaw in January 1945 and then Berlin in May, when he signed the German surrender in the city. Reputed never to have been beaten, he was awarded the Order of Victory, the five pointed star immediately below his collar, which is commemorated by the card. The five dots between the points are diamonds. The Order is the highest decoration for army officers and is awarded for outstanding military achievement. The Gold Star also commemorated by the card is given for actions contributing to the honour and development of the U.S.S.R. *Prime Minister's message on the reverse reads: 'This is a time for everyone to stand together and hold firm.' British: (Pub. Tuck) Circa 1945. Value B*

97 *'Marshal of the Soviet Union Rodion Malinovsky.'* Rodion Y. Malinovsky joined the Tsarist army at 16 and served as a machine gunner in the Russian Expeditionary Force in France during the First World War. In World War II, his forces, with those of General Tolbukhin, liberated Odessa (his home town) and Southern Ukraine, leading to the defeat of large German formations in Eastern Ukraine. In 1944, he accepted the German surrender in Rumania and led the Russian thrust from Budapest to Vienna. By the end of the war he was fighting the Japanese in Manchuria. An outspoken commander, Malinovsky was a favourite with his

troops and a close friend of Nikita Khruschev. *Prime Minister's message on the reverse reads: 'We have to gain the victory. That is our task.' British: (Pub. Tuck) Value B*

98 *'President Roosevelt.'* One of a series of at least five cards drawn by the same artist (unknown), which includes Stalin, de Gaulle and Montgomery. *Dutch: Circa 1945. Value C*

99 *'Prime Minister Winston Churchill.'* While the cigar and tie are right enough, the hat is quite wrong. But the spirit is clear. *Dutch: Circa 1945. Value C*

100 *'Umberto di Savoia.'* Umberto was the son of the King of Italy, Victor Emmanuel III of the House of Savoy. He commanded Italy's Army of the Alps, attacking France in 1940. The three-pronged invasion by 32 Italian divisions on 21 June was repulsed by six French divisions, the one bright spot in France's tarnished military prowess that year. It could not prevent France's capitulation, however, which officially took place on 25 June 1940.

Umberto assumed the Regency in 1944 when the Allies entered Rome and after the war he reigned for a brief 35 days from May 1946 (when his father abdicated in his favour) to June 1946, as Umberto II. The Italians then voted to abolish the Monarchy, and the rule of the House of Savoy, which had begun in the 11th century, came to an end.

Caption (translated) reads: 'With unshakeable faith and the heroic vision of past triumph, the unfailing destiny of Imperial Italy is again on the march.' *Italian: Artist F. Spoltora. 1941. Value C*

101 *'Il Duce.'* The Italian Fascist Party, the P.N.F., was founded in 1919 when Benito Mussolini, the man who was to lead the party to its greatest achievements and excesses, was still flirting with socialism. Seeing the emerging force as a tool for his ambition, Mussolini threw in his lot with the Fascists during the period of industrial unrest in 1920. His rise through the party was little short of meteoric and in October 1922 King Victor Emmanuel asked Mussolini to form a Government. He was granted extraordinary powers to deal with the widespread anarchy and gradually he adopted the power and behaviour patterns of a dictator. In 1925 a law was passed granting him 'greater power of parliamentary initiative' and limiting the King's effectiveness. Mussolini was surrounded by weak, incompetent subordinates in comparison with whom he appeared strong, decisive and intelligent. Hitler was shrewd enough to realize that by playing on Mussolini's colossal vanity he could make an Ally of him for Germany. Mussolini at one time feared, however, that Hitler would despise the Italians as 'non-Aryans,' and Italian scholars were set to work to prove that the Italians were of Nordic stock. *Italian: (Pub. R. Questura di Bergamo) Artist F. Spoltora. March 1941. Value B*

102 *'The Duke of Aosta.'* In 1922, as Mussolini's Fascists began to gain power in Italy, the popular Emanuele Filiberto, Duke of Aosta and hero of the First World War, sympathized with the Fascists. As cousin of the King, he was proposed as a prospective Fascist Pretender to the Italian throne. His son Amadeo, pictured here, was also to earn his place in Italian history. When World War II broke out he was Governor General of Italian East Africa, Viceroy of Ethiopia and was appointed Commander-in-Chief of Italian forces in the area. His force was numerically strong, although it consisted largely of colonial troops trained and equipped for security only, and he used its strength to force the British out of British Somaliland. The British then launched a campaign to reclaim East Africa, which converged in a huge pincer movements on Amba Alagi, where the Duke made an heroic last stand. His eventual surrender was to save further useless loss of life and the British accorded him 'The Honours of War' for his gallantry. He died in British captivity in Nairobi in 1942. *Italian: (Pub. S. A. Grafitalia, Milan) Artist A. Porni. 1941. Value C*

103 *'Kurt Student.'* As Guderian was Germany's 'tank man,' so Student was their 'airborne man' *par excellence*. He commanded

Con fede incrollabile e visione eroica dei trionfi passati, marciate ai nuovi immancabili destini dell'Italia Imperiale.

Umberto di Savoia

100

101

102

103

104

AIR COMMODORE VALIN : National Commissioner for Air.
Le GENERAL VALIN : Commissaire National à l'Air.

105

GENERAL de LARMINAT : Deputy Commander in Chief in the Levant.
Le GENERAL de LARMINAT : Adjoint au Général d'armée Commandant en
Chef dans le Levant.

106

REAR ADMIRAL C. THIERRY D'ARGENLIEU : National Commissioner
without Portfolio.
CONTRE AMIRAL C. THIERRY D'ARGENLIEU : Commissaire National
sans Département.

107

the German airborne forces throughout the war, forming separate parachute divisions. In 1938, on being promoted Major General, Student created the first secret battalions of para-troopers. He was wounded in the fighting to take Rotterdam and was out of action until he planned the airborne operation in Crete in May 1941, a campaign that was

extremely costly in German casualties. Student was bitterly frustrated when Hitler cancelled his proposed invasion of Malta, but he was a calmly philosophical man and remained loyal to Hitler throughout the war. In 1944 Student was appointed G.O.C. 1st Parachute Army and with Model organized the defence of Arnhem. In

December 1944 the Ardennes attack floundered and he was again disappointed when his proposed thrust to Antwerp was put off. In April 1945, Keitel and Jodl sought to have Student put in charge of the defence of Berlin, but the move came too late to be implemented. *Caption on reverse reads: 'General of Airborne Forces Student.'*

German: *(Pub. for the National League for Germans Abroad) Artist W. Willrich. 1941. Value C*

104   *'Il Duce and Victor Emmanuel III: After Toil, Strength in Arms.'* In his delusions of grandeur, Mussolini saw himself recreating the glory that was the Roman Empire. 'The 20th Century will be the

Century of Fascism, of Italian Power, during which Italy will return for the third time to be the directing force in human civilization,' he proclaimed in 1932.

The main target for his Imperialist expansion plans was East Africa. In 1935, Italy had 250,000 men under arms in East Africa and Eritrea was made the base for the conquest of Ethiopia. In 1936 Eritrea was declared a province of the new Italian Empire with Tigre. When Addis Adaba fell on 5 May, Mussolini declared Victor Emmanuel (without consulting him) Emperor, to mark the establishment of Italian suzerainty over Abyssinia. This postcard celebrates the event. Pursuing a policy of what appeared to the world to be, 'if you can't beat 'em, join 'em,' Victor Emmanuel acquiesced with Mussolini and his Fascist policies, signing decrees that virtually eliminated his own power and the freedom of the press.

When the Allies entered Rome in June 1944, Victor Emmanuel named his son, Crown Prince Umberto, Lieutenant General of the Realm and, while retaining the title of King, formally relinquished all power. On 9 May 1946 he finally abdicated in favour of Umberto, whose reign lasted only one month.
Italian: (Pub. 'I.G.A.P.,' Roma) Artist Lalia. 1936. Value C

105   *'Air Commodore Valin, National Commissioner for Air.'*
French (probably): Value A

106   *'General de Larminat.'* Edgard de Larminat brought the French Congo into the Free French orbit in 1940.
French (probably): Value A

107   *'Rear Admiral C. Thierry D'Argenlieu, National Commissioner without portfolio.'*
French (probably): Value A

108   *'Marshal Stalin.'* Joseph Stalin came to power after the death of Lenin and consolidated his position by a series of purges in which he liquidated more Army officers than were killed during the whole four years of war with Nazi Germany. During what the Russians call 'the Great Patriotic War,' Stalin skilfully exploited the fact that his country had far more men in combat than the other Allies combined in order to influence President

Marshal Stalin

108

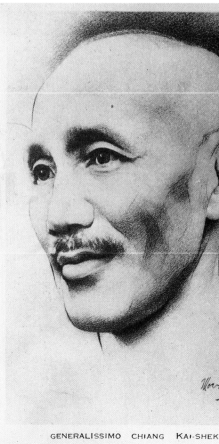

GENERALISSIMO   CHIANG   KAI-SHEK

109

Roosevelt towards Russian, rather than British, strategy. An official U.S.S.R. version of the D-Day landings reads, 'In June 1944 when it had become obvious that the Soviet Union was capable of defeating Hitler's Germany with her forces alone, England and the U.S.A. opened the Second Front.' Overlord and all operations in Western Europe that followed are dismissed in a few lines with the simple explanation that while the Germans had 60 divisions on the Western Front, they had 259 on the Eastern. *Prime Minister's message on the reverse reads: 'This is a time for everyone to stand together and hold firm.' French caption versions exist without the message. British: (Pub. Tuck) Value B*

109 *'Generalissimo Chiang Kai-Shek.' Prime Minister's message on the reverse reads: 'Let us all strive without failing in faith or in duty.' British: (Pub. Photochrom) Artist Morris J. Kellern. Circa 1943. Value A*

THE BRITISH ROYAL FAMILY

110 *'His Majesty the King'—Portrait by Hugh Cecil—As Fieldmarshal of the British Army. British: (Pub. Tuck) Circa 1940. Value A*

111 *'His Majesty the King'—Portrait by Karsh, Ottawa.* The famous Canadian photographer, Otto Karsh, catches George VI's quiet resolution as Admiral of the Fleet. *British: (Pub. Photochrom) Circa 1943. Value A*

112 *'His Majesty the King'—Portrait by Hugh Cecil—As Marshal of the Royal Air Force. British: (Pub. Tuck) Circa 1940. Value A*

113 *'H.R.H. Prince George, Duke of Kent.'* When war broke out the Duke of Kent cancelled his planned appointment as Governor General of Australia and served the Admiralty, first in London, and then at a northern base. In 1940 he transferred to the Ministry of Labour, and then the Royal Air Force, laying aside his titular rank of Air Vice-Marshal to become Group Captain. He worked tirelessly on the welfare front in the service and his promotion to Air Commodore in July 1941 was regarded as strictly

on merit. He toured Canada to inspect their air-training scheme, also making a brief visit to Washington. He was on a visit to Iceland when his 'plane crashed and the Duke was killed. He was given a Royal Military funeral at Windsor. He left a widow, Princess Marina (Duchess of Kent), and three children, Edward, Alexandra and Michael, who was born only seven weeks before his father's death in 1942. *British: (Pub. Tuck) No. 3982. 'Real Photograph' Postcard. Value B*

114 *'Queen Elizabeth.'* The Palace set its own standards of frugality and endeavour during the war. The ordinary basic rations (at the most supplemented by the rare game bird from a royal estate) were served to surprised guests on the usual gold plate. The Queen wore for the duration of the war the wardrobe which had been designed for her pre-war Tour of Canada. The Palace was itself bombed a total of nine times during the war and after the first hit, Elizabeth was recorded as saying, 'Now at last I can look the East End in the face.' They genuinely loved and were loved as few monarchs were before or since. *British: (Pub. Tuck) Portrait Cecil Beaton. Value A*

115 *'H.R.H. Princess Elizabeth.'* The Princess became 'bos'n' to a crew of Sea Rangers recruited from her friends and daughters of the Palace Staff on her 16th birthday. At 16 she also registered at the Labour Exchange and started her own list of engagements: inspecting youth organizations, receiving the Appointment of Colonel in Chief of the Grenadier Guards. At 19 she finally persuaded the King to allow her to join the A.T.S. She received an honorary commission as a second subaltern and learnt to drive at a training centre in Camberley, returning home triumphant through the thick of rush hour in an army car. *British: (Pub. Tuck) Portrait by Dorothy Wilding. 1942. Value A*

HIS MAJESTY THE KING

110

Portrait by Karsh, Ottawa

His Majesty the King

111

HER MAJESTY THE QUEEN

114

HIS MAJESTY THE KING

112

H.R.H. PRINCE GEORGE

113

H.R.H. THE PRINCESS ELIZABETH

115

CHAPTER THREE

Machines in the Air

117

116 *'Stuka Dive Bombers.'*
The Junkers Ju87 was the first
bomber used in the war and
led the air assault on Poland,
where its great accuracy was
useful in breaking up any
concentrations of Polish
forces that did manage to
gather together. Apart from
the effectiveness of its
weapons, the aircraft's
angular appearance and
high engine scream when in
its dive, added to the
terror it inspired. The name
Stuka comes from
'Sturzkampfflugzeug,' meaning dive bomber. Like the
He111, the He112 and other
new machines, it saw service
in Spain where at least three
examples were tried out.
*German: (Pub. Grieshaber
and Sauberlich. Stuttgart)
Artist Lotschke. 1940. Value C*

117 *'Fascist Wings
Command the Sky from
Gibraltar to the Red Sea.'*
The aeroplanes are probably
the artist's interpretation of
the three engined Savoia-
Marchetti SM79 bombers
with their distinctive bump

A s the First World War was essentially a struggle between men,
reported by the newspapers in
terms of thousands of casualties, so
World War II was a contest of
machines in which each side's score
was recorded by aeroplanes shot down, tanks
destroyed or ships sunk.

The major advances in weapon systems were in
the air, and every nation made massive use of the air
weapon. Prior to the outbreak of war it had been
supposed that strategic bombing would be a prime
factor in deciding the outcome of any European
conflict, and the threat of the Nazi's Luftwaffe
played an important part in the capitulation of
Chamberlain and Daladier at Munich. After the
defeat of France, the Third Reich took its first
preparatory step in Operation Sea Lion, the invasion
of England. That step was to obtain mastery of the air
across the Channel and over Southern England. The
fighting that followed was known as the Battle of
Britain and the men and machines of the Royal Air
Force became heroes to their people. The Spitfire
and Hurricane were drawn in every schoolboy's exercise books. So, too, were the angular, threatening
lines of the Stuka dive bomber. The aeroplane
represented the highest achievement of technology, life and death.

As each new machine was announced the
public eagerly scanned the published performance
figures to see if the latest model flew a little faster
than its predecessor. And the men who drew the
planes for magazines were almost as busy as the
flyers themselves. One man, whose wartime drawings will bring sharp tasting memories to anyone
who lived under the vapour-trailed skies of southern
England in the Summer of 1940, is A. F. D. Bannister.
He produced superb pictures for the old established
postcard company of J. Salmon Limited of Seven-
oaks, for whom he had been drawing since the early
1930's.

On 13 August (named *Adlertag* — Eagle day)
more than 1400 German planes initiated 24 hours of
bombing that continued at the same level for
another ten days. Fighter Command almost collapsed. Neither new pilots nor new planes were
coming in fast enough to replace losses, and without
radar and Ultra to help the R.A.F. the Luftwaffe
might well have been victorious.

However, on 7 September, Hitler switched the
attack to London — probably in reaction to the
R.A.F.'s raids on Berlin — and so saved Fighter
Command. Thus began the London 'Blitz,' which
reached its height on 15 September, when 56
German planes were shot down. In support of her
army, though, the Luftwaffe was more successful.

The German's *'Blitzkreig'* used the air arm in
close co-operation with ground forces right from the
beginning with the invasion of Poland and it was not
until the desert war of North Africa that Britain was
able to emulate that performance. But the Luftwaffe
had developed its fighter and fighter-bomber forces
at the expense of long range strategic bombers and
ultimately this was to prove a fatal weak link in
Germany's ability to carry the war to England.
Initially, the air war was conducted in an almost
gentlemanly fashion, with 'legitimate targets' being
confined to warships for fear of harming civilians.
Despite the Nazi invasion of Poland both sides spent
the Phoney War period hoping that peace might
somehow come about. Aircraft and air warfare
techniques developed rapidly. The fallacy of the
theory (adopted by both Britain and Germany) that
fast, lightly armed bombers could outpace enemy
fighters, was quickly proved. The Americans produced the Flying Fortress, a bomber supposedly
able to defend itself, and the Allies undertook
massive retaliation bomber raids by night and day
against German cities. In a last desperate attempt to
save the Third Reich, Hitler unleashed his V
weapons — the Flying Bomb and the V2 rocket.

In a little under six years air warfare had progressed from the 250mph Gloster Gladiator biplane
to the 3,000mph ballistic missile.

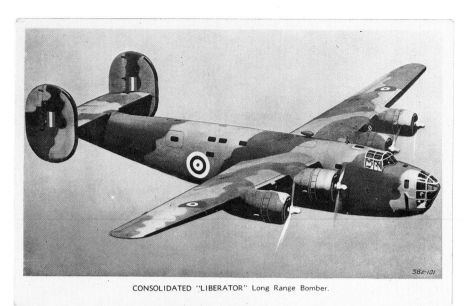

CONSOLIDATED "LIBERATOR" Long Range Bomber.

118

VICKERS WELLESLEY LONG RANGE BOMBER.

119

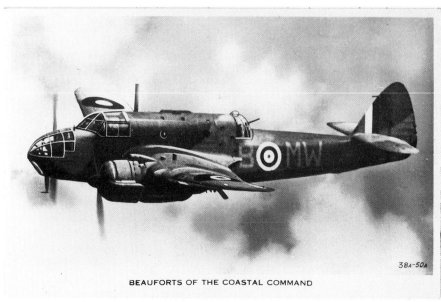

BEAUFORTS OF THE COASTAL COMMAND

120

above the pilot's compart-
ment. The backward facing
weapon in the bulge was a
12.7mm calibre machine
gun and fixed weapons were
fitted elsewhere. Known as
the Sparrowhawk, the SM79
established five world speed
records in 1938, but the
Italian Air Force (*Regia
Aeronautica*), which was
thought to be one of the
world's best before the war,
failed to keep up with
accelerating technical
development and was soon
outmatched by both
Germany and Britain.
Despite the proud boast on
this card, the *Regia
Aeronautica* was unable to
subdue Malta, and after
December 1940, when the
R.A.F. destroyed some 250
Italian planes in Libya, the
Italians never again posed
any serious threat. The
caption at the bottom reads:
*'To our fighting comrades
from the directors and
workers of the Carlo Erba
Company, Milan.'* Probably
the card was sponsored by
the Carlo Erba Company and
given free to servicemen to
use as a field postcard.
*Italian: (Official PNF Field
Postcard) Artist Boccasile.
Value C*

118 *'Consolidated
Liberator.'* Design on the
B24 Liberator began in 1939
with the aim of producing an
aircraft capable of carrying a
heavier load further than a
B17 Flying Fortress. The
Liberator's first operational
bombing mission with the
American 8th Air Force was
in the autumn of 1942.
24 machines set out for Lille
and 14 turned back due to
mechanical problems
(shades of the first use of
tanks in the Battle of the
Somme in 1916). The aircraft
fought in Europe, the
Mediterranean and in the
Pacific.
*British: (Pub. Valentine's)
No. 38A-101. Value B*

119 *'Vickers Wellesley Long
Range Bomber.'* The
Wellesley first flew in 1935
and stayed on active service
until 1941. It was one of the
earliest planes to use Barnes
Wallis' economical geodetic
construction, where a metal
skeleton was formed, over
which a fabric skin was
stretched. Top speed was
230 mph; armament: two
machine guns firing fore and
aft and the range was 1,100
miles.
*British: (Pub. Valentine's)
No. 38A-36. Value B*

120 *'Beaufort.'* The Bristol
Beaufort, made both in
Australia and in Britain, was
the standard Coastal Com-
mand torpedo bomber until
replaced by the Beaufighter
in 1943. It had a top speed of
260 mph and a range of
1,100 miles.
*British: (Pub. Valentine's)
No. 38A-50A. Value B*

121 *'Curtiss SBC-4 Dive
Bomber.'* This American
Navy plane served with the
Royal Navy early in the war
under the name
'Cleveland.'*British: (Pub.
Photochrom) No. 34. 'Britain
Prepared' scenes. Value A*

122 *'Supermarine Spitfires.'*
Of all British aeroplanes the
Spitfire became the prime
symbol of victory. Its elegant
lines and superior per-
formance over all German
aircraft during the Battle of
Britain made its name and
shape familiar to every
citizen of the land. If
machinery could qualify for
the Victoria Cross, the
Spitfire would have been
awarded dozens. The plane
derived from the
Supermarine Schneider
Trophy winners, and the
designer, R. J. Mitchell,
incorporated eight machine
guns at the behest of the Air
Ministry. Over 20,000 planes
were delivered to the R.A.F.,
some post war, and more
than 20 variants entered
service. It was not until the
FW190 appeared in 1942
that the Spitfire was seriously
challenged.
*British: (Pub. Photochrom)
No. 35. 'Britain Prepared'
series. Value B*

123 *'Buffalo 1 Fighter
Plane.'* The Buffalo turned
out to be something of a
disaster. It was innovatory in
that it was the first
monoplane fighter produced
for carrier use by the U.S.
Navy, but when it failed to
live up to expectations it was
quickly exported—to Finland
and to Britain. It had a top
speed of 320 mph and
carried four '50 calibre
machine guns. Prime
Minister's message on the
reverse reads: *'Let us all
strive without failing in faith
or in duty.'*
*British: (Pub. Photochrom)
No. 46. 'Britain Prepared'
series. Value A*

124 *'Fairey Battle.'* The
Battle first flew in 1936 and
in September 1939 claimed
the first German fighter kill of
the war. However, with a

121

122

123

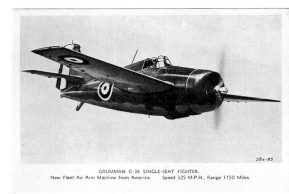

"HARVARDS," New American Planes in Service with the R.A.F.

128

124

125

126

GRUMMAN G-36 SINGLE-SEAT FIGHTER.
New Fleet Air Arm Machine from America.   Speed 325 M.P.H., Range 1150 Miles.

129

127

HAWKER "OSPREY" FLEET FIGHTER
H.M.S. "EAGLE" IN BACKGROUND

130

maximum speed of only 240 mph and one forward and one aft machine gun it was too slow and too lightly armed for the new warfare. *British: (Pub. Photochrom) No. 34. 'Britain Prepared' series. Value A*

125 *'Fairey Albercore.'* This aeroplane was the 'Albacore' and not as misspelt on the postcard. It was produced in order to replace the ageing Swordfish and while it flew faster and carried a slightly heavier bomb than the Swordfish, the latter was still in service when the Albacore was phased out in 1943. *British: (Pub. Photochrom) No. 38. 'Britain Prepared' series. Value A*

126 *'Boeing Flying Fortress B17F.'* The Fortress was used by the British in 1940 and 1941 and was progressively up-gunned. The American

8th Air Force used the Flying Fortress as the mainstay of their daylight bombing raids over Germany and the 17F model began to arrive in Britain in August 1942. It carried a crew of ten, had a maximum speed of 300 mph and a range of 2,000 miles. At the Chelveston base of the 301st Bombardment Group of the 8th Air Force was the English cartoonist Bruce Bairnsfather, acting as official artist to the Americans. On one B17 he painted his famous character 'Old Bill' and when the 'plane flew back from a mission with half its nose missing, it was left in front of the hangers to frighten newcomers into listening to their briefing instructions. Prime Minister's message on the reverse reads: *'This is a time for everyone to stand together and hold firm.'* *British: (Pub. Photochrom)*

No. 138. *'Britain Prepared' series. Circa 1942. Value B*

127 *'Handley Page Harrow.'* The Harrow had originally been a transport plane, but, with the prospect of war ahead, was converted to a bomber. However, in 1939 the Wellington replaced the Harrow in the offensive role and it returned to being a transport. *British: (Pub. Photochrom) No. 33. 'Britain Prepared' series. Value A*

AMERICAN SUPPORT
Not one American-made aeroplane fought in the First World War. Yet in World War II American-designed and manufactured machines were in combat even before the United States herself was at war. The moral and practical support given by the Americans was widely publicized—including via postcards.

HAWKER "NIMROD" FLEET FIGHTER

131

132

135

133

"HAMP

136

"BLENHEIM" FIGHTER-BOMBER

134

HURRIC
MES

137

MBER

ND
1ITT ME 109s

128 'Harvards. New American Planes in Service with the R.A.F.' British: (Pub. Valentine's) No. 39A-89. Value B

129 'Grumman G-36 Single-Seat Fighter. New Fleet Air Arm Machine from America. Speed 325 mph. Range 1,150 miles.' British: (Pub. Valentine's) No. 38A-85. Value B

FLEET AIR ARM

In 1924 a Fleet Air Arm was established with naval personnel who operated and specified machines built by the R.A.F. establishment. In 1938 the Navy took over total control of the Fleet Air Arm. Many F.A.A. aircraft were hybrids of pre-war R.A.F. designs for Navy use and increasingly whole-Navy concepts. The Osprey and Nimrod were typical Fleet 'planes, the latter also being used by the Danish Naval Service during the war.

130 'Hawker Osprey with H.M.S. Eagle in Background.' British: (Pub. Valentine's) No. 38A-64. Posted 1941. Value B

131 'Hawker Nimrod.' British: (Pub. Valentine's) No. 38A-63. Value B

132 'Hawker Hart Day Bombers.' These were the standard R.A.F. bombers of the 1930's with a top speed of 170 mph. There were a considerable number of variations developed from the basic design, such as the Hector and Demon. British: (Pub. Salmon) No. 4437. Artist Bannister. 1935. Value B

133 'Handley Page Heyford.' The mainstay of the R.A.F.'s night bomber squadrons in the 1930's, the Heyford had two Rolls Royce Kestrel engines and managed a top speed of 150 mph. The bombs were carried in the centre section of the lower wing. British.: (Pub. Salmon) No. 4439. Artist Bannister. 1935. Value B

134 'Bristol Blenheim.' Based on the Bristol transport 'plane, the Blenheim fighter bomber entered service in 1937. It was an all metal machine, carried a crew of three, had a range of 1,900 miles and a top speed of 290 mph. Blenheims were present in the first two British air missions of the war. Later versions had an extended

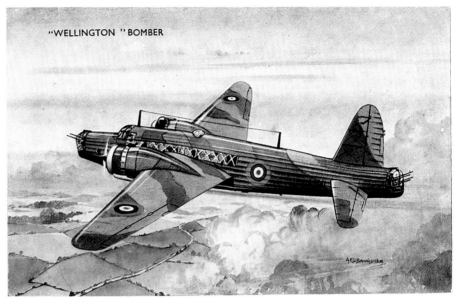

"WELLINGTON" BOMBER

138

"BRISTOL BEAUFORT" BOMBER.

139

WESTLAND "LYSANDERS"

140

bombardier's nose with a rearward firing, single gun turret below. The Blenheim 1F night fighter had airborne radar fitted as early as 1940. Caption on the reverse reads, *'Fighter bombers making machine gun attack on German aerodrome.'*
British: (Pub. Salmon)
No. 4849. Artist Bannister.
1940. Value B

135 *'Fairey Hendon.'* This aeroplane was introduced into R.A.F. service in 1936. It had a bomb load of 1,660lbs and a range of 1,300 miles. It might just have been able to fly to the 1936 Olympics, drop its bombs and return.
British: (Pub. Salmon)
No. 4440. Artist Bannister.
1935. Value B

136 *'Handley Page Hampden.'* This machine, one of the replacements for the Heyford, formed together with the Armstrong Whitworth Whitley and the Vickers Wellington, the trio of bombers with which the R.A.F. went to war in 1939. It was powered by two Bristol Pegasus XVIII's, and achieved a maximum speed of 265 mph, and a range of 1,700 miles.
British: (Pub. Salmon)
No. 4851. Artist Bannister.
1940. Value B

137 *'Hurricanes and Messerschmitt Me109's.'* The caption on the reverse reads: *'Down in flames. A Messerschmitt Me109 goes down under the guns of a*

Hurricane.' In 1940, schoolboys were either 'Spitfire men' or 'Hurricane men' and both machines could often be seen in action overhead. The Hurricane, designed by Sydney Camm, carried eight .303 calibre machine guns. It was credited with destroying more German aircraft than all the other British 'planes put together. The main strength of Fighter Command lay with the Hurricane which was the first R.A.F. fighter capable of exceeding 300 mph, and below 20,000ft it could outmanoeuvre the Me109E. More Me109's were made during World War II than any other type of aircraft. (The ex-schoolboy of the two of us was a 'Spitfire man.')
British: (Pub. Salmon)
No. 4866. Artist Bannister.
Circa 1940. Value B

138 *'Vickers-Armstrong Wellington.'* The Wellington 1 came into service in 1936 with a range of 2,500 miles and a bomb load of 4,000lbs. The geodetic design was conceived by Barnes Wallis, who had designed the R100 airship, would create the bouncing bombs for the Dam Busters, invent the swing-wing aircraft and work on the Concorde supersonic airliner. The Wellington was the best of the R.A.F.'s bombers at the beginning of the war.
British: (Pub. Salmon)
No. 4842. Artist Bannister.
Circa 1943. Value B

139 *'Bristol Beaufort.'* At the end of 1942, the Beaufort torpedo bomber was much used from Malta in raids on the Axis convoy routes, and thus played a part in the successful outcome of the battle of El Alamein by depriving the Afrika Korps of much needed supplies. However, when U.K. based Beauforts set out to bomb the *Scharnhorst* and *Gneisenau* as they steamed through the Channel in February of the same year, they didn't score even one hit. The basic design is similar to the Blenheim and the aeroplane remained in service until 1943.
British: (Pub. Salmon)
No. 4838. Artist Bannister.
Circa 1943. Value B

140 *'Westland Lysander.'* In 1938 the R.A.F. Army Co-operation Unit received its first monoplane—the

Lysander. The aircraft accompanied the B.E.F. to France, and with little Luftwaffe opposition to cope with, rendered valuable tactical support to the ground forces. The Lysander also saw service against the Japanese in the Far East. The card caption on the reverse claims a range of 600 miles and a top speed of 230 mph.
British: (Pub. Salmon)
No. 4852. Artist Bannister.
1940. Value B

141, 142, 143 *'Sunderland Flying Boats.'* These three cards show how the postcard changed to meet new circumstances. 141 shows the earliest version of the picture, full out with a brief caption. 142 shows the second printing of the card, now with the R.A.F. wings on the front plus a descriptive caption. (Most Salmon war 'plane cards were reprinted in this way.) 143 shows the white flying boat camouflaged for war. In sequence the cards were probably issued around 1939, 1940 and 1941. The last edition carries the Prime Minister's message on the reverse: *'This is a time for everyone to stand together and hold firm.'* All cards have the number 4844.
British: (Pub. Salmon) 141, 142 Value A, 143 Value B

144 *'Vickers-Supermarine Scapa.'* This is a fairly typical flying boat of the type used for maritime patrols between the wars. The two Kestrel engines developed 525 hp.
British: (Pub. Salmon)
No. 4436. Circa 1935.
Value A

145 *'Hudson Reconnaissance.'* This British specified American Lockheed-built 'plane was in service with R.A.F. Coastal Command in 1938 as a navigational trainer, but it replaced the Avro Anson (Faithful Annie) on anti-submarine duties and maritime patrols. It was a Hudson which spotted the German ship *Altmark* in February 1940, leading to its interception and the release of the British prisoners of war on board. The Hudson is also claimed to be the first aircraft to sink a U-boat with rockets—in May 1943. Some 2,000 Hudsons, a mixture of outright purchase and Lend-Lease, were eventually taken by the R.A.F. Late models were used by the U.S. army air force and navy.

British: (Pub. Salmon)
No. 4847. Artist Bannister.
Circa 1940. Value B

146 *'Gloster 1V. Racing Seaplane.'* The First World War forced the development of the aeroplane as a hot-house forces plants, and as the military and commercial potential of flying machines became clearer, so nations which could afford to do so, set up their own civil and military flying organizations. The air was the place where the frontiers of science could be explored, and individuals and nations competed to fly the highest, fastest and farthest. One of the most famous international competitions was the bi-annual Schneider Trophy Race for maritime aircraft—hence 'Racing Seaplane.' The R.A.F. entered for the first time in 1927 and won with a world speed record of 281 mph. In 1929 they won again with a Supermarine S6, reaching 328 mph and then took the Trophy permanently in 1936 with an S6b at 340 mph. The designer of the S6 was Reginald Mitchell and from his experience in designing these racing seaplanes he created the Spitfire.
British: (Pub. Salmon)
No. 3506. Circa 1935.
Value A

147 *'Hurricanes and Messerschmitt Me110's.'* The Me110 was developed in order to accompany bombers well into enemy territory, since machines like the Dornier 17, the Heinkel He111 and the Ju88 all relied upon their speed rather than upon their defensive armament, for protection. The Me110 was slower and less manoeuvrable than the Hurricane and fared very badly in the Battle of Britain, which led to its withdrawal from service. However, when Me210 production stopped in April 1942 the G and H models of the 110 were stepped up, the latter version doing well as a night fighter. Caption on reverse reads: *'Dive attack by Hurricanes on two Messerschmitt Me110's.'*
British: (Pub. Salmon)
No. 4867. Artist Bannister.
Circa 1940. Value B

148 *'Blackburn Skuas.'* The Skua was the only British dive-bomber to sink a major German ship—the light cruiser *Konigsberg* in Bergen. At the time the Skuas

141

142

143

involved in the action were land based, but the British-designed aircraft was a Fleet Air Arm machine, the first monoplane to join that Service. In action from 1939 to 1941 the Skua carried one 500lb bomb, presumably the one heading for the German warship in the drawing which conveniently has a swastika on its deck to identify it as a legitimate target.
British (Pub. Salmon)
No. 4865. Circa 1940.
Value B

149 *'The Pterodactyl.'*
A 1930's version of the aeroplanes of the future. The delta-wing in the background eventually turned into the post war V bombers. The Pterodactyl in the foreground is described on the reverse as *'An all metal biplane with . . . automatic stability . . . and four propellors. The engines are mounted in a central engine room in the fuselage.'*
British: (Pub. Salmon)
No. 3510.
Artist possibly Bannister.
Value A

150 *'Spitfire and Heinkel 111K.'* The He111 saw its first operational use in the Spanish Civil War and by 1939 was the Luftwaffe's standard level bomber. It was used in the invasion of Poland and then onward in a variety of modifications until almost the end of the war. The bomber, called 'The Spade' by its crews, was produced in larger numbers than any other German machine and was able to carry torpedoes in external racks.
British: (Pub. Salmon)
No. 4868. Artist Bannister.
Circa 1940. Value B

151 *'Roc Fleet Fighter.'*
Blackburn set out to combine the qualities of the Skua air frame and the Defiant (Boulton Paul) four gun powered turret. The result was the Fleet Air Arm Roc, which in theory was supposed to be able to pull alongside an enemy bomber and kill it with a broadside. The concept was not a success. Like the Defiant, the Roc was extremely vulner-able to head-on attack. Less than 150 models were built and production ceased in 1940.
British: (Pub. Salmon)
No. 4848. Circa 1940.
Value B

152 *'Armstrong Whitworth Whitley.'* This twin engined heavy bomber carried a crew of five, one more than the Hampden, had a range of 1,250 miles and a top speed of 254 mph. Its bomb load of 8,000lbs was almost twice that of the other R.A.F. 'planes in its class. As with most aeroplanes, there were a good few variations on a basic airframe—sometimes occasioning the addition of a letter to the identification number as with the American Flying Fortresses, e.g. B17B, 17C, 17D, or earning a different 'Mark' number. This drawing, complete with what may be the Ruhr under attack, is probably meant to be the Whitley Mark V.
British: (Pub. Salmon)
No. 4850. Artist Bannister.
1944. Value B

153 *'Spitfires and Dornier Do215's.'* The Do215 was an export version of the civilian Luftwaffe Do17, which had been designed in 1934 as a mail-cum-passenger carrier. Although rejected by the civilian authorities in its original form because of inadequate passenger accommodation (it was so thin that it became known as 'the Flying Pencil'), it was developed into a fast bomber, which saw action in Spain and then throughout the war. The Spitfire's major enemy in the Battle of Britain was the Me109 which it could out-manoeuvre if not out-run, although the Me109 could climb and dive faster. Caption on reverse reads: *'Spitfires breaking up a formation of Dornier Do215's'.*
British: (Pub. Salmon)
No. 4869. Artist Bannister.
Circa 1940. Value B

154 *'Defiants and Junkers 88K's.'* The Boulton-Paul Defiant had all four of its .303 calibre machine guns contained within the single power-driven turret which can be seen in the picture. Because of its close resemblance to the Hurricane, whose guns could only fire forward, the Defiant was at first attacked from the rear and ran up a splendid score at Dunkirk until the Luftwaffe realized what was happening. The Defiant was not produced after 1943 but the Junkers 88, probably the most versatile German aircraft of all, continued throughout

144

"HUDSON" RECONNAISSANCE

145

146

HURRICANES AND
MESSERSCHMITT ME 110s

147

149

BLACKBURN SKUAS

148

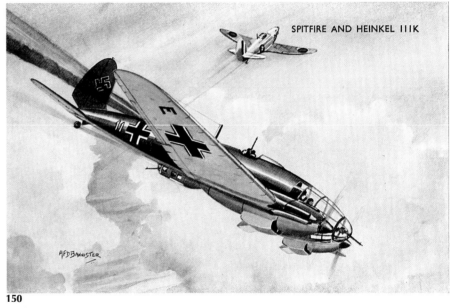

SPITFIRE AND HEINKEL 111K

150

"ROC" FLEET FIGHTER

151

the war. The Defiant served as a bomber for day and night operations, a night fighter, and a maritime bomber. Later versions achieved maximum speeds of over 400 mph.
British: (Pub. Salmon) No. 4870. Circa 1940. Value B

FIVE BATTLE SCENES. On 4 September 1939, 24 hours after Britain declared war, 29 Bristol Blenheims set out to bomb German naval vessels near Kiel. Seven machines were lost and the General Purpose bombs used did not cause much damage. It was the first air raid of the war and was dramatically, if un-Britishly, recorded on mock photo postcards. There were other firsts too. The Avro Anson, Faithful Annie, remained in production for 17 years and, though near obsolescence and supposedly on recon- naissance duties at the beginning of the war, it was credited with the first aerial attack upon a German submarine.

155 *'Bristol Blenheims Raid Kiel.'*
British: (Pub. Valentine's) No. 38W-1. Circa 1939. Value B

156 *'Bristol Blenheims Raid Kiel.'*
British: (Pub.Valentine's) No. 38W-2. Circa 1939. Value B

157 *'Avro Anson Sinking a German Submarine.'*
British: (Pub. Valentine's) No. 38W-4. Circa 1939. Value B

158 *'Bristol Blenheims Raid Borkum.'*
British: (Pub. Valentine's) No. 38W-3. Circa 1939. Value B

159 *'Westland Lysander Shooting Down a Heinkel.'*
British: (Pub. Valentine's) No. 38W-8. Circa 1939. Value B

160 *'Heinkel He112.'* Produced before the war as a rival to the Messerschmitt Me109, the He119 had no special qualities that made it of particular value. However, it was tried out in Spain and its main claim to fame is as the first experimental vehicle for Ernst Heinkel and Wernher von Braun, who were perfecting their rocket engines. This was done as early as 1937 but the Luftwaffe showed no interest.
British: (Pub. Valentine's) No. 38A-74. Value B

152

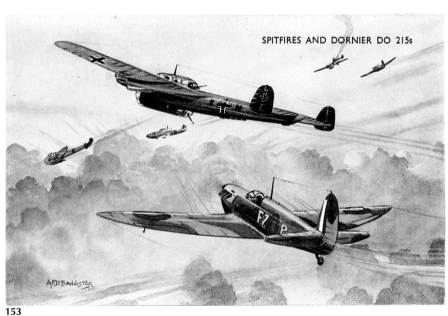

153

154

"BRISTOL BLENHEIMS" RAID KIEL.
THE FIRST AIR RAID OF THE WAR.

155

"BRISTOL BLENHEIMS" RAID KEIL.
THE FIRST AIR RAID OF THE WAR

156

AVRO "ANSON" SINKING
A GERMAN SUBMARINE.

157

"BRISTOL BLENHEIMS" RAID AN
ENEMY SEAPLANE BASE AT BORKUM.

158

"WESTLAND LYSANDER" SHOOTING DOWN
A GERMAN HEINKEL 'PLANE

159

GERMAN "HEINKEL" HE.112
SINGLE SEAT FIGHTER

160

161 'Junkers Ju88.' The picture shows a Ju88 being refuelled in Denmark. The location may well be Aalborg where part of Luftflotte 5 was based. The remainder of the Air Fleet, all commanded by General Stumpff, was based in Norway. Luftflotte 5 only took part in the Battle of Britain for one day— 15 August 1940—and its losses were so high that 'planes from such a distance were not employed again. The Ju88 was probably Germany's most versatile aeroplane, serving as a bomber, ground support and reconnaissance aircraft, and as a day/night fighter. *German: (Pub. Carl Werner. Reichenbach) Danish text for consumption by occupied Denmark. Value C*

162 'Bombing-up a Wellington.' More than a little 'Two-Six' would be needed to load this monster bomb even though it has its own wheeled trolley. 'Two-Six' was the R.A.F. call meaning 'All hands to help.' The 2,000lb MC (Medium Capacity) was dwarfed in 1941 by the 4,000lb HC (High Capacity), 'Dangerous Dustbin,' which in turn was made to look small by the 20,000lb Grand Slam. *British: (Pub. G.P.D.) No. 445/2/5. Value B*

163 'Royal Air Force Balloon Barrage.' A popular catch question during the war was, 'What is a barrage balloon for?' The correct answer was, 'To hold up its wire.' The danger to the aircraft was the invisible steel hawser, which could slice 'plane and pilot in two. Thus the balloons acted as deterrents to low flying attack, and, particularly in the early part of the war when high level precision bombing was poorly developed, balloons provided a formidable defence for targets such as power stations and airfields. *British: (Pub. Valentine's) No. 38A-22. Value B*

164 'Savoia Bomber.' This photograph shows the front end of a Savoia-Marchetti SM79 bomber which was captured in North Africa and put on public display in Cairo and Alexandria. *Egyptian: Explanatory text on reverse in French, English and Arabic. Posted 10 October 1940 in Cairo, the month by which the*

Italians had consolidated their advance into Egypt by establishing camps at Sidi Barrani and eight weeks before Wavell threw them out again. *Value C*

165 'British Stirlings and Their Bomb Loads.' British bombers were capable of larger bomb loads than their American counterparts and could often carry a more effective mix of types. There were four major categories of bombs: incendiary, fragmentation, armour-piercing and general effect. The proportion of each type carried by any bombing formation was related to the desired result, and as more experience was obtained so effects could be accurately forecast. By the end of the war the formula for an incendiary raid would be: first general purpose bombs to create the blast effect, then incendiaries to start the fires followed by more general purpose bombs to spread the flames. The Stirlings' bomb bay configuration, however, prevented it from carrying bombs larger than 4,000lbs, but its bomb load was 14,000lbs compared to the Flying Fortresses' 6,700lbs. *Nationality and Pub. uncertain, probably British sponsored: Caption in English, Spanish and Portuguese. Value B*

Tysk Kamp- og Styrtkampflyvemaskine Ju 88 bliver forsynet med Benzin

161

"BOMBING-UP" AN R.A.F. "WELLINGTON" An R.A.F. "Wellington" waits to be loaded with this 2,000 lb. bomb, one of the weapons which are devastating Germany's capacity for making war.

For Freedom

162

ROYAL AIR FORCE BALLOON BARRAGE.   38A-22

163

164

British "Stirling" aircraft with part of their enormous bomb-load.
Bombardeiros britânicos "Stirling" metendo parte do formidavel carregamento de bombas.
Un avión británico "Stirling" con parte de su enorme cargamento de bombas.

165

CHAPTER FOUR

Machines on the Land

167

166 *'Anti-Aircraft Guns in Action.'* This Italian card was posted on 4 June 1943, hardly a month before the Sicily landings and in the same year that Italy and Germany became enemies. There was plenty of action ahead for the Italian Sixth Army quite as dramatic as this picture.
Italian: (Official Field Postcard) 1943. Value B

167 *'Air Defence Display.* The gun pictured resembles the 40mm Bofors, which threw 2lb high explosive shells into the air at the astounding rate of two per second, and which with the 20mm Oerlikon was the mainstay of Allied anti-aircraft defence. The normal mounting was on a four-wheeled trailer, but the two-wheeled units were produced for airborne use. Here the searchlights have 'acquired' their targets and the guns have already shot

s the importance of air power grew, so the defences against attack from the air had to develop to keep pace with the increasing threat.

Anti-aircraft guns were linked to sophisticated prediction devices which calculated, from the direction, speed and height of attacking enemy planes, where the guns should be aimed to score a hit.

Coastal areas were liberally sprinkled with detector stations using the newly perfected device of radar. It had been discovered quite independently and almost simultaneously in America, England, France and Germany in the 1930's. Britain was the first to put into effect a system of working radar early warning stations. Called 'Chain Home' (CH) stations, they incorporated the revolutionary British discovery of the powerful multicavity magnetron transmitting tube from its invention in 1940, and it was this device which made possible the long range effectiveness of Chain Home. Indeed, so efficient were the stations that attacking enemy formations were detected as they assembled to cross the Channel, and Fighter Command had sufficient warning to enable it to position its forces to maximum effect. The name of the device is an acronym, coined by the U.S. Navy in 1942, from the initials for 'Radio Detecting And Ranging.'

On the land warfare scene, the weapon which developed most dramatically during World War II was undoubtedly the tank which probably reached its apogee in the desert warfare in North Africa. There Rommel, 'The Desert Fox,' and his Afrika Korps, gave the tank a romantic image. This was furthered by General Patton in his dashing use of the tank in the race with Montgomery towards Berlin in 1944-45.

In contrast to the modernity and mobility of the tank was the static defensive 'line,' which was the main characteristic of the First World War, with its system of trenches and fortified dugouts. A defensive 'line' was maintained by the Germans and the

French along their common border. The German side was known as the 'Siegfried Line,' and the French as the 'Maginot Line.' The Allies anticipated a repetition of the Schlieffen Plan, which had been ineffectually altered by Kluck in August 1914, and they planned to counter it by pivoting the First Army Group from the northern tip of the Maginot Line.

When Germany invaded in May 1940, the Belgian fort at Eben Emael on the Albert Canal, thought to be impregnable, fell due to a daring assault by gliders, and the Belgians abandoned their line of the Meuse. The Germans broke through at Sedan and Guderian's tanks raced forward, virtually cutting off the Allied force in the Maginot Line.

The months of planning and construction and the vast expense of the Maginot Line had proved totally ineffectual against the German's strong, mobile, swift initiative.

168

171

169

172

173

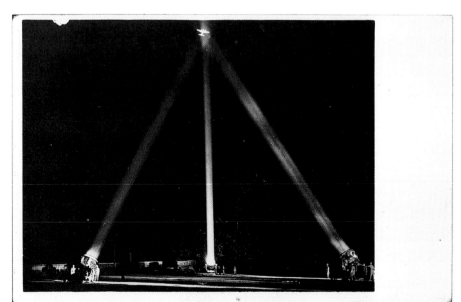

170

174

one down. All this apparently happened at the Royal Tournament for which this card was a souvenir. The guns, however, would not have fired live ammunition into the air because what went up had to come down.
British: (Pub. Fleetway Press (1930) Ltd.) Value A

168 *'V2.'* The *Vergeltungswaffe* (Reprisal) weapons were planned by Hitler as retaliation for the bombing of Germany. The V1 flying bomb, or 'doodlebug,' began its life as the FZG-76 at the Peenemunde research station. It was driven by a pulsating flow duct motor and carried an 1,850lb explosive warhead. When it ran out of fuel the engine stopped and the machine fell to earth. Although V1's were not used until after June 1944, over 30,000 were produced. The V2, or A-4 rocket, was first launched successfully on 3 October 1942 and production then began at Peenemunde. It was a ballistic missile fuelled by liquid oxygen, which carried one ton of high explosive. Its first operational firing was against Paris on 6 September 1944—the missiles exploded before they reached their target.
Dutch: (Pub. Foto Stevens, Haarlem) No. 1045. Circa 1945. Value D

169 *'V2.'* The V1 weapons were launched from coastal sites which were progressively over-run as the Allied invasion forces spread out. Although an Allied air raid in August 1943 had made production at Peenemunde impossible for the V2, by moving operations to an underground factory in the Harz mountains, a rate of 900 rockets a month was reached. Unlike the V1, the V2 could be launched from a mobile platform which made it difficult to locate, and since the missile's speed was supersonic there was no warning of its approach. About 10,000 V2's were produced altogether, and when the first explosions occurred in London their origin was a complete mystery. The missile was 46ft long and weighed over 13 tons at launch.
Dutch: (Pub. Foto Stevens, Haarlem). No. 1045 (probably a series number). Circa 1945. Value D

170 *'Caught.'*
German: (Pub. B. Mitschke, Oberhof) 1941. Value B

171 *'Predictor, Height Finder and 3.7 A.A. Gun.'* The heavy ack ack guns were generally controlled by electromechanical devices, which enabled the weapon to change its aim according to directions fed into it. At the beginning of the war, although the Chain Home radar stations had been completed, most detection of enemy aircraft for gunfire purposes was done visually or by sound detectors. Once an enemy aircraft had been located, its distance, altitude, speed and direction were 'fed' into the Predictor. The apparatus then calculated where the aeroplane would be by the time a shell got to it and the gun was aimed and fired accordingly. This picture shows the complete ack ack system—the Height Finder visually determines the aircraft's position, the Predictor calculates where to point the gun and the gun shoots the shell.
British (Pub. Valentine's) No. 38-E4. 1938. Value B

172 *'3.7in Anti-Aircraft Gun.'* The chances of hitting an aeroplane with a shell are very slim indeed. One veteran anti-aircraft man who served with a Bofors unit throughout the war said that the only 'plane he ever hit was one of our own. Heavy guns, therefore, were equipped with sophisticated ammunition, carrying time or proximity fuses so that an explosion could be produced in the vicinity of a target. This would often be sufficient to damage the 'plane and cause it to crash. Arrangement of guns in patterns in order to produce barrages through which enemy 'planes had to fly, improved the hit rate enormously but the fall-out of lead from the sky onto the population below was horrendous.
British: (Pub. Valentine's) No. 38-D2. 1938. Value B

173 *'Predictor.'* This early form of artillery computer worked on the assumption that aeroplanes flew in straight lines at a fixed height. Thus, if it were told where an aeroplane was, it could work out where the aeroplane was going to be shortly afterwards. Knowing the flight time of the ack ack shell, the future position of

the aeroplane at the end of that time was obtained and the gun pointed and fired there. The information was initially fed into the Predictor (having been obtained from the Height/Range Finder) by small constant velocity handwheels. At least three of the five men in the picture are winding handles. World War II wags would say that the other two were there to hold the horses.
British: (Pub. Valentine's) No. 38-D8. Value B

174 *'90cm AA Searchlights.'* At night, detection of enemy aircraft relied on sound detectors until, as the war progressed, radar was developed. Having found out roughly where the enemy was, searchlights would sweep the sky seeking their targets. Often barrage balloons would be used in an attempt to channel the enemy into areas where anti-aircraft barrages were set up and waiting. Once the searchlight 'acquired' its target it would 'track it' and this tracking information would be fed to the Predictor. The message on this card reads: *'Dear Laddie, Here's some more soldiers with a searchlight—one of those things that send up beams of light after dark to pick out aeroplanes. . . . I expect your page of Rules for Monopoly will come soon. I have written for it. . . . Love Daddy.'*
British: (Pub. Valentine's) No. 38-E5. Posted 6 November 1939. Value B

175 *'A Mobile Column (Somewhere in France).'* Those old enough to remember the war will say 'Bren Gun Carriers' when they see this picture. The tracked vehicle is actually the British Universal Carrier. It was designed for a wide range of roles: reconnaissance vehicle, cross country ambulance, forward support vehicle and . . . bren gun carrier. This column appears to be of Mk 1 carriers armed with bren guns. Their function was mobile fire support, but often they ended up retrieving infantiers from positions under enemy fire. The leading vehicle has a driver, four men, a portable bren gun and a fixed, forward-firing, weapon.
British: (Pub. Photochrom) No. 21. 'Britain Prepared' series. Value B

175

176

177

178

LEICHTE FLAK GEGEN TIEFFLIEGENDE FLUGZEUGE

179

POSTKARTE

KdF.-Sammlergruppen, Abgabepreis 20 Rpf.

MIT UNSEREN FAHNEN IST DER SIEG!

180

ANTI-AIRCRAFT ARTILLERY

BOMBARDIER
(FIELD DRESS)

N.C.O.
(WALKING-OUT) DRESS

OFFICER
(FIELD SERVICE DRESS)

3·7 ANTI-AIRCRAFT SECTION IN ACTION

181

176 'Bren Gun Carriers (Somewhere in France)'. German reports often referred to the carrier as a tank, a mistake perhaps prompted by the fact that some carriers did have small anti-tank guns, such as the Boys rifle and the 2-pounder. *British: (Pub. Photochrom) No. 14. 'Britain Prepared' series. Value B*

177 'Passing Through a Village (Somewhere in France).' After the Nazi *Blitzkrieg* on Poland, the war settled into an eight month lull, jocularly called the 'Sitzkrieg.' Correspondents from Britain flocked to the Continent in organized parties and sent back their reports from 'Somewhere in France.' *British: (Pub. Photochrom) No. 24. 'Britain Prepared' series. Value B*

178 'Light Tanks (Somewhere in France).' On 4 May 1940 seven Panzer Divisions punched across the frontiers of Belgium and Luxembourg and the 'Sitzkrieg' was over. Just two weeks later the B.E.F. was being ferried back to England by the Little Ships, and by 4 June the last of the 338,000 British and Belgian soldiers had landed in Britain. These tanks, indeed all of the B.E.F.'s equipment was left in France and oddly the loss of so much armour spurred the British to come to terms with modern warfare and to accelerate the development of new armoured fighting vehicles. *British: (Pub. Photochrom) No. 15. 'Britain Prepared' series. Value B*

179 'Light Anti-Aircraft Defence Against Low Flying Aircraft.' Both the 20mm Oerlikon and the 40mm Bofors, numbers of which were captured in Poland and France, were used by the Germans. Light weapons, such as this one, were used for close-in defence and fired solid shot, tracer and incendiaries. In order to damage a target, direct hits had to be obtained, and to achieve a hit, light guns had to be used in clusters, firing at a very high rate. The aimer is sitting behind the gun looking through a telescopic sight and the man holding what appears to be a horizontal tube to his face is looking through a range finder.

German: (Pub. 'Die Wehrmacht' (Illustrated War Magazine)) Value B

180 'With Our Flag is Victory.' The flag is that of the Luftwaffe and it can be argued that the failure of Goering's boys to win the Battle of Britain lost the war for Germany. Searchlights—like barrage balloons and ack ack guns—were generally positioned to give interlocking beams, thus creating the effect of a barrier to oncoming aircraft. *German: (Official Card) Artist von Axel-Heudtlass. Value C*

181 'Anti-Aircraft Artillery.' This picture is very similar to those produced in millions during the First World War where dramatic, colourful if simple, designs promoted the image of the Fighting Forces. The guns depicted are 3.7in heavy ack ack weapons. *British: (Pub. Valentine's) Artist Bryan de Grineau. Circa 1939. Value A*

RUSSIA
In 1942 the tide of war turned against the Nazis. Not only were they defeated in North Africa at Alamein, but the battle for Stalingrad was lost. In Russia over 1,000 tanks were captured or destroyed and by December the strengthening Russian Army and the freezing weather were forcing the Germans westwards. The picture magazine *Signal*, which until now had reported events reasonably accurately, found itself having to cover up and repeat past glories. Dramatic pictorial propaganda be-came even more important to sustain the will of those at home to continue to bear the hardships of daily life.

182 'In a Russian Wood.' *German: (Pub. Erich Gutjahr. Berlin) Artist Hermann Schneider. 1942. Posted February 1943. Value C*

183 'Destroyed Russian Tank.' *German: (Pub. Erich Gutjahr. Berlin) Artist Hermann Schneider. 1942. Value C*

184 'Assault Gun Action in Russia.' This is an artist's impression of the SdKfz assault gun which carried a 7.5cm weapon with a limited 12° left and 12° right traverse. Assault guns were designed to provide im-mediate direct fire artillery support for infantry attacks,

182

184

183

185

186

VORSTOSS UNSERER TRUPPEN IN NORD-AFRIKA

particularly in the reduction of fortifications. The self-propelled versions, such as this, were cheap substitutes for the tank, much used by the Germans and the Russians. The SdKfz 142 went into Russian territory in June 1941 with the 6th Assault Artillery Battalion. *German: (Pub. Friedrich Ebert) No. 38. One of a series entitled 'The War Victims Wall Calendar,' which was sold to raise funds for Party members injured in the war. Circa 1941. Value C*

185 *'Motor Convoy.'* This splendid artist's impression has as its centre piece the SdKfz 232 heavy armoured radio car. The grid-like contraption on top is the frame antenna for the long-range radio. The car saw service in Austria and Czechoslovakia prior to the war and took part in the Polish and French campaigns. However, the vehicle had very limited mobility off the road and was withdrawn from front line service in 1940. It had six wheels, weighed around 5.5 tons and managed a top speed of 45 mph. *German: Artist Gotschke. No. 34. 1940. Value C*

186 *'Our Troops Punch Forward in North Africa.'* The Germans did not intend to become involved in North Africa because it was in the agreed area of Italian political influence. However, following the failure of the Army after its first advance into Egypt, Mussolini asked his friend, Hitler, for help. Eventually Hitler agreed, and despatched the 5th Light Division and 15th Panzer Division, the combined force to be known as the Deutsches Afrika Korps and to be commanded by Erwin Rommel. Amongst the deliveries which arrived at Tripoli early in 1941 were PzKpfw III's, one of which is seen here. The German General Staff had decided upon two types of tank—a light one and a medium one, both of which were to have good cross-country performance. The PzKpfw III began as a compromise between these requirements, but successive variants produced an effective tank. Initially there was a crew of five, a top speed of 20 mph and for armament a 37mm cannon and three machine guns. Within a few weeks of his arrival in North Africa and before the whole of his

187 British Army " Valentine " (Mark III) tanks drawn up in imposing array for an inspection by King George **VI.**
Uma impressionante concentração de tanks " Valentines," do exercito britânico que foi passada em revista pelo Rei Jorge **VI.**
Tanques " Valentine " del Ejército Británico dispuestos en una formación imponente para ser revistados por el Rey Jorge **VI.**

" Valentines " (Mark III), Britain's new infantry tanks, advance to attack during training.
Uma formação dos novos tanks de infantaria " Valentines," avançando para o ataque durante uns exercícios.
Avance de unos " Valentine," nuevos tanques británicos de infantería, durante unas maniobras.

188

British cruiser-tanks moving over rough ground at Tobruk.
Tanks pesados britânicos avançando em terreno acidentado em Tobruk.
Tanques cruceros británicos avanzando sobre terreno abrupto en Tobruk.

189

forces arrived, Rommel attacked, driving the British back into Egypt. He and the Afrika Korps dominated the African scene until the end of 1942.
German: (Pub. 'Die Wehrmacht' (Illustrated War Magazine)) Circa 1941. Value C.

187 *'Valentine Mark III Tanks Drawn Up For Inspection by King George VI.'* Pre-war tank tactics demanded two types of vehicle. One was to be a cruiser tank for use in open country by the cavalry and the other a slower more heavily armoured vehicle to support the infantry. The Valentine was a private venture by Vickers supposedly to meet the infantry, or 'I,' requirement. In fact it was rather more a slow, well-armoured cruiser. In July 1939, 275 were ordered for delivery in the shortest possible time and the first ones came into service in May 1940, though later, instead of being issued to Infantry Division Tank Brigades, many were taken by the cavalry to make up their losses incurred at Dunkirk.
British (though possibly published in Portugal): Text in English, Spanish and Portuguese. Value B

188 *'Valentines Advance to Attack During Training.'* The Valentine was destined for a long and varied career. Although the 2-pounder gun was virtually obsolescent when it was fitted, the engine and transmission were simple and reliable. Production continued until 1944 by which time over 8,000 had been made. It was converted to more roles than any other British tank: amphibian, SP gun, flame-thrower, minefield clearing, armoured recovery and so on. More than 1,000 were made in Canada and most of these, plus another 1,300 from Britain were sent to Russia. But the tanks' first action was in the Western Desert in 1941 and they fought right through the campaign which cleared the Axis from North Africa.
British: Text in English, Portuguese and Spanish. Value B

189 *'British Cruiser Tanks at Tobruk.'* Tobruk was once the main Italian fortress in Libya and a vital target for the British as a port through

which to supply their desert army. In January 1941 it was taken from the Italians in two days of fighting by the 16th Australian Brigade and the 19th Brigade, though the Italians fought determinedly, bringing their ack ack guns into use as field pieces. 30,000 prisoners, 236 guns and 87 tanks were captured. There were so many vehicles that nobody bothered to count them. In 1941 Rommel besieged the port from April to December and then recaptured it in June 1942. It was the last time. The 10th Corps of the 8th Army retook Tobruk in November—and kept it.
British: Text in English, Portuguese and Spanish. Value B

190 *'The Battle of Overloon.'* Following the failure of Operation Market Garden and the holding of XXX Corps at Nijmegen, the Germans strengthened their line, prompting Montgomery to ask for further assistance from Eisenhower. On 30 September the U.S. 7th Tank Division made a five point thrust towards the River Maas and the small town of Overloon to the south of Nijmegen and east of Veghel. The splitting of the armoured force into so many sub-units reduced its effect and though some ground was won, the Americans suffered heavy losses and were withdrawn from the battle on 8 October. The task was re-assigned to the 3rd (BR) Division who took the town on 12 October in a fiercely contested struggle that was called 'the second Caen.' This card shows a member of the 3rd Division entering the village, followed by Churchill tanks. Today Overloon is the site of the Dutch National War and Resistance Museum.
Dutch: Circa 1945. Value B

191 *'Light Scout Car.'* This is probably a variant of the SdKfz 222, which was in service with the German Army from 1938 to 1945, and gave good service in North Africa. These machines were issued to *Panzerspahwagen* squadrons of the Reconnaissance Battalions and accompanied the heavier armoured cars to provide covering fire as well as short range radio links. It had a road speed of 50 mph and in its basic form carried a 20mm cannon and a 7.92 machine gun. *German: (Pub. 'Die Wehrmacht' (Illustrated War Magazine)) Value B*

192 *'A Wehrmacht Tank.'* This is a PzKpfw 1 Light Tank which saw service from 1934 to 1944 in a variety of roles. It was introduced shortly after the Germans openly began to re-arm in 1933 as a base from which armoured tactics could be tried out and a wider range of equipment could be developed. It was a two man vehicle with a hand traversed turret plus two machine guns, both fired by the Commander. The PzKpfw 1 saw action in the Spanish Civil War, in Poland, the Netherlands, North Africa and Russia. It was one of the few armoured vehicles susceptible to the British 2-pounder, which destroyed a good many during the retreat to Dunkirk. As the war brought developments in armoured weaponry so **the PzKpfw became dated** and was employed in other than tank roles. The Commander standing in his turret is wearing the black uniform worn by all those serving in armoured vehicles. His hat is the large black beret, pulled backwards rather than

sideways, which was given up after the Polish campaign. *German: (Pub. Horn) No. 124. Value B*

193 *'Heavy Tanks on Patrol in the Western Desert.'* Doubtless the censor worked at altering the images shown on real photographs but these so-called 'Heavy Tanks' would appear to be Matilda A10's. The original Matilda was produced for under £6,000 a vehicle, and fought in France in 1940 where its only weapon was a machine gun. The A10 started out as an infantry tank charged with forming a protective screen for infantry, but her armour was insufficient to defeat the enemy's anti-tank weapons at close range and she reverted to the cruiser role. Engine power output was double that of the Matilda 1 giving a speed of 15 mph instead of 8 mph, and in addition to a 94mm cannon she carried two machine guns. After the early desert battles the Matilda was dropped from production. *British: (Pub. Valentine's) No. 38T-7. Value B*

194 *'Covenanter Tanks Going Into Action.'* A real publicity story this one, for the Covenanter never went

192

HEAVY TANKS ON PATROL IN THE WESTERN DESERT.

193

190

LEICHTER PANZERSPÄHWAGEN

191

A SQUADRON OF "COVENANTER" TANKS GOING INTO ACTION.

194

LA LIGNE MAGINOT
...en action. — Artillery towers in action.

195

LA LIGNE MAGINOT
20. Soldats arrivant aux casemates. — Troops entering a fort...

196

LA LIGNE MAGINOT
11. Transporteur aérien de munitions — Ammunition coming by aerial.

198

LA LIGNE MAGINOT
9.. Soldats sur le train souterrain. — Underground electric railway.

197

into action. Built by the London, Midland and Scottish Railway, it was used to equip Home Defence Divisions.
British: (Pub. Valentine's) No. 38T-4A. Value B

THE MAGINOT LINE
The Line, named after André Maginot, the French Minister of War during the First World War, stretched from the Swiss Border to Malmédy in the north. When constructed, it was thought to be stronger and safer than any other permanent fortification. Predominantly linear, with the odd circular fort system incorporated at intervals, it had air-conditioned living and recreation areas. A large series of posed photographic propaganda postcards were made just prior to the outbreak of war to show off the modern and comfortable amenities of this 'impregnable' fortification.

195 *No. 17. 'Artillery Towers in Action.'*

LA LIGNE MAGINOT
8. Porte d'entrée d'un bloc. — Iron gate of a block.

199

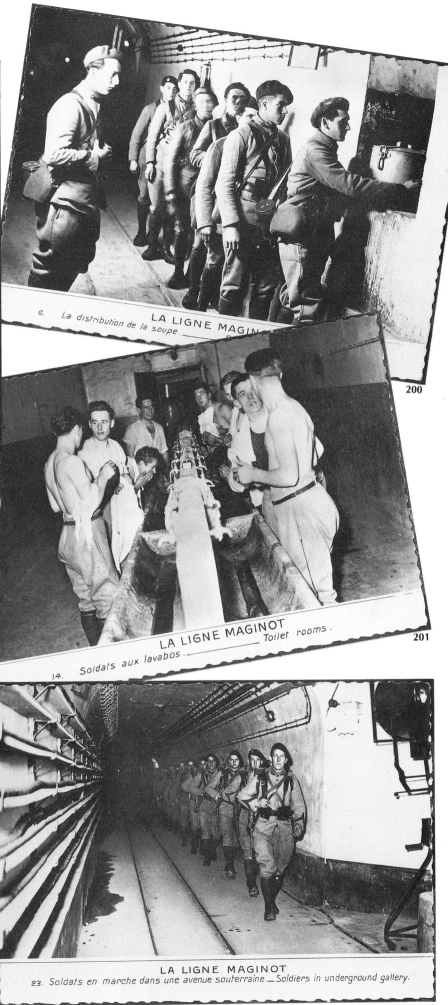

G. La distribution de la soupe.

LA LIGNE MAGINOT

200

LA LIGNE MAGINOT — Toilet rooms.
Soldats aux lavabos.
14.

201

LA LIGNE MAGINOT
23. Soldats en marche dans une avenue souterraine. — Soldiers in underground gallery.

202

French: (Pub. 'Photolumen'
Paris) Pre 1939. Value A

196 No. 20. 'Troops
Entering a Fortress.'
French: (Pub. 'Photolumen'
Paris) Pre 1939. Value A

197 No. 9. 'Underground
Electric Railway.'
French: (Pub. 'Photolumen'
Paris) Pre 1939. Value A

198 No. 11. 'Ammunition
Coming by Aerial (sic).'
French: (Pub. 'Photolumen'
Paris) Pre 1939. Value A

199 No. 8. 'Iron Gate of a
Block.'
French: (Pub. 'Photolumen'
Paris) Pre 1939. Value A

200 No. 6. 'Distribution of
Food.'
French: (Pub. 'Photolumen'
Paris) Pre 1939. Value A

201 No. 14. 'Toilet Rooms.'
French: (Pub. 'Photolumen'
Paris) Pre 1939. Value A

202 No. 23. 'Soldiers in
Underground Gallery.'
French: (Pub. 'Photolumen'
Paris) Pre 1939. Value A

Der FÜHRER am Westwall

203

KÜSTENFLAK AUF EINER DEUTSCHEN INSEL

204

WEST WALL

This was the German line of fortifications along her western border with France, nicknamed 'The Siegfried Line' by the Allies. It ran along the Saar, opposite the Maginot Line, but was later extended to cover the Swiss and Dutch borders. The West Wall was master-minded by Dr. Fritz Todt and it was as thorough a defensive system as had been the Hindenburg Line in the Great War. Three miles deep and comprising of 3,000 interconnecting chambers, thick concrete blockhouses and troop shelters, it was vaunted to be impregnable. The pillboxes were supplemented by rows of menacing 'Dragon's teeth' tank obstacles

203   *'The Führer at the West Wall.'* The line of fortifications was neglected after the successful invasion of France, but Hitler always maintained that it could be held. In fact it was not pierced in its entirety until the German failure in the Battle of the Bulge in the spring of 1945.

German: (Photo Hoffmann, Munich) Value C

COASTAL DEFENCES

204   *'Coastal Anti-Aircraft on a German Island.'* This is probably one of the 'Ostfriesische Inselen' in the North Sea.
German: (Pub. 'Die Wehrmacht' (Illustrated War Magazine)) Photographer Lonse, Berlin. Circa 1942. Value B

ATLANTIC WALL

The Germans built strong defences along the French and Belgian coast lines once they had occupied these countries, in order to repel an Allied invasion.
A series of Belgian cards showing German coastal defences, with captions in Flemish, French and English.

205   *'In the Barbed Wire.'* More wire and blockhouses.
Belgian: (Pub. and photographer, Luc, Coxyde) Circa 1945. Value B

206   *'On the Defense (sic) Wall of the Coast.'* Rolls of barbed wire, wiring crosses, concrete pillboxes and guns.

Belgian: (Pub. and photographer, Luc, Coxyde) Circa 1945. Value B

207   *'Bastion to the Fore.'* A massive concrete block-house right on the beach.
Belgian: (Pub. and photographer, Luc, Coxyde) Circa 1945. Value B

208   *'Mine and Post at Low Tide.'* The post would be concealed underwater at high tide and the mine would explode on contact with any landing craft.
Belgian: (Pub. and photographer, Luc, Coxyde) Circa 1945. Value B

209   *'Obstacles Spread on the Shore.'* Most of these ugly looking obstacles and traps would be concealed at high water.
Belgian: (Pub. and photographer, Luc, Coxyde) Circa 1945. Value B

210   *'A Mine Among Thousands.'* This is actually an H.E. shell, fixed on concrete, pointing out to sea.
Belgian: (Pub. and photographer, Luc, Coxyde) Circa 1945. Value B

205

208

206

209

207

210

CHAPTER FIVE

Machines at Sea

212

211 *'Italy breaks the chains which jeopardize her hold on her seas.' From the Workers of the Franco Tosi-Legnano to their fighting comrades.'* (The card was probably sponsored by the workers of the company and given free to servicemen to use as a Field Postcard). *Italian: (Pub. 'E.P.O.C.A.' Milan/Rome) Field Postcard. Artist Boccasile. Circa 1940. Value C*

212 *'Fortune guides the brave.'* The Italian Navy was more conspicuous for its panache than its staying power. *Italian: (Pub. V. E. Boeri, Roma) Artist Manlio D'Ercoli. Circa 1940. Value C*

THE BRITISH NAVY. *Derek Bannister was as proficient at drawing ships the way people wanted to see them as he was at 'planes. For J. Salmon Ltd., he produced some fine series of Britain's Fleet. Each postcard bears a*

B
etween the wars the development of air power was so rapid and dramatic that many 'experts' felt that action on and from the sea would be made obsolete. In fact, naval warfare played an immensely important role in the conduct of World War II.

The one revolutionary type of warship produced with effectiveness as a weapon in World War II was the aircraft carrier, which linked the modern element of air warfare with the traditional waging of war from the sea.

The submarine also became a vastly more versatile weapon during World War II. It functioned as a mine layer and was equipped with deck guns as well as firing powerful and deadly torpedoes. Submerged speeds increased, as did the length of time a submarine could remain under water.

The lethal effect of German U-boats led to an early development of one of the features of World War II at sea – the convoy system, to protect the Allies' Merchant and military supply fleet.

The British Navy
As a result of the traditional British policy of maintaining a fleet equal to any two possible opponents, the British Navy was, in 1939, the largest in the war and thanks to the massive re-armament programme in 1937, new stock was being brought into use by 1939-40. The estimates of Britain's effective strength at the outbreak of war vary wildly. A reasonable summary was 7 aircraft carriers, 15 capital ships, 181 destroyers, 54 escorts, 15 heavy cruisers, 46 light cruisers and 59 submarines. The Home Fleet was based at Scapa Flow, the Channel Fleet at Portsmouth and a smaller fleet in the Mediterranean.

The French Navy
At the outbreak of the war, the French Navy, under Admiral Darlan, was strong and vigorous. Its expansion programme had progressed smoothly since

1932, with a good proportion of its planned new battleships, six new cruisers and a number of destroyers, coming into service by 1939.

The German Navy
Drastically limited by the terms of the Treaty of Versailles, the German Navy was reduced after the First World War to six battleships and cruisers (with two of each in reserve); 12 destroyers and torpedo boats (with four of each in reserve). Personnel were limited to 15,000 men, including 1,500 officers.

This had the effect of producing an élite corps of high calibre men who had to beat tough competition to get in – there were over 30 applicants for each post in the 1930s. Although submarines were not permitted by the Treaty, much under-cover development work was done in Holland. Radar was produced, and so was Germany's ingenious answer to the limit of 10,000 tons imposed upon her shipbuilders. She invented the 'pocket battleship'.

Germany's strength was still well below that of the Royal Navy, She did, however, possess a crack fighting force of highly skilled sailors and a lethal nucleus of U-boats.

The Italian Navy
The Italians began the war with a large fleet of modern ships, including six battleships, seven heavy cruisers, 14 light cruisers, 122 destroyers and torpedo boats, and 119 submarines. Most vessels were designed for speed at the expense of armament.

One of the most original naval weapons of the war was the Italian 'Maiale' (pig), a human torpedo guided by two men, which was used with other unorthodox craft with great success against the British in Alexandria harbour, where the battleships *Valiant* and *Queen Elizabeth* were disabled.

In 1943, when Italy signed an Armistice with the Allies, the fleet escaped from the Germans by sailing to Malta, pursued en route by the Luftwaffe.

213

Battleship, NELSON Class. Completed 1927. Length 710ft. Beam 106ft. *H.M.S.* **RODNEY**
Displacement 33,900 tons. Main armament nine 16-in. and twelve 6-in. guns. Two
24.5-in.torpedo tubes. 2 Aircraft. 45,000 h.p. Speed 23 knots. Complement 1,314.

214

Battleship, KING GEORGE V Class. Completed 1942. Length 739ft. *H.M.S.* **DUKE OF YORK**
Beam 103ft. Displacement 35,000 tons. Main armament, ten 14-inch and sixteen
5.25-inch guns. 4 Aircraft. 152,000 h.p. Speed over 30 knots. Complement 1,500.

Aircraft Carrier, ILLUSTRIOUS Class. Completed 1941. Length 753ft. *H.M.A.C.* **FORMIDABLE**
Beam 95ft. Displacement 23,000 tons. Armament sixteen 4.5-inch guns.
110,000 h.p. Speed 32 knots. Complement 1,600.

215

detailed caption describing the ship's dimensions and capabilities and on the reverse is a stirring quotation from the Prime Minister. Some designs are unsigned.

213 'H.M.S. Rodney.' The *Rodney* was launched in 1927. Displacing 33,900 tons, she was 710ft long and was fitted with three triple 16in turrets forward and twelve 6in guns aft. She had a small turning circle and her tall tower made her rather unwieldy, but she was well armed and protected.

From September to December 1939 she patrolled the North Sea and the Atlantic; in April 1940 she took part in the Norwegian campaign, being hit by a dud bomb on 9 April. In May 1941 she took part in the search for *The Bismarck*, helping to sink her, and in 1942 covered the landings in North Africa, Sicily and Salerno. In 1944 the *Rodney* took part in the D-Day Normandy landings and, having survived the war with honour, was scrapped in 1948.
British: (Pub. J. Salmon Ltd) No. 4603 (unsigned design). Value B

214 'The Duke of York.' In the George V class, the *Duke of York* was completed in November 1941. Her first mission was to take Mr Churchill to America in December. In March 1942 she was involved in the search for the *Tirpitz* and again from May to December 1943, as Flagship for the Home Fleet, took part in her pursuit and final sinking. In December 1943 she destroyed the German battleship, *Scharnhorst*. In 1945 she was Flagship of the British Pacific Fleet and was in Tokyo Bay for the Japanese surrender.

Having survived the war with glory she remained as Flagship of the Home Fleet from 1946 to 1949 and was scrapped in 1958.
British: (Pub. J. Salmon Ltd) No. 4902. Artist Derek Bannister. Value B

215 'H.M.S. Formidable.' An aircraft carrier of the Illustrious Class, the *Formidable* was built by Harland and Wolf in Belfast and completed in November 1940. In the battle of Cape Matapan in March 1941 one of her aircraft hit the Italian battleship *Vittorie Veneto*, which managed to escape.

In May 1941, the sole British aircraft carrier in the Mediterranean in an area dominated by 500 enemy aircraft, the *Formidable* was dive bombed and put temporarily out of action.

Like the other five ships in her class—the *Illustrious*, the *Victorious*, the *Indomitable*, the *Indefatigable* and the *Implacable*—she was hit by a Japanese Kamikaze aircraft in the Pacific but was soon back in action. She was finally scrapped in 1955.
British: (Pub. J. Salmon Ltd) No. 4901. Artist Derek Bannister. Value B

216 'H.M.S. Sussex.' A cruiser of the London Class, completed in 1928/9, the *Sussex* was one of the first British warships to have a production radar set. The 'Counties' (also Kent, Norfolk, Dorsetshire, Berwick) were designed for Pacific operations, had an excellent range and were equipped with power-worked twin turrets. Their 8in guns had 70° elevation and good penetration of German heavy armour. The *Sussex* was partially rebuilt after being bombed and was scrapped in 1948.
British: (Pub. J. Salmon Ltd) No. 4602 (Unsigned design.) Value B

217 'H.M. Submarine Pandora.' The 'P' class submarines, like the 'Counties' cruisers, were designed for long range work in the Pacific. Because of the shortage of British submarines, they had to be used in the Mediterranean in 1940, where they proved too large and difficult to manoeuvre. In 1940 11 out of 15 of them were lost.
British: (Pub. J. Salmon Ltd) No. 4904. Artist Derek Bannister. Value B

OTHER ARTISTS FOR J. SALMON

218 'H.M.S. Tartar.' The Tribal class destroyers were built in the late 'Thirties to combat the 'super-destroyers' being built by other Powers. Brought into service at the beginning of the war they served with distinction in the Mediterranean and in the North Sea. They were large, complex and expensive ships and somewhat lacking in anti-aircraft fire as their 4.7in guns were short on elevation.
British: (Pub. J. Salmon Ltd) No. 4759. Artist Bernard W. Church. Circa 1940. Value B

216

H.M.S. **SUSSEX**
Cruiser, LONDON Class. Completed 1929. Length 633ft. Beam 66ft.
Displacement 9,830 tons. Main armament eight 8-inch and eight 4-inch guns.
Eight torpedo tubes. 1 Aircraft. 80,000 h.p. Speed 32 knots. Complement 650.

ONE OF BRITAIN'S LATEST BATTLESHIPS.

219

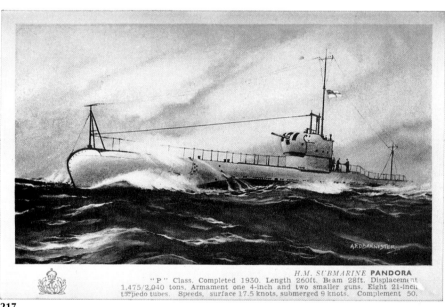

217

H.M. SUBMARINE **PANDORA**
"P" Class. Completed 1930. Length 260ft. Beam 28ft. Displacement
1,475/2,040 tons. Armament one 4-inch and two smaller guns. Eight 21-inch
torpedo tubes. Speeds, surface 17.5 knots, submerged 9 knots. Complement 50.

H.M. BATTLESHIP NELSON

220

H.M.S. ROYAL OAK

221

218

H.M.S. **TARTAR**
Destroyer, Tribal Class. Completed 1939. Length 355ft. Beam 36ft.
Displacement 1,870 tons. Armament eight 4.7-inch guns and four multiple M Gs.
Four 21-inch torpedo tubes. 44,000 h.p. Speed 36.5 knots. Complement 190.

H.M.S. ARK ROYAL

222

'Britain Prepared.'   By permission of H.M. Admiralty

FIRING 15-in. GUNS FROM H.M.S. 'QUEEN ELIZABETH'   [Reference No. 15

223

L'Angleterre prête à frapper   Avec l'autorisation de l'Amirauté

SALVES DES PIÈCES D'UNE BORDÉE   5

224

PASSED BY PRESS AND CENSORSHIP BUREAU

GUNS OF H.M.S. "RODNEY" WITH GIBRALTAR IN BACKGROUND   "BRITAIN PREPARED" 3

225

219 'One of Britain's Latest Battleships.' The censor's office had periods of being coy about naming new items in Britain's armoury—both aeroplanes and tanks as well as ships. Then 'artist's impressions' of anonymous machines had to be printed which did not exactly represent any particular model.

This ship looks like a compromise between H.M.S. Hood and the George V Class.

Printed on reverse: 'An Artist's Impression of ONE OF BRITAIN'S LATEST BATTLESHIPS. Publication authorized by the Admiralty.' British: (Pub. J. Salmon Ltd) No. 4754. Artist Bernard W. Church. Circa 1940. Value B

220 'H.M. Battleship Nelson.' The Nelson, sister ship to the Rodney, was an extremely powerful battleship built with stronger protection than later models. She had triple 16in turrets forward, and six twin 6in turrets aft. Later in the war the Nelson was camouflaged on the hull, turret and bridge sides to break up her silhouette. She was also fitted with radar. She was damaged by a magnetic mine early in the war and torpedoed by an Italian bomber while on escort duty to Malta.

The Italian surrender was signed on her decks off Salerno. She provided fire support in the Normandy Landings and finished the war with the Eastern Fleet in the East Indies.
British: (Pub. J. Salmon Ltd) No. 3684. Artist Leslie Carr. Circa 1940. Value B

221 'H.M.S. Royal Oak.' This gallant old battleship had fought in the battle of Jutland in 1916 and had been little modernised by the outbreak of World War II. On the night of 14 October 1939 she was daringly attacked at anchorage in Scapa Flow, by the German U-boat, U-47, commanded by Kapitän Leutenant Gunther Prien. The first salvo of three torpedoes missed and a single torpedo hit, but only partially detonated. A second salvo of three torpedoes, nearly an hour later, detonated her magazine and the old warship sank with the loss of 833 men, one of the earliest major military casualties of the war.

British: (Pub. Valentine's) No. 4774. Artist P. A. Vicary. Circa 1939. Value B

222 'H.M.S. Ark Royal.' Caption on reverse reads: 'H.M.S. Ark Royal'—the largest and the newest edition to the Navy, the aircraft carrier named after Howard's Flagship of Armada fame. The crew consists of 138 officers and 1,355 other ranks, 6 squadrons of fighter aircraft and 4 of torpedo spotter reconnaissance. The ship is well-armed with anti-aircraft guns, which are set in sets of 8, and sixteen 4.5 dual purpose guns in twin mounts.'
British: (Pub. Valentine's) No. 4772. Artist P. A. Vicary. Circa 1939. Value B

BRITAIN PREPARED
A large section of this vast and important propaganda series featured ships. The Photochrom Co. Ltd. had secured exclusive permission from H.M. Government to reproduce the pictures as postcards. They produced them in two styles—coloured and sepia—and some were also reproduced for the French market with the text in French. The coloured versions date from the mid-thirties as they are presented under the gracious patronage of King George V and Queen Mary.' The series continued to be added to after World War II had broken out.

223 No. 15. 'Firing guns from H.M.S. Queen Elizabeth.' 'Britain Prepared.' By permission of H.M. Admiralty.

The Elizabeth had seen service in the First World War in the Dardanelles and as Flagship of the Fleet from 1917. She covered the evacuation of Crete in June 1941 and was damaged by Italian human torpedoes in Alexandria Harbour in December 1941. She was finally scrapped in 1948.
British: (Pub. Photochrom) Circa 1935. Value B

224 No. 5. 'Firing a broadside.' 'England Ready to strike.' By permission of the Admiralty.
British: (Pub. Photochrom) Circa 1935. Value A

225 No. 3. 'Guns of H.M.S. Rodney with Gibraltar in Background.' 'Britain Prepared.' Passed by Press and Censorship Bureau. On reverse: 'The Fighting Services.' H.M. Royal Navy.

British: (Pub. Photochrom) Copyright Charles E. Brown. Circa 1940. Value B

226 No. 7. 'Smoke screen H.M.S. Wren.' 'Britain Prepared.' Passed by Press and Censorship Bureau. On reverse: 'The Fighting Services.' H.M. Royal Navy. British: (Pub. Photochrom) Copyright Charles E. Brown. Circa 1940. Value B

227 No. 9. 'H.M.S Malaya and Destroyers.' 'Britain Prepared.' Passed by Press and Censorship Bureau.

The Malaya was laid down in 1913 and completed in 1916. A battleship of the Queen Elizabeth class, she was paid for by the Federated Malay States. During World War II she saw extensive service until she was disarmed for use as an accommodation ship in 1944 and finally scrapped in 1948.
British: (Pub. Photochrom) Copyright Charles E. Brown. Circa 1940. Value B

228 'The Latest Aircraft Carrier: H.M.S. Ark Royal.' (Photographic) The Ark Royal was completed in November 1938. In 1939 she patrolled with the Home Fleet and on 14 September was narrowly missed by torpedoes from the German U-39. On 26 September she

was again missed—this time by bombs from German aircraft, but the Germans announced she had been sunk. She then joined the Renown in the hunt for the Graf Spee in the South Atlantic and in 1940 took part in the Norwegian campaign. After a variety of assignments, the Ark Royal joined in the search for the Scharnhorst and the Gneisenau in the spring of 1941 and in May her aircraft scored a hit on the Bismarck. She was involved in action off Genoa, Leghorn and La Spezia and in November was hit by a torpedo from the U-81 and sank off Gibraltar.
British: (Pub. Valentine's) No. 38B-19 Circa 1940. Value B

ANONYMOUS SERIES

229 'A British submarine going out on patrol in enemy waters after repainting and refitting at a base depot.'

230 'British 10,000 ton cruiser, Suffolk, patrolling off Iceland.' The Suffolk performed well in cold waters. In May 1941, amidst ice flows, rising sleet and rain, she shadowed the movements of the Bismarck. She also escorted convoys to Russia. In 1943 she sailed to the warm waters of the Indian Ocean and stayed there.

SMOKE SCREEN H.M.S. "WREN" "BRITAIN PREPARED" 7

226

H.M.S. "MALAYA" & DESTROYERS "BRITAIN PREPARED" 9

227

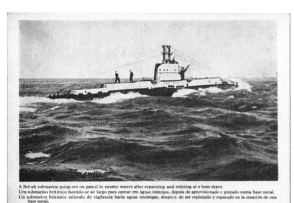

A British submarine going out on patrol in enemy waters after repainting and refitting at a base depot.
Um submarino britânico fazendo-se ao largo para operar em aguas inimigas, depois de aprovisionado e pintado numa base naval.
Un submarino británico saliendo de vigilancia hacia aguas enemigas, despues de ser repintado y reparado en la estación de una base naval.

229

British 10,000 ton cruiser "Suffolk," patrolling off Iceland.
O cruzador britânico de 10.000 toneladas "Suffolk," em serviço de patrulha ao largo da Islândia.
El crucero británico de 10.000 toneladas "Suffolk" en servicio de vigilancia frente a Islandia.

230

THE LATEST AIRCRAFT CARRIER, H.M.S. ARK ROYAL. 38B-19

228

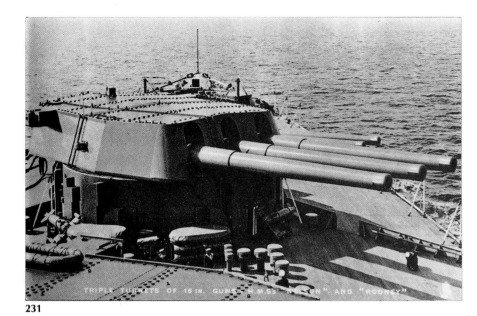

231

232

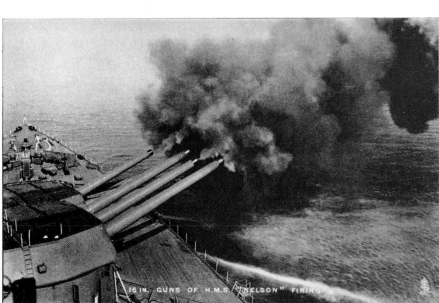

233

British (probably): Captions also in Portuguese and Spanish. Circa 1939. Value B

TUCK'S 'OUR NAVY' SERIES. A photogravure series of sepia photographic postcards of ships of the British Navy circa 1939.

231 *'Triple Turrets of 16in Guns. H.M.S.'s Nelson and Rodney.'*
British: (Pub. Tuck) 'Our Navy.' Circa 1939. Value B

232 *'Destroyers of the Second Flotilla at Speed.'*
British: (Pub. Tuck) 'Our Navy'. Circa 1939. Value B

233 *'16in Guns of H.M.S. Nelson Firing.'*
British: (Pub. Tuck) 'Our Navy.' Circa 1939. Value B

234 *'Aerial View of H.M.S. Nelson.'*
British: (Pub. Tuck) 'Our Navy.' Circa 1939. Value B

235 *'Aircraft Carrier H.M.S Courageous.'* The *Courageous* was completed during the First World War and converted to a flush deck aircraft carrier between 1924 and 1929. She was torpedoed and sunk by the German U-boat, U-29, in the Western Approaches on 17 September 1939. The *Courageous* was the Royal Navy's first loss in the war and went down with over 500 officers and men. Her Captain, W. T. Makeig-Jones, went down saluting the flag, alone on the bridge. This gallant but futile waste of trained and vital personnel

234

235

236

was soon officially discouraged by the Admiralty in London. *British: (Pub. Tuck) 'Our Navy.' Circa 1939. Value B*

236 *'County Class Cruisers—H.M.S. London.'* London was completed in 1929 and rebuilt between 1939 and 1941 with a tower bridge, two funnels and improved AA armament. The reconstruction was not a success as the extra weight from the new superstructure caused tremendous strain. *London* was rebuilt again in 1946 but scrapped in 1950. *British: (Pub. Tuck) 'Our Navy.' Circa 1939. Value B*

THE FRENCH NAVY
This series of coloured pictures of ships of the French Fleet was drawn by artist Paul Igert in 1942. Each design incorporates a portrait of the famous French personality who gave their name to the ship.

237 *'Richelieu.'* A battleship of 35,000 tons armed with eight 380mm guns and 15 152mm guns, she entered into service in 1940 and effectively contributed to the defence of Dakar in September 1940. In the same year, she was hit by aircraft from the *Hermes* and repulsed attacks by the British and Free French. She was taken to U.S.A. and rebuilt. In 1943 she was attached to British Home Fleet and took part in operations in Norway, bombarding Sabang in 1944 and '45. She was eventually scrapped in 1968. Caption on reverse reads: *'Richelieu (1585–1642) Great Statesman. He was the first to understand the importance of the sea in the life of the nation. He constructed and organized the first navy worthy of the name that France had ever possessed. French: (Pub. Giraud-Rivoire, Lyon) 1942. Value C*

238 *'Montcalm.'* A cruiser of 7,600 tons, armed with eight 152mm guns, she entered into service in 1937 and survived the war, to be scrapped in 1970. Caption on reverse reads: *'Montcalm (1712–1759). This name symbolizes the glorious defence of Canada against the English. Montcalm was killed in the siege of Quebec.'*
French: (Pub. Giraud-Rivoire, Lyon) 1942. Value C

Bâtiment de ligne **RICHELIEU**

RICHELIEU. — Cuirassé de 35.000 tonnes armé de 8 canons de 380 ‰ et 15 canons de 152 ‰. Entré en service en 1940. A efficacement contribué à la défense de Dakar en Septembre 1940.

237

Croiseur **MONTCALM**

...ur de 7.600 tonnes ... Entré en service en

238

Contre-Torpilleur **VOLTA**

239

VOLTA. — Contre-torpilleur de 2.800 tonnes armé de 8 canons de 138 et 10 tubes lance-torpilles. A pris part au combat de Mers-el-Kébir.

JEAN DE VIENNE. — Croiseur de 7.600 tonnes armé de 8 canons de 152. Entré en service en 1937.

240

Croiseur **DUQUESNE**

DUQUESNE. — Croiseur de 10.000 tonnes armé de 8 canons de 203. Entré en service en 1928.

241

Sous-marin
ARCHIMÈDE

ARCHIMÈDE. — Sous-marin de 1.5...
armé de 11 tubes lance-torpilles. Entré...
en 1932.

242

Ravitailleur
JULES VERNE

JULES VERNE. — Ravitailleur de sous-marins
de 6.000 tonnes. Entré en service en 1932.

243

Croiseur-Ecole
JEANNE d'ARC

...RC. — Croiseur de 6.500 tonnes
...ons de 152 m/m. Entré en service
...vire-école d'application des offi-
...aisait chaque année le tour du
...motion sortant de l'école navale.

244

PASTEUR. — Sous-marin de 1.500 tonnes,
1 canon de 100, 11 tubes lance-torpilles. Entré
en service en 1932.

245

Aviso
C* RIVIÈRE

COMMANDANT RIVIÈRE. — Aviso dragueur
de 600 tonnes. Entré en service en 1940.

246

COMMANDANT TESTE. — Transport d'aviation de 10.000 tonnes. Entré en service en 1932.
A échappé au guet-apens de Mers-el-Kébir.

247

239 'Volta.' A torpedo boat destroyer of 2,800 tons armed with eight 138mm guns and ten torpedo tubes, she took part in the Battle of Mers-el-Kebir. Caption on reverse reads: 'Volta (1745–1827). Physician famous for research and discoveries on electricity.' French: (Pub. Giraud-Rivoire, Lyon) 1942. Value C

240 'Jean de Vienne.' A cruiser of 7,600 tons, armed with eight 152mm guns, she entered into service in 1937. The sister ship of the Montcalm, she was scuttled on 27 November 1941 at Toulon, then salvaged by the Italians, renamed the FR-11 and finally sunk on 24 November 1943. Caption on reverse reads: 'Jean de Vienne (1341–1396) Admiral of the Galleys. At the head of the French Flotilla he had organized, he distinguished himself in The Hundred Years War, spreading terror along the English coast.' French: (Pub. Giraud-Rivoire, Lyon) 1942. Value C

241 'Duquesne.' A cruiser of 10,000 tons armed with eight 203mm guns, she entered into service in 1928. (A modern French Guided Missile destroyer now bears this name.) Caption on reverse reads: 'Duquesne (1610–1688). One of the most glorious figures in our French maritime history. He annihilated the Spanish Fleet and inflicted severe damage on the Dutch Fleet.' French: (Pub. Giraud-Rivoire, Lyon) 1942. Value C

242 'Archimède.' A submarine of 1,500 tons, armed with 11 torpedo tubes, she entered into service in 1932. Caption on reverse reads: 'Archimède (287–212 BC). Illustrious physician. His discovery of the famous principle of the pressure of water on a submerged body is the basis of submarine technology.'

243 'Jules Verne.' A submarine supply ship of 6,000 tons, she entered into service in 1932. Caption on reverse reads: 'Jules Verne (1828–1905). Celebrated adventure writer who, with ingenious imagination, foresaw the majority of modern inventions, particularly submarines.' French: (Pub. Giraud-Rivoire, Lyon) 1942. Value B

244 'Jeanne d'Arc.' A cruiser of 6,500 tons armed with eight 152mm guns, she entered into service in 1931. This training ship for Naval Officers sailed around the world each year with the graduates of the Naval College. Caption on reverse reads: 'Jeanne d'Arc (1412–1431). National heroine born in Domrémy, a small village in Lorraine, who kicked the English out of France. Wounded in the Siege of Orleans, she perished in Rouen, burnt alive by the English.' French: (Pub. Giraud-Rivoire, Lyon) 1942. Value C

245 'Pasteur.' A submarine of 1,500 tons, one 100mm gun, 11 torpedo tubes, she entered into service in 1932. Caption on reverse reads: 'Pasteur (1822–1895). Learned French chemist born in Dôle. We owe the invention of vaccination to him.' French: (Pub. Giraud-Rivoire, Lyon) 1942. Value C

246 'Commandant Rivière.' A despatch boat-dredger of 600 tons, she entered into service in 1940. Caption on reverse reads: 'Commandant Rivière (1827–1883). The name of Captain of Vessel Rivière is, with that of Francis Garnier, associated with the conquest of Tonkin—to which they both gave their lives.' French: (Pub. Giraud-Rivoire, Lyon) 1942. Value C

247 'Commandant Teste.' An aircraft carrier of 10,000 tons, she entered into service in 1932, and escaped ambush at Mers-el-Kebir. Caption on reverse reads: 'Commandant Teste. Daring aviator, one of the hardy pioneers of maritime aviation. Killed in an air crash.' (No dates given). French: (Pub. Giraud-Rivoire, Lyon) 1942. Value C

FREE FRENCH NAVY

The Free French Navy was organized by Admiral Emile Muselier from England from June 1940. On 3 and 4 July a British squadron appeared off Oran, Algiers, where the bulk of the French warships was harboured and gave them three choices: either to join the Free French Navy and help the Allies to fight Germany; to turn into a British port to be interned; or to scuttle itself in the harbour at Oran. The French refused all the alternatives and the British, under Vice Admiral Sir James F. Somerville, opened fire, sinking three battleships. Also on 3 July, Admiral Sir Andrew Cunningham ordered the French squadron at Alexandria to disarm itself. Two submarines were in English ports and joined the Free French Navy, which was gradually built up with British and American help.

248 'A Sloop Leaving Harbour.' French: Red and blue Cross

248

TORPEDOBOOTE LAUFEN AUS

249

KREUZER "NÜRNBERG" — (IM HINTERGRUND "ADMIRAL SCHEER")

250

251

of Lorraine, Free French symbol, on reverse. Circa 1941. Value B

GERMAN NAVY

249 'The Torpedo boat run is over.' German World War II torpedo boats were small, fast destroyers; many of them were motor boats, known as 'Schnellboote.'
German: (Pub. 'Die Wehrmacht' (Illustrated War Magazine) Circa 1942. Value C

250 'The Cruiser Nürnberg. (The Admiral Scheer in the background).' The *Nürnberg* was completed under Germany's 'Plan Z' in 1935. She operated from Kiel and was the flagship of the Reconnaissance Forces. Early in the war she was hit by the British submarine *Salmon* and was out of action till mid-1940. At the end of the war she was commissioned in the Russian Navy and re-named *Admiral Makarov*. The *Admiral Scheer*, a pocket battleship, was very active in the Atlantic after her refit in 1940. She sank *H.M.S. Jervis Bay* (an auxiliary cruiser), captured the freighter *Duquesa* and the Norwegian tanker *Sandefjord*. Early in 1941 she eluded H.M.S. *Hermes* and six cruisers. By the time she reached Bergen again she had sunk 14 ships, one auxiliary cruiser and captured two other vessels. On 10 April 1945 she was bombed and capsized as she headed towards Kiel from Pillau with 1,000 wounded and refugees aboard.
German: (Pub. 'Die Wehrmacht' Illustrated War Magazine) Circa 1942. Value C

251 'The Bismarck *in Battle off Iceland against superior hostile forces.'* The hunt for and sinking of the great battleship the *Bismarck* was one of the most exciting maritime episodes of the war, the subject of many books and films. The *Bismarck* was commissioned on 24 August 1940 and became the Fleet Commander's Flagship. With the heavy cruiser *Prinz Eugen*, she sailed on 'Operation Rheinübung' to break out into the Atlantic. As they sailed through the Denmark Strait, they were spotted by H.M.S. *Hood* and H.M.S. *Prince of Wales*. A fierce battle ensued during which the *Hood* was sunk. The *Bismarck* then ducked her

British pursuers, but a report radioed to Germany was picked up by the Royal Navy and she was located by aircraft from the carriers *Ark Royal* and *Victorious*. She was then attacked by the *Rodney* and the *King George V*. When her position became hopeless, in the tradition of the German Navy she was scuttled by her own crew and went down with the loss of nearly 2,000 men.
German: (Pub. Friedrich Ebert, Berlin). Artist Schnürpel. For the famous 'War Victims Wall Calendar'. This was sold to raise funds for N.S.D.A.P members injured in the war. Circa 1941. Value C

252 , 252 A 'Small Boats.' The rugged coastline behind the boats could be Norway. The Germans operated a Kriegsmarine in Norway and had over 50 naval bases of varying size, from Oslo in the south to Vardo in the north. The three men in the foreground may have been rolling cannister depth charges from the stern.
German: (Field Postcard) 1942. Value B

253, 253A 'Small Boat At Speed.' The forward mounted anti-aircraft gun can just be seen against the sky and is probably a 37mm. The same guns were used on land where Navy gunners were responsible for defending their own installations. At one time it was proposed that U-boats be prepared as underwater anti-aircraft platforms. The idea was to entice an aeroplane into thinking that it had an easy kill and then suddenly produce an array of weapons to shoot it down. An experimental version did shoot down an attacker, but was so badly damaged itself that the idea was abandoned.
German: (Field Postcard) 1943. Value B

254 'Destroyers.' 'With the approval of the Supreme Command for War Defence.
German: (Pub. Carl Werner) Artist Kaklo. 1939. Value C

ITALIAN NAVY

255 'Customs Officials. *Official story of the award of the silver Medal for Military Valour on board ship to a Customs Official.'* The citation on the reverse details a customs patrol's bravery on duty in the

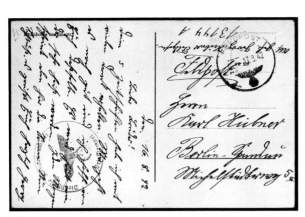

252A

Mediterranean from 10 June
1940 to 8 September 1943
and in the Adriatic from
9 September to 8 May 1945.

*Italian: (Pub. Vecchioni and
Guadagno) Artist Antonio
Ventiorini. 1945. Value C*

254

252

253

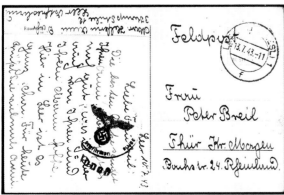

253A

255

Nicht Du bist der Maßstab! Sondern die Front!

CHAPTER SIX

The Men

A British Grenadier Guardsman—new style!
Un soldato britannico di granadiere—nuovo stile!
Un Granadero de la Guardia británica | nuevo estilo!

257

256 *'Are You Not the Standard—Especially at the Front.' Card overprinted on reverse: Day of NSDAP in General Government 13–15 August 1943 and posted in Krakau with a special commemorative postmark and stamp of the 'Grossdeutsches Reich Generalgouvernement.' German: Artist Will Tschech. 1943. Value D*

257 *'A British Grenadier Guardsman—New Style.' The thought of a posse of motorcyclists all blazing off with their Tommy guns as they rode along would certainly have frightened the Duke of Wellington. The motorcyclist is likely to be a despatch rider or perhaps the member of a forward patrol unit, probably controlled by a battalion or regimental H.Q. The 'Tommy' gun was not named after the soldier, but after John T. Thompson who invented it in 1920. It weighed around ten pounds*

As in the First World War, World War II provided, to many of the men serving in it, an episode of excitement, of heightened sensation and affectionate comradeship that they would never manage to recreate in civilian life. It seems extraordinary, in view of the likelihood of being killed or maimed, or being separated from loved ones, and of existing in conditions of extreme discomfort and danger, that men should regard the war in this way in their heart of hearts. Certainly, when a country has not engaged in active warfare for several years, its male youth resorts to vandalism, hooliganism and active physical demonstrations to fulfil its natural feelings of aggression. It would be sad to conclude that man is more fulfilled and contented when fighting — and of course there are many pacifist exceptions — but there can be no disputing the fact that to many men (and to a large number of women) World War II was 'their finest hour.'

Another parallel with the First World War was in the size and quality of Britain's professional fighting force at the outbreak of World War II. At the beginning of both wars, the British Expeditionary Force (B.E.F.) was a small, crisp and disciplined fighting machine. By another coincidence, both B.E.F.'s were forced by the Germans to retreat or withdraw as the first phase of their respective wars drew to a close. In 1914, the B.E.F. retreated from Mons in a superbly controlled action. In 1940, the B.E.F. was evacuated from Dunkirk in a magnificently organised and executed action. Both defeats were sold by the propaganda machine to the public — who eagerly bought the story — as triumphs. As military exercises they were undoubtedly triumphs. Victories they certainly were not. But such was the spirit and pluck of the British soldiers taking part in these two historic events, 20 years apart, that they have passed into history as victories. It was a spirit that was to continue throughout the war. A Gunner, serving in Benghazi, Greece, Crete, Tobruk,

Alamein, Sicily, Normandy, Holland, the Rhine Crossing and the Ardennes from 1940 to 1945, summed up his experience 40 years later as 'happy and sad memories to me — but I'm glad I was there.'

In contrast to the tiny British force (five regular and five territorial divisions in May 1940) the French had a pre-war standing army of 900,000 men. On the outbreak of World War II, she mobilised 89 divisions, which comprised one armoured, three light mechanised, five cavalry and 80 infantry. Relying, as she had traditionally done, on defences like the Maginot Line, France was extremely deficient in armoured, mobile forces. By May 1940, conscription had increased France's forces to 115 divisions, 23 in her colonies.

In September 1939, the French advanced along a 100 mile stretch of the shared frontier with Germany, between the Rhine and the Luxembourg border. When Poland collapsed, the French Command decided to withdraw its forces to the safety and shelter of the Maginot Line, where they stayed for the next seven months.

Pressed by Paul Reynaud, (the Minister of Finance, who succeeded Daladier as Premier in March 1940), the Commander-in-Chief, General Maurice Gamelin, planned to continue on the offensive by advancing through Belgium and Holland to the Lower Rhine. Belgium preferred to preserve her neutrality, however, and the French and the British were forced into the period of stagnation that the French called the *'Drôle de Guerre.'* It was a time spent in hatching and reforming plans, most of which the Allies did not have the resources to put into operation.

When the war burst into life with the German invasion of Belgium and France, French resistance was weak and unco-ordinated. On 15 May, Reynaud told Churchill, 'We are beaten, we have lost the battle,' and General Gamelin admitted he had no strategic reserve.

By 14 June, victorious German forces marched down the Champs Elysées in Paris, and on 22 June the Armistice was signed. It was all over for France.

The successful German Army was a large and effective force of disciplined, dedicated men. Hitler expanded his army until it reached about two million men in 1939. By the Invasion of France it had reached three million men, in 150 divisions. Ten of these were armoured — thanks to the insistence of Guderian and other 'tank-minded' senior officers. Four divisions were motorised and one was airborne.

The German system of command owed much to the early Prussian format which had proved so successful for most of the First World War. German officers and men were encouraged to use their own initiative whenever expedient, to an extent that was unheard of in the British Army. Morale, efficiency and skills were generally of a high quality. Equipment too, if not always plentiful, was generally of good quality, with tanks, guns and machine guns of a powerful and reliable standard that made them highly respected by their opponents.

Perhaps the greatest lack in the German Army, during World War II, was of motorised transport, which hampered the mobility of their infantry.

Hitler was both titular and actual head of his army, being Chief of the High Command of the Armed Forces (Oberkommando der Wehrmacht, OKW). From the beginning of 1942 he appointed himself Commander-in-Chief of the Army, the first civilian to do so in German history.

In America, as in Germany, one man was the main architect of the structure, policy and strategy of the armed forces. That man was General George C. Marshall, Chief of Staff. In 1942, before Pearl Harbour forced America into the war, he reorganised the army into three branches: Army Ground Forces, Army Air Forces and Services of Supply. During World War II, American troops fought in 34 campaigns and by V-E Day all but two army divisions had seen combat action. Their casualties were proportionately high, totalling about one million, of which almost one quarter were deaths. 1,400,409 decorations were awarded, exclusive of the Purple Heart, the medal originated by George Washington, and awarded to all U.S. Army, Navy and Coast Guard personnel killed or wounded by enemy action. The Americans were remembered in Europe not so much for their military prowess as for their effect on the culture and the female population. 'Got any gum, Chum?' was a phrase that passed into the vocabulary of wartime Britain.

Whatever their differences in training and attitude, in conduct and style and the surface differences that national characteristics imposed, the armed forces of all the combattant nations shared the same human feelings. Men on each side performed acts of incredible bravery, or soiled their trousers in utter fear, loved their pals, missed their mums and girls and wrote home. Many of them used the convenient postcard, that required only a few words to complete the link between home and station, to express their feelings of loneliness or worry or joy in victory. Their messages are simple and banal, but through the everyday clichés of the war which, like every war, produced its own slang and vocabulary, their humanity shines. Not only did the soldiers use the postcard, but the designers of the postcard (the artists and the photographers) used the soldiers as subject matter. They portrayed them in action, in training, in their leisure moments and as straight portraits.

and the circular drum magazine contained 50 rounds. The weapon gained notoriety as the favourite 'persuader' of Chicago gangsters during Prohibition. The motorcycle has been painted overall—doubtless khaki—and the headlight has been covered, leaving just a small slit to provide essential illumination.
British (probably): Caption in British, Spanish and Portuguese. Value C

THE 'BRITAIN PREPARED' SERIES (SOMEWHERE IN FRANCE)

During the Phoney War period from October 1939 to May 1940 the B.E.F. built up to five regular and five territorial divisions. There was time to train, to fraternize and to enjoy the open-air life. There was also time to produce postcards showing the public back home how well our lads were looking and doing.

258 *'Here We Are Again.'* Many older soldiers were back in the areas they had known so well in the First World War 20 years earlier. This time their stay would be much briefer.
British: (Pub. Photochrom) No. 13. 'Britain Prepared' series. Value B

259 *'Getting Ready for the Troops.'* This field kitchen has a foot pump clearly visible on the left-hand side. Its function was to provide pressure to drive an air-fuel mixture into a line of burners stationed underneath the dixies. On the right, the receptacle with its lid open, which seems to fascinate the soldier in the background, is a 'haybox'—an insulated container in which hot food could be carried to the troops unable to 'come and get it.' Message on the reverse reads: *'Some of our lads use cooking tins like these but not in the open air. . . . Love from Dad-Dad.'* It is dated 23 April 1941 so the writer is talking about an experience in England, not France.
British: (Pub. Photocrom) No. 20. 'Britain Prepared' series. Value B

260 *'Making Sure of Their Soles.'* Despite horse and mechanization, feet were still the Army's staple method of movement. Regular 'foot parades' were standard.

British: (Pub. Photochrom) No. 18. 'Britain Prepared' series. Value B

261 '9.2in Coast Defence Gun.' Close inspection of this card reveals that the man on the left is a Royal Artillery officer in riding breeches, Sam Browne and Service Dress top—plus a knobbed swagger stick tucked under his left arm. British Home Defence became the responsibility of reserve forces, often composed of old campaigners more tuned to the hostilities of 20 years before. The general principle of building massive static defence positions, as shown here, or the 'Lines' like the Maginot and Siegfried, was soon disproved. That such 'Coastal Defence' could be

overcome was ultimately proved in June 1944 in Normandy.
British: (Pub. Valentine's) Circa 1938. Value A

262 '6in Howitzer and Tractor.' The howitzer is a weapon designed to throw a shell into a high trajectory, thus enabling a bombardment to be made upon an enemy concealed just beyond a hill. The infantry had close support small calibre howitzers known as mortars and usually this sort of weapon was un-rifled. These posed pictures by 11 Medium Battery R.A. give away their theatricality by the freshly painted equipment. Even the tyres were painted, and the mud sticking to the parts foolish

261

258

259

262

260

263

WHERE THEIR FATHERS FOUGHT.   WAR OFFICE PHOTOGRAPH B.1747

264

THE MODERN ARMY

Bren Gun

267

AUXILIARY MILITARY PIONEER CORPS IN FRANCE.   War Office Photograph No.B.1475.

265

THE MODERN ARMY

Apprentice Tradesmen at an Army Technical School

266

THE MODERN ARMY

Apprentice tradesmen at an Army Technical School

268

enough to touch the ground can be clearly seen. The towing vehicle is probably a Scammel 6×4 later used by the Royal Electrical and Mechanical Engineers as a general purpose recovery vehicle.
British: (Pub. Valentine's) No. 38E-13. Circa 1938. Value B

263 *'6in Howitzer.'* The man on the left is the Sergeant of the gun section and he is holding the ram-rod with which the charge is pushed up into the breech. There is obviously no intent to fire the gun for the spade at the left-hand end of the trail has not been sunk into the ground. If the gun were to be fired the whole device would travel backwards and cause the Sergeant irrepar-able harm. Gun howitzers usually had short barrels because the range of shot was not normally a major factor, nor was pin point accuracy, although single targets could be successfully engaged.
British: (Pub. Valentine's) No. 38-D9. Posted June 1938. Value B

264 *'Where Their Fathers Fought.'* Caption on the reverse reads: *'During training in France, Welsh Guards used a partially destroyed building at a spot where their fathers, who served in the Regiment, fought in the last war.'* In the B.E.F. actions early in the war, prior to Dunkirk, the 1st Battalion Welsh Guards was charged with the defence of General Headquarters, which was initially at Arras, while the 2nd Battalion was rushed from England in May 1940 to assist in the defence of Boulogne. One soldier in the picture is wearing puttees, which were worn by most armies in the First World War (except the German). The long strip of cloth which formed the puttee was said to serve as an auxiliary bandage when needed. Puttees were replaced by anklets, or gaiters, as worn by the soldier on the right.
British: (War Office Photograph) No. B.1747. Circa 1940. Value B

265 *'Auxiliary Military Pioneer Corps in France.'* The A.M.P.C. was formed in 1940 to provide a labour force to support the growing administrative organization in France. It consisted mostly

of civilians without previous military experience, often men who had volunteered as a welcome change to being on the dole. They had very little military training and only one in four had a rifle. It is doubtful if even that quarter knew how to fire their weapons. They were commanded by a skeleton force of mostly senior non-commissioned and veteran officers.
British: (War Office Photograph) No. B.1475. Circa 1940. Value B

THE MODERN ARMY SERIES
This series has an odd selection of pictures, some of which look as if they originated in the First World War. The cards may have been produced by the Services to encourage recruiting for some bear an Army number and others are printed on the reverse in a style unused since 1910.

266 *'Apprentice Tradesmen at an Army Technical School.'* These young soldiers are watching a non-commissioned officer with a 'scriber'—a sharp metal rod used to mark other metals for cutting or machining. The transition from man-war to machine-war increased the need for better educated soldiery. The Army set out to produce its own, eventually forming a complete Corps responsible for the maintenance and repair of most military equipment—The Royal Electrical and Mechanical Engineers.
British: Value B

267 *'Bren Gun.'* Originally a Czech weapon, this gun was taken up by the British in the 1930's. The name is derived from a combination of *Brno* (the town where it was developed) and *Enfield* (the town where it was produced in England by the Royal Small Arms Arsenal). The gun became the staple light machine weapon of the British Forces although it was not much employed in the anti-aircraft role, as it apparently is here. The use of machine guns against aeroplanes was an American habit.
British: Value B

268 *'Apprentice Tradesmen at an Army Technical School.'* The rapid development of motorized transport between the wars led to the need for more

extensive radio communica-tion in order that command instructions could be given to widely scattered forces. Effective wireless systems depended upon tuned aerials and specially chosen sites, technical qualities requiring a new breed of soldier to understand them. Long-range communication (for example ship to ship or ship to shore) still depended upon the use of signal codes—such as Morse—but tactical systems increasingly used speech.
British: Army Form B2556-7. 1910 layout on reverse. Value B

269 *'Winter on the Western Front.'* Although Belgium and Holland were threatened by the Nazis following the invasion of Poland, the only countries whose armed forces could hope to stop the Germans were France and Britain. Overall Commander of the Allies was General Maurice Gamelin, a Frenchman, and subordinate to him was Lord Gort, who commanded the B.E.F. Although Gort was prepared to follow orders he was not enthusiastic about the plans (D & E) which Gamelin had made to meet a German invasion of Belgium.
National rivalries began to show an increasingly similar condition to that of the N.A.T.O. alliance in the 1970's and early '80's, where French secular interest prevailed over international co-operation.
British: (War Office Photograph) No. B1508. Value B

270 *Auxiliary Military Pioneer Corps in France.'* Although poorly armed and with much of their strength virtually untrained, the Pioneers gave a good account of themselves in the fighting that led to Dunkirk. However, even though many of them had joined in response to an appeal by the War Minister, Hore-Belisha, they were intended for use as labourers rather than soldiers. Perhaps they had some compensation when Hore-Belisha was forced to resign in 1940.
British: (War Office Photograph) No. B1490. Circa 1940. Value B

271 *'Dorsets Out of Battle Dress.'* Mobile units provid-ing bathing and laundry facilities travelled behind the battle areas and, ideally,

WINTER ON THE WESTERN FRONT. WAR OFFICE PHOTOGRAPH B.1508.

269

AUXILIARY MILITARY PIONEER CORPS IN FRANCE. War Office Photograph No.B.1490.

270

DORSETS OUT OF BATTLE DRESS. WAR OFFICE PHOTOGRAPH B.1728.

271

H.M. THE KING WITH THE R.A.F. IN FRANCE. AIR MINISTRY PHOTOGRAPH C.63.

272

MACHINE GUNNER ON B & P 'OVERSTRAND'   "BRITAIN PREPARED"

273

274

275

soldiers would not only have a bath (or more usually a shower) but also a change of clothes. Sometimes decontamination procedures accompanied the wash and brush up.
British: (War Office Photograph) No. B1728. Circa 1940. Value B

272 'H.M. the King with the B.E.F. in France.' Once the immediate scare following the invasion of Poland was over, dignitaries ventured out to France to see the B.E.F. The War Minister, Hore-Belisha, went out in November 1939 for a two day visit; Ironside, the C.I.G.S., went out on 30 November followed by the King. On his return to England he told Chamberlain that the Army was resentful of Hore-Belisha's implied criticism. So Chamberlain went out and wrote to Gort that he appreciated '. . . the great progress that has been made in so short a time.' Hore-Belisha was forced to resign.
British: (Air Ministry Photograph) No. C63. Circa 1940. Value B

273 'Machine Gunner on B & P Overstrand.' The 'one man, one gun' open-cockpit idea of aerial warfare faded fast. The Overstrand was a 'between the wars' aeroplane and by the time that battle was truly joined in 1940, pilots, let alone gunner/navigators, sometimes had as many as eight guns under their control.
British: (Pub. Photochrom) 'Britain Prepared' series. Posted October 1940, the month that the R.A.F. knew that they had won, and Goering knew he had lost, the Battle of Britain. Value B

274 'Crashed German.' This downed Me109 is carrying very little marking and is therefore probably a very early casualty in the Battle of Britain. A popular place to record the number of kills and the *Jagdstaffel* (Hunting Squadron) emblem was on the tail rudder, although in this case the painting may be on the other side. Judging by the comparatively intact state of the plane the pilot may have made a safe forced landing.
British: Value C

275 'Rescued Briton.' Official and unofficial small boat rescue services operated off the south coast.

By early September 1940, the R.A.F. was losing 'planes and pilots so fast that some airfields could not be kept in action. Written note on reverse reads: '*Descent of parachutist at Bognor Regis. 26 August 1940.'*
British: Value C

THREE HAMPER CARDS
Service morale was a subject that commanded a great deal of attention. Tactical successes and the prospect of ultimate victory were fundamental ingredients to the maintenance of good spirits. However, a continuing contact with 'home' was almost as important. To the troops it meant that they were not forgotten, while those at home felt they were 'doing their bit.' Some men had no one with whom to correspond and 'gifts from home' were distributed by voluntary organizations so that no one should feel too left out. Inside the parcel would be placed a pre-addressed postcard which the lucky soldier could send to the donor with his thanks.

276 'Sudanese Donor.' This card was included in hampers packed and despatched by Fortnum and Mason of Piccadilly under the auspices of donors to the Overseas League Hamper Fund. What a splendid war—for a brief period anyway!
British: Value A

277, 277A 'Navy, Army, Air Force.' Tobacco parcel card. Caption on reverse reads: '*Dear Mrs. Field. My hearty thanks for your Great Kindness for gift of ciggarettes (sic) which was given to me soon after I returned from Normandy—your Sincere Mr. G. Daniel Worcester.'* As the card is dated August 1944 it requires little imagination to figure out what Mr. Daniel had been doing in Normandy.
British. No. W537B. Value B

278, 278A 'We're All Lit Up' Tobacco parcel card from the Overseas League Tobacco Fund. Caption on reverse reads: '*My dear Mrs. Field, I wish to acknowledge with many thanks your gift of cigarettes which is greatly appreciated. Driver R. Beales.'* The censor has obliterated the details of Driver Beales' unit.
British: No. W541. Value B

279 'Letters to the Folks at Home (Somewhere in France).' The retention of a

276

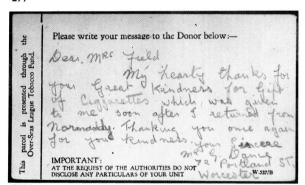

277

Please write your message to the Donor below:—

Dear Mrs Field
My hearty thanks for
your Great Kindness for Gift
of Cigarettes which was given
to me soon after I returned from
Normandy. Thanking you once again
for your kindness. Your sincere
Mrs G Davis
72 Portland St
Worcester

IMPORTANT:
AT THE REQUEST OF THE AUTHORITIES DO NOT
DISCLOSE ANY PARTICULARS OF YOUR UNIT W-537/B

This parcel is presented through the Over-Seas League Tobacco Fund.

277A

POST CARD

This parcel has been presented by

Mrs Joy Field,
10 West Rocke Rd.,
Norwalk, CONN. U.S.A.

Sketch by Crime

WE'RE ALL LIT UP—
LET BATTLE COMMENCE 2.

278

Please write your message to the Donor below:—

My Dear Mrs. Field,
I wish to acknowledge
with many thanks your
gift of cigarettes which is greatly
appreciated
DRIVER R. BEALES

IMPORTANT:
AT THE REQUEST OF THE AUTHORITIES DO NOT
DISCLOSE ANY PARTICULARS OF YOUR UNIT W.541

This parcel is presented through the Over-Seas League Tobacco Fund.

278A

soldier's link with home was a major plank in the regimental officers platform of morale. Following upon the experience of trench warfare, where because of the static nature of the fighting there was time to experiment with, and develop, administrative support organizations for the forward troops, the B.E.F. had a proven system of mail collection and delivery. Post Offices were established at most headquarters and their operation was undertaken by the Royal Engineers.
British: (Pub. Photochrom) No. 23. 'Britain Prepared' series. Value B

TWO MESSAGES
280 *'North Africa to England. Cancelled 21 March 1943.' '. . . I have just*

279

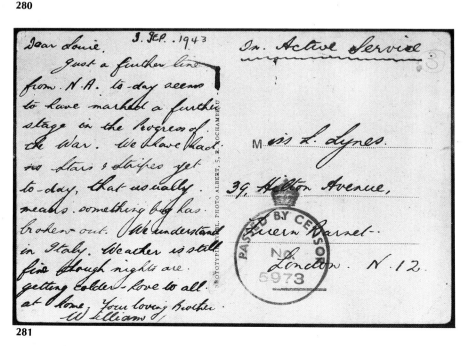

280

281

AVEC LES TOMMIES

20. — Un détachement de troupes de l'Armée anglaise vient d'arriver dans un port français.

282

AVEC LES TOMMIES

21. Les Tommies saluent joyeusement les côtes de France, pendant leur traversée de la Manche.

283

284

285   **286**

returned from another leave, again very enjoyable and extremely interesting, this time to Luxor. . . . Now hard at work again and wondering where next. However, I'm doing quite well and cannot grumble. . . . L.A.C. James. R.A.F. M.E.F.' Not a bad war! Egyptian: (Pub. E. Landrock, Cairo) Value B

281   'North Africa to England. Dated 3 September 1943.' 'Dear Louise, Just a further line from N.A. Today seems to have marked a further stage in the Progress of the War. We have had no Stars and Stripes yet today, that usually means that something big has broken out. We understand in Italy. Weather is still fine though nights are getting colder. Love to all at home, Your loving Brother William.' Odd that the absence of an American service magazine should mean so much. On 3 September, Montgomery's 8th Army invaded Italy across the Straits of Messina. So much for Censor No. 5973!
Nationality unknown: (Pub. Photo Albert) Value C

282   'A Detachment of English Troops Arrive at a French Port.' These soldiers are wearing the pre-war uniform of service dress tunic, pantaloons and puttees. Their Mark 1 steel helmets, also descendants of First World War equipment, are covered with a string net into which strips of hessian have been inserted for camouflage purposes. By May 1940 most soldiers had been issued with the new 'BD'—battledress.
French: (Pub. M. Lescuyer, Lyon) No. 7961. Value B

283   'Tommies Waving at the French Coast as They Cross the Channel.' This cheerful crowd appear to be wearing the old four-pocket service dress with brass buttons. Normal headgear for this uniform was the field service cap, known as the sidecap or 'fore and aft.' Some regiments had dispensations to wear other hats and these soldiers could be Foot Guards as they are wearing khaki service dress caps similar to those of the Guards.
French: (Pub. M. Lescuyer, Lyon) No. A.490. Value B

284   'Japanese Sentry.' To the British in Europe the Japanese war was too far

away to rouse much interest and the troops in South-East Asia came to call themselves the Forgotten Army. When Malaya and Singapore fell the next target was Burma and Orde Wingate's Chindit operations there, which began in 1943, raised the interest value of the campaign followed later by the American Merrill's Marauders who were similar to the Chindits.
Japanese: Value B

285 *'Burma.'* The two soldiers are members of the 14th Army, and the one on the left has a Crossed Keys symbol on his bush hat, the symbol of the 2nd Division. In the spring of 1944 two crucial battles in the Japanese invasion of India were fought around two Indian towns—Imphal and Kohima. Opposing the Japanese General Renya Mutaguchi's force of 100,000 men were three Indian Army Divisions, one East African Division and the British 2nd Division. The Japanese were stopped, and written on the 2nd Division's memorial is:
'When you go home
Tell them of us and say
For your tomorrow
We gave our today.'
British: (Pub. Gale and Polden) No. 11/G&P/35. 1945. Value B

286 *'Commandos.'* Caption on reverse reads: *'Invasion Exercise—Commandos make an Assault Landing.'* The idea for a special force of highly trained volunteers arose in 1940. It was proposed that small, effective cross-Channel operations against the enemy would raise British morale. What Churchill described as 'the iron hand from the sea' impressed General Marshall, the U.S. Chief of Staff, so much that he sent American soldiers to Britain to be trained by the Commandos. Those Americans became the 1st U.S. Ranger Battalion. The Special Forces quickly extended their activities from small specialist assaults to supporting large scale amphibious landings, as at Salerno and Normandy, and it is a measure of their contribution to the war effort that the Commandos won over 470 individual decorations including eight V.C.'s.
British: (Pub. Gale & Polden) No. 8/G&P/32. 1945. Value B

287   **288**   **289**

FIVE JAPANESE CARDS
287, 288, 289, 290 & 291
The Japanese soldier was as fond of his home as any European fighting man. Nevertheless, writing home was something which under the pressure of war all soldiers found difficult to do, and the authorities made the act as easy as possible. Usually postage was free and postcards were provided with the rations, often with alternative messages printed upon them. Postcards with already written messages on them, which require the addition of just a few words by the sender, are called 'Write-Aways.' These Japanese cards are an oriental version of a write-away. The sender drew, or stuck a photo of, his own face upon them. The comic situations contrast strongly with the contemporary European image of the Japanese soldier.
Japanese: Each card value C

292 *'Signal Corps in Action.'* The U.S. Signal Corps had a much wider experience of radio and line communication between the wars than the British Royal Signals, established in 1920. The vast size of America and the extraordinary distances between Army bases prompted the development of telegraph and wireless communication systems. These Service networks were operated by the Military, while British equivalents were civilian systems.
American: (Pub. Tichnor Bros., Boston) No. 69989. Value B

290

291

292

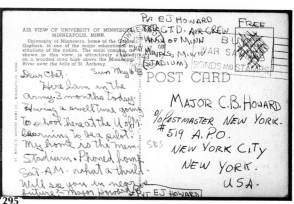

295

293

296

297

294

298

293 'Gas Mask Drill Camp Croft South Carolina.' Printed caption on reverse reads: 'Camp Croft was named after Maj Gen Edward Croft, a native of nearby Greenville S.C. who died in 1938. Army recruits assigned to Camp Croft Infantry Replacement Training Center for their basic military initiation are put through a rigid course of training, which enables them to be fit for duty with permanent service units upon completion of program here.' American: (Pub. Curteich—Chicago) No. L-31. Posted 5 April 1943. Value B

294 'Signal Corps Soldiers Laying Telephone Lines.' A message on the reverse reads: 'Hello, Carry, Sorry, I didn't see you before I left, but you understand when I say that I was tied up that last week as a civilian. Wrote Jack today and I hope to get an answer before I move from here. I expect I'll be here for four weeks after which I'm going to school. Army life is the berries. Believe me, I like it. Regards to the family. Write. Leo.' American: (Pub. Curteich—Chicago) Posted 29 March 1943. Value B

295 The message reads: 'Sun. 16 May '43. Dear Chet, Here I am in the Army three months today. Having a swell time going to school here at the U of M (University of Minnesota) learning to be a pilot. My home is the Mem (Memorial) Stadium. Phoned home Sat A.M.—what a thrill. Will see you in near future Major Howard. As ever, Pvt. E. J. Howard.' The card is addressed to Major C. B. Howard, New York. Obviously son to father. Successive generations were to fight in Europe, like it or not. American: (Pub. Gopher News Co) Value B

296 'The Infantry Advances.' This card depicts the 'First Army War Maneuvers 1939' and the message on the back, dated 17 August 1939 reads: 'Hello, They are trying to make a soldier out of me, some fun, huh. It is beautiful country up here. Warm in the day and cool nights. No mosquitos. Joe.' Joe must have been a volunteer soldier, because conscription was not authorized until 16 September 1940, when President Roosevelt signed the Selective Training and

Services Act. Even then another 14 months would pass before America was at war. American: (Pub. Santway Photo-Craft) No. 82793. Value B

297 'Clearing and Assembling 75mm Guns.' During the First World War the Americans had used French built 75mm guns and then later made their own, based on the French design. These were in service at the beginning of World War II but the general increase in calibre of the whole range of artillery weapons led to the replacement of the 75mm by the 105mm howitzer. Apart from the destructive power of larger calibre weapons, another reason for the size escalation was that artillery pieces no longer depended upon horses for their mobility. One 75mm had required a team of at least six horses. The card was posted on 10 March 1943 and in addition to a printed slogan which reads: 'For Victory BUY United States War Bonds—and Stamps,' the written message includes: 'Hi Charles. . . . I'm feeling pretty good here at Fort Dix. It's a pretty nice place . . . don't write till you here (sic) from me again cause we might be shipped out of this camp . . . Irving.' The Americans were preparing to invade Sicily. Irving might have gone off to join Patton. American: (Pub. W. R. Thompson, Richmond) Value B

298 'Kings of the Broad Highway.' This may be a reference to what the British call 'The Poor Bloody Infantry' or sometimes 'The Queen of the Battlefield.' These American soldiers are marching either pre-war or early in it, because they are still wearing their First World War steel helmets. American: (Pub. Marshall Davis) Value B

299, 300 & 301 'W. Morgan Drawings.' Artists, who were themselves servicemen and therefore had experienced the situations which they depicted, naturally produced much genuine and effective work. Sadly few details of such artists were recorded and, except for the giants like Bairnsfather in the First World War and Mauldin in World War II, little is known about them. No information is at hand about W. Morgan,

BULL SESSION

299

FIRST CLASS PRIVATE

300

"FURLOUGH"

301

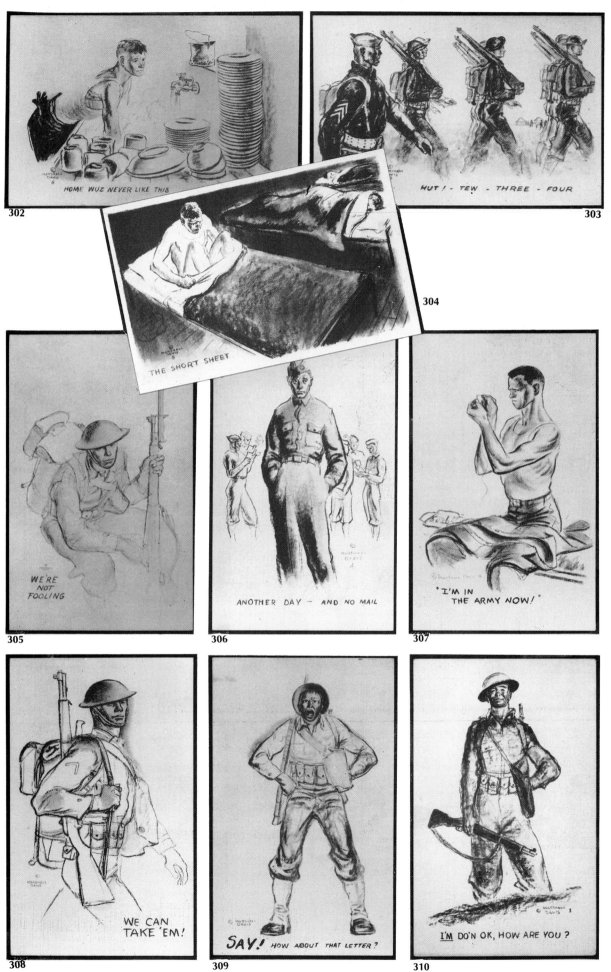

302

HOME WUZ NEVER LIKE THIS

303

HUT! - TEW - THREE - FOUR

304

THE SHORT SHEET

305

WE'RE
NOT
FOOLING

306

ANOTHER DAY - AND NO MAIL

307

'I'M IN
THE ARMY NOW!'

308

WE CAN
TAKE 'EM!

309

SAY! HOW ABOUT THAT LETTER?

310

I'M DO'N OK, HOW ARE YOU?

but it looks as if he knew what he was drawing from personal experience, because no captions are needed for his postcards. *American: All the cards were published by A. D. Steinbeck & Sons of New Haven, Conn.) Each card value B*

302, 303, 304, 305, 306, 307, 308, 309 & 310
'Marshall Davis Drawings.' The American postcards of the war parallel in their variety the British cards of the First World War. American First World War cards were of appallingly bad quality, judged both on content and material. In World War II, however, they made much more use of the medium than the British. **These cards by Marshall Davis**, again an unknown artist/publisher, carry the usual message about the importance of mail, but they also are not embarrassed to say, *'We Can Take 'Em!'* The British hid their pride, their belief in Victory, behind a mask of humour, but their more direct Transatlantic cousins had no such inhibitions. Message on reverse reads: *'US Armed Forces FREE.'*
American: Each card value B

311, 312, 313, 314 & 315
'American Red Cross Service Clubs.' During the First World War the American Red Cross staffed and operated the hospitals of the United States Armed Forces, and when this function was taken over by the Military, the Red Cross was able to concentrate upon its social services. More than 1,500 overseas clubs were set up during the war and these not only offered recreational facilities, but often provided meals and accommodation. These latter were frequently of a higher standard than those of the civilian population—as indeed were the normal service pay and rations of American soldiers. So there was great competition amongst British girls to be invited to an American club. These cards were probably freely available in the club, which would have a quiet corner where a soldier could write home and regular entertainment, such as dances and shows. This club is probably in London and the cards are published by the American Red Cross.
American: Each card value B

AMERICAN RED CROSS SERVICE CLUBS.

"THERE'S ROOM FOR YOU ALL—SIGN RIGHT HERE." C. 7.

311

AMERICAN RED CROSS SERVICE CLUBS.

"SATURDAY NITE"—WITH A G.I. BAND. C 10

312

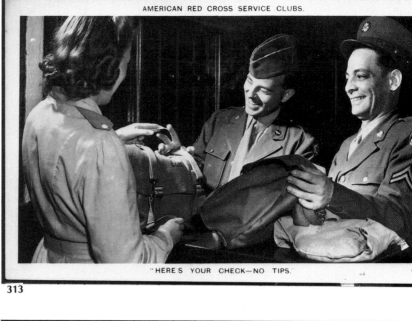

AMERICAN RED CROSS SERVICE CLUBS.

"HERE'S YOUR CHECK—NO TIPS." C 6.

313

AMERICAN RED CROSS SERVICE CLUBS.

"DEAR FOLKS; I'M FEELING FINE . . . . ." C. 3.

314

AMERICAN RED CROSS SERVICE CLUBS.

"NOW, WHERE WOULD YOU LIKE TO GO TONIGHT?" C. 4.

315

THE AMERICAN THEATRE WING STAGE DOOR CANTEEN

As part of the continuous effort to maintain the morale of the fighting forces, well known showbusiness personalities were prevailed upon, or volunteered, to visit the troops in the field and entertain them under the direction of the British E.N.S.A. (Entertainments National Service Association) and the American U.S.O. (United Services Organization). The armed forces had their own newspapers and even their own radio programmes. The Americans beamed out the World-Wide Armed Forces Radio Service and the Voice of America broadcasts to Europe. Back in the United States the sponsors of commercial radio patriotically subsidized programmes designed to cheer up the fighting services and produced postcards to prove it.

316 'The American Theatre Wing Stage Door Canteen.' This card was published by the Stage Door Canteen itself and the printed caption says that it '. . . gives a welcome to all men in the uniformed services of the United Nations without distinction of rank, race, creed or color.' The card was actually posted in New Jersey, U.S.A., on 31 May 1945. It was addressed to a Miss Clark in Sutton, Surrey, England. It reads: 'Dear Doris, Thanks a lot for your letter received just as I left. Please give my regards to Bobby and explain that I am not yet in any danger area. We are all having a really terrific time. Gags of food, ices, sweets etc. Might see you next year but will write. John.' The odds are that John never saw Doris again. The American postal officials who censored mail from Normandy after D-Day calculated that one in eight letters were to girl friends in England.
American: (Pub. Stage Door Canteen) No. 491. Artist Barney Tobey. Value B

317 'The American Theatre Wing Stage Door Canteen.' The caption on the reverse reads, 'Tune in! Stage Door Canteen. Columbia Network every Friday night 10.30 to 11.00 Eastern War Time. Corn Products Refining Company producers of— dextrose sugar. Karo syrup. Mazola salad oil. Linit starch. Kre-mel dessert.'
American: (Pub. Corn Products Refining Co.) No. 491 Artist Barney Tobey. Value B

318 'The American Theatre Wing Stage Door Canteen.' Caption on the front reads: 'Stars of stage, screen, radio, vaudeville and music worlds provide food, dancing and entertainment to servicemen —all free nightly.'
American: (Pub. Corn Products Refining Co.) No. 491. Artist Barney Tobey. Value B

319, 320, 321 & 322
'American Write-Aways.' One method of encouraging soldiers to communicate was to enlist the help of popular cartoon characters. Cartoon strips were a major feature of American newspapers and commanded massive audiences. American papers tended to be local publications, primarily because communities were so far apart and to distribute a national newspaper to the whole country was impossible. Cartoonists had agents who sold their work for them around the country to different newspapers—the expression was 'syndicated them'—and one of the most important agencies was the King Features Syndicate.

THE AMERICAN THEATRE WING STAGE DOOR CANTEEN.
Stars of stage, screen, radio, vaudeville and music worlds provide food, dancing and entertainment to service men—all free nightly

316

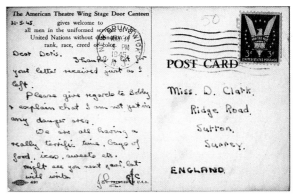

316A

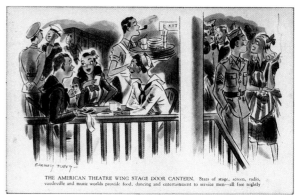

THE AMERICAN THEATRE WING STAGE DOOR CANTEEN. Stars of stage, screen, radio, vaudeville and music worlds provide food, dancing and entertainment to service men—all free nightly

317

THE AMERICAN THEATRE WING STAGE DOOR CANTEEN. Stars of stage, screen, radio, vaudeville and music worlds provide food, dancing and entertainment to service men—all free nightly

318

319

323

320

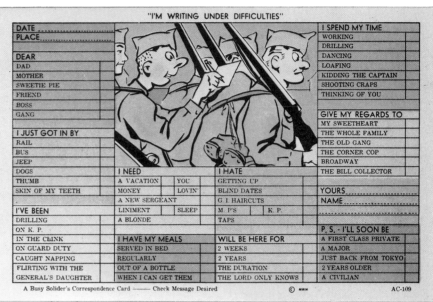

324

321

322

325

326

327

329

328

330

King handled Popeye, Wimpy & Snuffy, while Famous Artists handled Chester Gould's Dick Tracy. All the cards are were probably issued free at service clubs and on the reverse have spaces for 'Name and Rank, Serial No., Branch of Service, Approved Address.'
American: Each card Value B

LETTERS
The American soldier was further from home than most. There were no opportunities to nip home on a '36,' '48' or '72' (the number of hours of leave). Thus even more important to the U.S. soldier than to the British was the letter from home, and the authorities' concern that a steady two-way flow of correspondence across the Atlantic should take place is reflected in the variety of ways to put across the message.

323 *'Enviously.'* The man with the mail is popular, so folks at home write to me.
American: (Pub. Curteich—Chicago) No. USA-17 1B-H2. Value B

324 *'Officially.'* A copy of the First World War Field Postcard.
American: (Pub. Asheville Post Card Co.) Value B

325 *'Poetically.'*
'The mail clerks are busy sorting mail
With a crowd of soldiers on their tail
Those who get letters leave with a smile
The rest who are there just linger awhile
So please send a letter if you care
The soldier who wants it is waiting there.'
American: (Pub. E. C. Kropp. Milwaukee, Wis.) No. C174. Author Pvt. James V. Cerullo. Value B

326 *'Grammatically.'* An obvious, and therefore possibly effective, pun.
American: (Pub. Colourpicture. Cambridge, Mass.) No. 336. Series S. Army Life Comics. Value B

327 *'Sexily.'* Look what can happen at home if you don't write!
American: (Pub. Asheville Post Card Co.) No. 74340. Value B

328 *'Aggressively.'* 'Halt!'
American: (Pub. Colourpicture. Cambridge, Mass.) No. 335. Series S. Army Life Comics. Value B

331

332

333

334

3   *Sur le Front. - Remise de décorations*

335

8   *Sur le Front. - Un Observatoire.*

336

4   *Le Général Gamelin au G. Q. G. Britannique*

337

10   *Deux Allemands viennent d'être faits prisonniers.*

338

6   *La D. C. A. - Pièce en action.*

339

13   *Aux Armées. - L'Heure du Courrier.*

340

329 *'Belgium Leave Section U.S. Army.'* Allied Forces reached Belgium on 3 September 1944 and their actions were greatly assisted by the activities of the armed underground resistance movement. The period following Liberation was one of comparative affluence, due to an excess of dollars from U.S. Lease-Lend. Doubtless, therefore, American soldiers on leave would find many a welcome, but whether this card is smiling upon fraternization or reminding soldiers of their obligations to the Girl back at home is not clear. *American. Presumably produced in Belgium. Artist Joop Geesink. Value C*

330 *'Happy Birthday to You.'* A simple message from the Leave Station. The Section may have been set up to advise American soldiers taking leave in Belgium on the customs of the country. *American: Presumably produced in Belgium. Artist Joop Geesink. Value C*

ARMÉE FRANCAISE
Series of coloured artist-drawn pictures of various branches of the French Army.

331 *'Moroccan Machine-Gunner.'* French Morocco was subdivided into Military districts governed by officers of the Regular French Army, and many Moroccans fought in the seven Colonial divisions in the French army. The Moroccans suffered economically when France capitulated in 1940. Trade was virtually paralysed, but they remained officially loyal to Vichy France. A token resistance was even offered to the Allied Invasion of November 1942 by General Vogues. *French: (Pub. André Leconte) Artist Paul Barbier. 1940. Value B*

332 *'D.C.A.'* (Sound Ranging Equipment). The four microphone dishes feed into the earphones of the operator who is listening for enemy aeroplanes or gunfire. The hand wheel which he holds rotates the microphone array until he gets the loudest sound. This is then taken to indicate the direction of the enemy activity. *French: (Pub. André Leconte) Artist Paul Barbier. 1940. Value B*

333 'Aeronauts.' Balloons, equipped with radio, were used for air defence and for observation purposes.
French: (Pub. André Leconte) Artist Paul Barbier. 1940. Value B

334 'Pigeon Handlers.' The pigeon has often been used to carry messages. During the First World War and World War II many messengers were eventually consumed by their starving handlers.
French: (Pub. André Leconte) Artist Paul Barbier. 1940. Value B.

C.A.P. SERIES
Sepia series of photographic views of the French Army of 1939/40 similar in subject matter and presentation to the British Photochrom 'Britain Prepared' series.

335 No. 3. 'On the Front. Awarding Decorations.' Note the First World War style uniforms of these World War II Poilus.
French: (Pub. 'C.A.P.') Circa 1939–40. Value B

336 No. 8. 'On the Front. An Observation Post.' As in the First World War, the French posed their military publicity photographs for civilian consumption.
French: (Pub. 'C.A.P.') Circa 1939–40. Value B

337 No. 4. 'General Gamelin at British Staff Headquarters.' Gamelin, the French Chief of Staff, with Viscount Gort, Commander of the B.E.F. and General Sir Edmund Ironside, Chief of the Imperial General Staff. Ironside replaced Gort as C.I.G.S., as the latter did not get on well with Hore-Belisha. Ironside, a man of action, would have preferred Gort's post.
French: (Pub. 'C.A.P.') Circa 1939–40. Value B

338 No. 10. 'Two Germans Have Just Been Taken Prisoner.' This picture looks more authentic and unrehearsed than most in the series. The photographer was particularly fortunate in being present when some of the very few German prisoners were taken by the French in World War II.
French: (Pub. 'C.A.P.') Circa 1939–40. Value B

339 No. 6. 'Aircraft Detection machine in Action.' This is an anti-aircraft gun which works in co-operation with the sound-ranging equipment. It would be laid according to the information obtained by the sound ranger.
French: (Pub. 'C.A.P.') Circa 1939–40. Value B

Un défilé de troupes. — Het défilé van de troepen.

343

L'Armée motorisée. — Het gemotoriseerde Leger.

344

14 Dans la Montagne. - Les Éclaireurs-Patrouilleurs.

341

11 Avant-Poste sur le Front.

342

Prêts au départ. — Gereed voor het vertrek.

345

346

347

340 No. 13. *'With the Army—Letter-writing Time.'* Contact with home was a vital aid to morale, especially when soldiers were as bored as those kicking their heels behind the Maginot Line in the Drôle de Guerre. *French: (Pub. 'C.A.P.') Circa 1939—40. Value B*

341 No. 14. *'In the Mountains. Scout Patrol.'* The *'Chasseur Alpins'* were amongst France's most famous fighting men. In the battle for France the strongest French resistance was offered in the Alpes Maritimes on 21 June by six Divisions who heroically repulsed the attack of 32 Italian Divisions. *French: (Pub. 'C.A.P.') Circa 1939—40. Value B*

342 No. 11. *'Forward Post on the Front.'* During the winter of 1939 the Front stretched the length of France's border with Germany. France relied on Belgium's neutrality and the B.E.F. to protect her border with Belgium. *French: (Pub. 'C.A.P.') Circa 1939—40. Value B*

THOSE WHO ARE ON THE LOOK OUT SERIES

343 *'A March Past of Troops.'* When the Germans attacked in May 1940, the strength of the Belgian Army was about 600,000 men. It was commanded by King Leopold—as his father Albert had commanded the Belgian forces in 1914. *Belgian: (Pub. NELS) Captions in Belgian and French. 1939. Value B*

344 *'The Motorized Army.'* The conscript force of the Belgian Army had been on full war footing since August 1939. Its cavalry corps consisted of two cavalry divisions and a motorized cavalry brigade. Seven infantry corps, consisted of 12 active divisions, six territorial divisions, two divisions of *Chasseurs Alpins* and a brigade of cyclist frontier guards. *Belgian: (Pub. NELS) Captions in Belgian and French. 1939. Value B*

345 *'Ready to Move Off.'* The Belgian Army had no tanks of its own. This impressive array appears to be of the AMR 33VM type of light tanks made in France by Renault. *Belgian: (Pub. NELS) Captions in Belgian and French. 1939. Value B*

THE GERMANS

346 *'Anti-tank Gun in Action.'* From an original by V. Mundorff, Chemnitz. *German: (Pub. 'Traditionspflege,' Berlin) Value C*

347 *'Pioneers.'* From an original by V. Mundorff, Chemnitz. *German: (Pub. 'Traditionspflege,' Berlin) Value C*

348 *'Our Tank Forces. A Motorcyclist.'* The motorcycle troop would be attached to the Panzer Division for reconnaissance purposes. During the Battle for the River Meuse in the Invasion of France by the Germans in May 1940, the French attacked the German motorcycles at Wastia and achieved one of the few French successes of the campaign. It was, however, shortlived, as the French tank crews became nervous at night and withdrew from the heights they had captured on 14 May. Card overprinted on reverse: *'German People's Fund for Fallen Comrades. German Youth September 1941.' German: Postcard in aid of the Fund for Germans Abroad.*

349 *'Our Tank Forces. A Tank Engineer.'* By 1940 Germany had ten Panzer Divisions. Each division was a complicated mixture of self-contained battle groups, consisting of Rifle Regiments, Signals Battalions, Engineers and an Artillery Battalion to back up the main Panzer Regiment. After the invasion of Poland, several cavalry divisions were converted to Panzer Divisions. *German: Postcard in aid of the Fund for Germans Abroad. Artist W. Willrich (the name just visible on the picture is that of the subject). Circa 1940. Value D*

350 *'The Police in Frontline Duty.'* Caption on reverse reads: *'Day of the German Police 1942. Patrol of the Constabulary and the Security Police in the East.'* This postcard is dated by hand—15 February 1942— right in the middle of the Russian winter offensive when at points from Finland along the Front to the Crimea, the Soviets were making deep penetrations into the German defences. If the owner of the card was on the Eastern Front, he would have been feeling worried. *German: (Official postcard) Value D*

348

349

350

351

352

Lieb' Vaterland magst ruhig sein!

355

Kanonier am Rundblickfernrohr

353

Flammenwerfertrupp vor dem Angriff

356

In höchster Bereitschaft

357

Geschütz auf dem Marsch

354

Auf dem Schlauchboot wird der Fluß überquert

358

359

351 *'Day of the National Socialist German Workers' Party in General Government.'* When Germany invaded Poland, Hitler divided the land into two zones. The Provinces that had once been ruled by Prussia and parts of Central Poland were incorporated into the Reich on 19 October 1939. The remaining territory was organized as 'General Government,' one year of which is celebrated on this card.
German: Printed and posted in Krakow, Poland. Artist W. Hoeck. Value C

352 *'Our Army Marching in Step.'* As the infantry were short of vehicles, they had to rely on foot power for much of their movements. This column appears to be singing to help them on their way.
German: (Pub. Amag) Value B

GERMAN SERIES 'WEHRMACHT BILDSERIE' (Army Pictures) Scenes photographed by Heinz Schröter, probably during exercises. Caption on reverse (translated) reads: *'Published with the permission of the Army Supreme Command.'*

353 *'Gunner Looking Through Telescopic Sight.'*
German: No. 5194/4. Value B

354 *'Guns on the Move.'* The Artillery had to rely on horse power for much of its transport throughout the war.
German: No. 5172/2. Value B

355 *'Dear Fatherland Rest Assured!'*—the power of Germany's great guns is protecting her.
German: No. 7266. Value B

356 *'Flame Thrower Troop on the Offensive.'* The World War II flamethrower had changed little from its First World War prototype.
German: No. 7156. Value B

357 *'In Highest State of Readiness'*—rarin' to go!
German: No. 7316. Value B

358 *'The River is Crossed by Rubber Dinghy.'* Note the 'pudding basin' haircuts. The Unteroffizier wields an oar.
German: No. 5354. Value B

359 *'Our Army. Artillery Battle in the East.'*
German: (Pub. E. A. Schwerdtfeger, Berlin) No. 379. Foto H. Müller-Brunke. (A branch of the Schwerdtfeger company operated as postcard publishers in Britain between the wars.) Value B

360

Unser Heer
Nachrichtentruppe: Am Funkgerät

361

362

PK-Aufnahme Quart (PBZ)

363

Unser Heer
Infanterie: Granatwerfer

364

360 *'Our Army. 15cm Gun Put in Position.'* Postcard from soldier on active service posted in March 1941.
German: (Pub. Foto-P1/2) No. D3413. Value B

361 *'Our Army. Communications Section. On the walkie-talkie.'*
Geman: (Pub. in Berlin) Value B

362 *'Gas Training.'* The Germans introduced both chlorine and mustard gas during the First World War and so European armies prepared themselves for its use in the new conflict. However, during World War II, gas was not used, probably because each side was fearful of the enemy's power of retaliation, particularly in view of the new 'nerve' gases which had been developed.
German: (Pub. Amag) Value B

363 *'The N.C.O. in Battle.'* On the reverse (translated): *'The N.C.O. and his men safeguard their foothold on the shore.'* Propaganda Company Photograph. N.C.O.'s in the war—a model German youth, N.C.O. Bewerber engaged for either a 4½ or a 12 year service.
German: (Pub. Amag) September 1944. Value B

364 *'Our Army. Infantry: a Grenadier.'* Posted by a soldier in Bremen in 1941.
German: (Pub. Ross-Verlag, Berlin) Value B

365 *'Helmets off in Prayer.'* Luftwaffe Junior Officers stand at the end of each row (which probably comprises a platoon) of privates and Junior N.C.O.'s at this large open air service. The photograph is reprinted from *Der Adler,* the Luftwaffe's Illustrated Magazine.
German: Value C

'DAY OF THE STAMP 1942' German series of Official Postcards, celebrating various branches of the German Army and Services, designed by Axel-Heudtlass. A tax of 25pf from the sale of each card went to the 'Kulturfonds.'

366 *'The Todt Organization.'* Dr. Fritz Todt (1891–1942) was the architect of the *autobahns* and the West Wall Defences, as part of his job as Chief of Germany's construction industry. He was killed on 8 April 1942 when his 'plane crashed after taking off from Hitler's East Prussian headquarters at Rastenburg —the 'Wolf's Lair.'
German: (Official card) Posted in Potsdam on 11.1.1942. Value B

367 *'Afrika Korps.'* The Afrika Korps was formed to assist the Italians in North Africa in 1941. Its first

Commander was Lieut-General Erwin Rommel.
German: (Official card) Posted in Strassburgiels on 11.1.1942. Value B

368 *'German Navy.'* Hitler 3pf Deutschesreich stamp, with Ukraine overprint. 1942 was one of the German Navy's most successful years, with U-boats sinking a total of 6,266,215 tons of Allied shipping (1,160 ships).
German: (Official card) Value B

369 *'In the Struggle for Liberty.'*
German: (Official card) Posted in Berlin on 12.1.1941. Value B

'DIE WEHRMACHT' Series of postcards reproduced from photographs printed in this Illustrated War Magazine, published in Berlin.

370 *'Memorial for Heroes.'* Hitler takes his Italian friend, Mussolini (in splendid

Ruritanian costume) to a ceremony at the *Neue Wache* (New Guard House). Hindenburg remodelled it in 1931 as a Tomb to the Unknown Warrior and a Memorial to the Fallen of the 1914–1918 War. Today it stands in East Berlin as a memorial to the Victims of Fascism and Militarism.
German: Photograph by 'Weltbild' (World Newspaper), Berlin. Value B

371 *'Heavy Howitzer.'* The great, heavy guns of World War II were towed by powerful tractors which gave them the all-important feature of mobility. The German 170mm gun had a range of 17 miles. Its Allied counterparts were the 155mm 'Long Tom,' which had a range of 14 miles, and the huge 8in gun, which weighed over 30 tons. It was so enormous that its mount had to be broken into two sections for transport over

366

365

368

367

369

bridges and along roads. It had a range of 20 miles. *German: Photographer Habedanck, Berlin. Value B*

372 *'Engineers at their Work in Rushing Water.'* As the complexity of mechanical warfare increased, so greater knowledge and wider skills were needed at all levels. 'Pioneers' once generally meant 'labourers,' while 'Engineers' meant skilled men. But engineers' skills were now needed well forward with fighting units, and so pioneers on regimental strengths were given additional training and then backed up by detachments of more specialized units. The preparation of river crossings, temporary road and bridge repairs, and emergency engineering works under fire were usually the province of the *Sturmpionier* (Assault Engineers) while at a higher command level were *Bruckenkolonnen* (Bridging Columns) *Sturmbootkommandos* (Assault Boat Units), *Bruckenbau-Batgaillone* (Bridge Building Battalions) and *Eisenbahn-Pionier* (Railway Engineers).

373 *'Music Corps of the Cavalry.'* Although this band is on Ceremonial Parade and therefore one would expect them to be on horseback, the use of the horse for transport and supply was much greater than is generally realized during World War II. This was especially true of the Germans who, because of their sheer numerical strength, simply did not have enough motorised transport to stretch. Gradually throughout the war, the Cavalry Regiments on both sides became mechanized and converted to tanks or armoured cars—the battle steeds of modern warfare. *German: 'Die Wehrmacht' (Illustrated War Magazine) Value B*

374 *'Motor Cyclist, Through Thick and Thin.'* From the 'Thirties, the Germans made more and more use of powerful motorcycles to transport their fighting force to battle. B.M.W. and Zundapp both made 750cc combinations of bike and sidecar, with engines that drove the wheels of both bikes and sidecars. The motorbikes

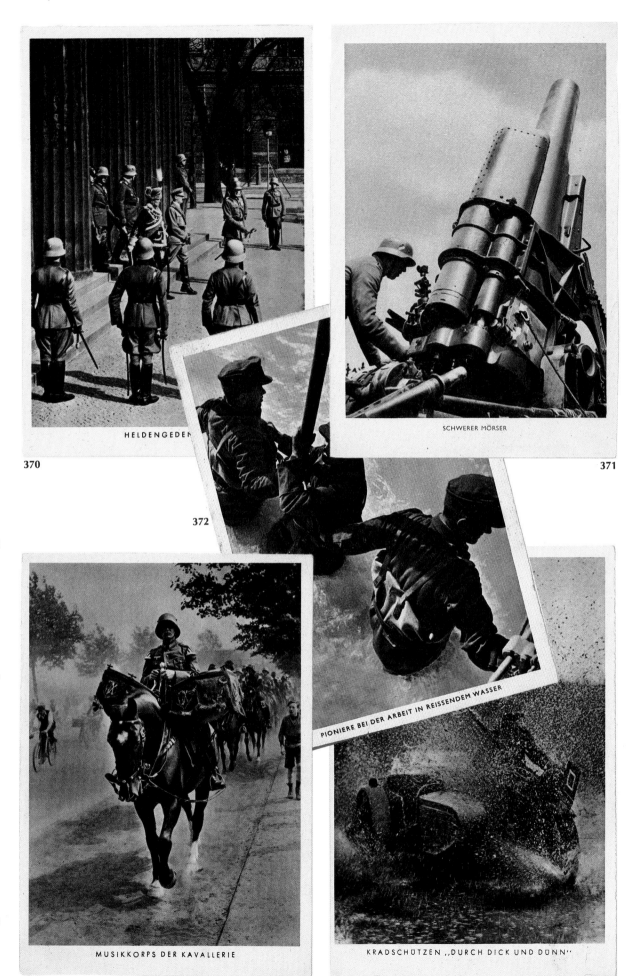

HELDENGEDEN

SCHWERER MÖRSER

370

371

372

PIONIERE BEI DER ARBEIT IN REISSENDEM WASSER

MUSIKKORPS DER KAVALLERIE

KRADSCHÜTZEN „DURCH DICK UND DÜNN"

373

374

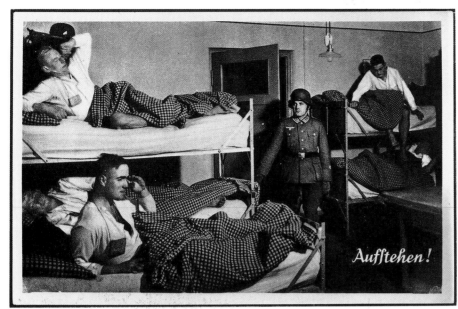

Aufftehen!

375

Urlaubszeit — schöne Zeit?
Auch für mich ist's jetzt so weit.
Ich werde nun bald bei Dir sein.
Erwarte mich! Auf immer Dein!

376

Tapfere kleine Soldatenfrau
Lied von Carl Sträßer

1. Als wir im August hinausgezogen sind, / Da hast
du mich zum Sammelplatz gebracht, / Du trugst auf
deinem Arm unser kleinstes Kind, / Und du hast mich
so fröhlich angelacht. / Du sagtest unserem Jungen:
„Schau, / Dort steht der Vater ja!" / Und du warst eine
kleine tapfere Frau, / Die ihren Liebsten scheiden sah.

1.—4. Tapfere kleine Soldatenfrau, / Warte nur, bald
kehren wir zurück. / Tapfere kleine Soldatenfrau, /
Du bist ja mein ganzes Glück. / Tapfere kleine Soldatenfrau, / Ich weiß, wie so treu du denkst an
mich. / Und so soll es immer sein. / Und so denk
ich ja auch dein, / Und aus dem Felde von ganzem
Herzen grüß' ich dich.

2. Als Abschied ich nahm, da war der Garten bunt, /
Viel Rosen waren ringsumher erblüht. / Du gabst mir
einen Kuß und dein roter Mund, / Der hat auch wie
ein Röselein geglüht. / Du drücktest mir die Hand so
fest, / Da hab' ich's tief gespürt, / Daß mit Stolz in
den Kampf du mich ziehen läßt, / Den Freiheitskampf,
den Deutschland führt.

3. Heut' bin ich so fern von dir und unserem Haus, /
Doch fühl ich deine Grüße mit mir gehn. / Ich rechne
mir den Tag bis zum Urlaub aus, / Werd' dann dich
und die Kinder wiedersehn. / Du stehst am Gartentore
dann; / Wie schön ist da die Welt, / Wenn die tapfere
Frau ihren feldgrauen Mann / In ihren Armen selig hält.
(wenden!)

377

378

379

were, however, always
accident prone and their
value was limited, recon-
naissance being perhaps
their most useful function.
*German: Photographer
Mitschke, Oberhof
(Thuringen). Value B*

375 *'Wakey, Wakey!'* This
obviously posed photograph
is designed to show the
comfortable sleeping
quarters of the wartime
soldier in his check quilted
bunk. The N.C.O. stands
gently by as his men
gradually come to!
*German: (Pub. Franckh,
Stuttgart) No. 214. Value B*

376 *'On Leave.'* The happy
moments of leave-time, of
being again with one's loved
ones, are the subject of this
verse. This soldier hopes his
girl will be waiting for him
when he arrives with his gift.
German: Circa 1940. Value B

377 *'Brave Little Soldier's
Wife.'* Song by Carl Strasser,
sent by a soldier in the
Artillery to his wife.
*German: (Pub. Robert Franke,
Hamburg) 1942. Value B*

378 *'Field Telephone.'* Line
communication was used
between forward observa-
tion posts and their reporting
headquarters throughout the
war. However, Artillery
forward observation, which
required secure and prompt
message passing in order to
bring accurate fire on to an
enemy position, tended to
use both line and radio. This
soldier, whose gas mask
container can just be seen
over his left shoulder, may
well be relaying the
instructions of an Artillery
Observation Officer.
German: Value B

379 *'Pilot.'* German pilot
training was rigorous and
thorough. Pilots in bomber
squadrons would have at

least 250 hours flying
experience. The Captain of
the bomber was the
Observer, not the Pilot, and
he would have at least 150
hours flying experience. In
1940 these highly trained
men frequently had to
double as pilots, and they
were awarded a special
'Double Badge.' Many of the
wearers of this mark of
exceptional skill and
experience were lost and the
standard of the Luftwaffe was
never again as high.
German: Circa 1942. Value C

SCAPA FLOW, NORWAY, NARVIK, AND CRETE
The phenomenal increase in
the mobility of the armed
forces of all the belligerents
led to many experimental
exploits designed sometimes
to raise morale, or achieve
specific military objectives.
The Germans used the
postcard as an additional
tool of the propaganda
machine.

380 *Scapa Flow.* At the end
of the First World War the
German Navy had been
interned at Scapa Flow in the
Orkney Islands, the main
base of the British Home
Fleet and there it had
scuttled itself. On
14 October 1939 U-boat
U-47, commanded by
Oberleutenant Gunther
Prien, slipped past the
harbour defences and sank
the battleship *Royal Oak*. It
evened the score. This
Luftwaffe card doesn't
mention the U-47. It reads
(translated): *'German
aeroplanes over Scapa Flow
—bombs rain on the British
cruisers and battleships.'*
*German: (Pub. Der Adler)
Circa 1940. Value C*

381 *Norway.* Hitler
coveted the long Norwegian
coastline. He saw it as a
safeguard against a sea
blockade of Germany's ports
and, in violation of the

country's professed neutrality, Nazi forces began landing from both air and sea on 8 April 1940. Each of the detachments was under 2,000 men and required rapid follow up of supplies and reinforcements. This card is titled on the reverse (translated): *'Our German infantry had just landed on a Norwegian airstrip—and the transport plane is about to take off again.'*
Der Adler (The Eagle).
German: (Pub. Der Adler) Circa 1940 Value C

382 *The Heroic Battle of Capitain Commodore S. Bonte at Narvik on 13 April 1940.* The British reacted quickly to the Nazi invasion of Norway on 8 April 1940. At Narvik, beyond the effective range of the Luftwaffe, five destroyers suddenly attacked the German vessels in the harbour early on the morning of the 10th. Three days later the battleship *Warspite* arrived with more destroyers, and despite what turned out to be an action costly to both sides, the Germans came off worst, with the loss of ten destroyers. The card was posted from the German Naval Academy by a cadet on 24 January 1944. His message (translated) reads: *'Dear Aunty Poja, I've been here for 2½ weeks now and I've learned all the instructions. Up to now I've not been getting mail, but otherwise everything is OK with me . . . many greetings and kisses from your Alex.'*
German: (Pub. Joh Thordsen, Hamburg) Value B

383 *'100 Against 10.'* After the British naval assault on Narvik, landings were made the following day, 14 April 1940, but it was not until 28 May that the 25,000 Allied soldiers had wrested control from General Dietl's force of 2,000 mountain troops. Dietl had fought well and skilfully, using the additional 2,000 sailors who had survived the naval battle. However, the Allies were unable to stay in Norway and began their evacuation early in June so that on 8 June Dietl was back in control of Narvik. Forgetting the sailors, the odds against him had been 120 against 10. Including the sailors they had been 60 against 10. The postcard, advertising the weekly 'Cologne Illustrated' which

was reporting the story, is justified in claiming '100 against 10'.
German: (Pub. The Cologne Illustrated) Circa 1940. Value D

384 *'Parachutists on Crete.'* The island of Crete had initially been seen by the British as a support base for operations in Greece, but when the Germans won the mainland battle, the island became important to them as a means of controlling the Eastern Mediterranean. On 20 May 1941 the German 7th Air Division with

supporting mountain troops totalling 13,000, dropped on the island from an armada of 1,400 aeroplanes—bombers, gliders, fighters and transports. Despite a valiant defence by General Bernard Freyberg's 28,000 troops, the Germans increased their strength to 30,000 and the British were forced to evacuate. Damage to both sides was severe and the Germans never again tried an airborne operation on such a scale.
German: (Pub. Joh Thordsen, Hamburg) Artist H. Gross. Posted 31 July 1942. Value D

380

381

382

383

Fallschirmabspringer auf Kreta

384

BLACK OUT!

385 *'Black Out.'* A full moon such as this made many people extremely nervous about bombing. It was generally expected after the Invasion of Poland that Hitler would launch an all out Blitzkrieg of aerial bombardment.

Nerves were intolerably strained when no bombs fell during the period of the Phoney War and it was almost a relief to the unbearable tension of expectancy when the Blitz finally started.
British: (Pub. Tuck) Artist Dinah. Value A

386 *'What we found in last night's blackout.'*
American: (Pub. Asherville Postcard Co.) Value A

387 *'Taking up positions for the Blackout.'* Possibly the only people who appreciated the enforced darkness were courting couples.
British: (Pub. Lychgate Ltd., Worthing) Artist E.M.C. Circa 1939. Value A

385

386

CHAPTER SEVEN

The Home Front– Women at War

388 *'I wouldn't trust my husband further than I could see him in a black-out.'* The artist, Reg Maurice, had been designing postcards since before the First World War. During that war he drew many comic series showing life in the army. *British: 'Humoresque' series. Artist Reg Maurice. Circa 1939. Value A*

Taking up positions for the Blackout.

387

388

I n World War II, for the first time since the Civil War, the British civilian population was involved as an active, suffering 'Home Front'. There had been some Zeppelin bombing raids, several serious explosions in munitions factories and a few cases of direct shelling during the First World War, but casualties were relatively few.

Anticipating an aerial bombardment, the Government instituted a plan for evacuating the children of London to the safety of the countryside. 827,000 school children reported at evacuation reception centres in September 1939 as well as 324,000 children under school age.

The town children mixed like oil and water with their country hosts. Cultural differences were enormous – in speech, eating and sleeping habits. Inevitably many unhappy and homesick evacuees returned home after only a few weeks – much to the relief of their foster parents. However, Dunkirk and the fall of France created a feeling of panic, and many mothers sent their children back to the country. It was a wise decision. Over 60,000 civilians were killed by air-raids.

Visiting their children was difficult for parents. Petrol was rationed, resulting in an active black market and some ingenious schemes for powering cars – including gas engines. Hitch-hiking was encouraged with Government 'Help Your Neighbour' free-lift programmes.

The populace responded to the hardships with the cheerful philosophical approach that had carried the Tommy through the First World War. They learned to 'Make do and Mend', to patch their patches, but to go to bed in their very best undies in case they should be bombed. They queued with patience and swallowed Lord Woolton's stories that carrots would make them see in the dark and that 'Woolton Pie' (a vegetable concoction in white sauce) was delicious.

Many British women 'joined up'. At the beginning of the war they were given traditional 'Women's jobs' – cooking, nursing, cleaning, serving – but later were put to more technical and skilled jobs, and the traditional subservient female role was subtly changed.

Their American sisters flocked to enlist too. The U.S.A. had active women's branches in all three of their services. The W.A.C. (Women's Army Corps) was established in May 1942, the first of the U.S. Women's Services. Its peak strength in April 1945 was 99,000. Its wartime Director was Colonel Oveta Culp.

The popular acronym for the American Women's Naval Service was W.A.V.E.S. (Women Accepted for Volunteer Service). It was established in July 1943 to allow women to enter the U.S. Naval Reserve. Its peak strength in July 1945 was 90,000. From 1944 it was known as 'Women Reserves' and its wartime Director was Captain Mildred McAfee.

W.A.S.P.S. was another name – Women's Airforce Service Pilots – for an organisation started by an energetic woman pilot, Jacqueline Cochran. Although it had to remain a civilian organisation, the W.A.S.P.S. reached a strength of 916 and fulfilled a useful function in delivering aircraft and towing targets for aerial gunnery training etc. It incorporated the Women's Airforce Service Pilots (W.A.F.S.) organised by the woman aviator, Nancy Harkness Love, in 1942. The Women Marines reached a peak strength in June 1945 of 18,409 personnel and its Director was Colonel Ruth Cheney Sweeter. Even the Free French had their own 'Corps Féminin' in response to a call from General de Gaulle, but they disliked seeing their women in uniform.

For many people, the war was a time when they found a deep inner sense of satisfaction – even joy – in the comradeship of 'pulling together'. It was the same feeling experienced by the soldiers in the trenches of the First World War and, like those soldiers did in 1918, civilians felt a strange sense of loss in 1945 when the war came to an end.

389

390

391

394

392

395

393

396

389 *'Is it worth two bits for a black-out?'*
Following Pearl Harbour, blackouts were rehearsed in America and a Civil Defense force was organized with volunteers after the pattern of the British A.R.P. (Air Raid Precautions) and Civil Defence.
American: 'A Mutoscope card.' Value A

390 *'Why didn't you black out like the rest of us last night?' 'Sorry brother, but when you gotta glow, you gotta glow!'* Ouch!
American: 'A Mutoscope card.' Value A

391 *'Newbury by night— our house marked X.'* On the reverse of this card an evacuee writes to his mother in Streatham from Newbury: *'Dearest Mum I arrived back safely but it was very dark going. . . . I spent a very happy weekend and I enjoyed everything I did and it was so nice to see you and I am waiting for Saturday now.*
British: (Pub. J. Salmon) December 1939. Value A

392 *'Silence Civilians.'* Everyone wanted to be in uniform. Many school O.T.C. (Officers' Training Corps) Groups helped the Home Guard and the A.R.P. (Air Raid Precautions).
British: (Pub. Tuck) Value A

393 *'And Let Our Dear Soldiers Conquer Hitler.'* As in the First World War, God was confidently assumed to be on both sides by the belligerents.
British: 'J.K. 115.' 1943. Value A

394 *'We had Haricot beans for dinner today.'* A typical Donald McGill joke. He was undisputed master of the innuendo and *double entendre.*
British: (Pub. D. Constance Ltd.) 'New Donald McGill comics.' Value A

395 *'But surely Darling, you're not going to bed in that thing on our Honeymoon?'*
'Well, Dearest, Mother told me that if I was a sensible girl I should take precautions.'
British: (Pub. D. Constance Ltd.) 'New World McGill comics.' Value A

396 *'Old Maid: "If there's a war I'm going to have six children."'* The billeting of children in safe areas was planned well before the official outbreak of war. During the first few days, 827,000 schoolchildren reported at evacuation reception centres, and 324,000 children under school age.
British: (Pub. Bamforth) Artist D. Tempest. Stamped 'Martime Mail' and sent by a sailor 'On active service.' 1938. Value B

397 *'The Home Front.'* During the period of the Phoney War the public was so bombarded with warnings of dangers—by invasion, by bombing, by gas attacks— that when virtually nothing happened for months, people became jittery. The first bomb fell in Britain on Hoy in the Orkneys on 17 October 1939. The first civilian was killed at Bridge of Waith, Orkney on 16 March 1940. At last, people began to feel that their efforts at civil defence were really necessary. During World War II 70,000 civilians were killed in Britain, 110,000 in France, 500,000 in Germany and an almost unbelievable 15,000,000 in Russia.
British: (Pub. Tuck) Artist Dinah. 1944. Value A

398 *'If You Can't Do Nuthin Else You Can Always Knit!'* Knitting circles were organized to produce woollies for the forces. Special knitting patterns were designed for each service and its particular requirements.
British: (Pub. Bamforth) No. K664. 'Tempest Kiddy' series. Artist D. Tempest. Value A

THE HOME FRONT

397

IF YOU CAN'T DO NUTHIN' ELSE YOU CAN ALWAYS **KNIT**!

398

TWO INTERESTING MESSAGES

399 *'From Elsie, having a day's outing in Colwyn Bay: ". . . I want G to send us some apples and Rations, Tea Butter and Marg. . . ."'* A main preoccupation—food!
British: (Pub. Valentine's) Viewcard of Colwyn Bay. Posted 17 September 1942. Value A

400 *'From Roz to Edie: "We have waited for Mr. Browse to return to work, but find that they have no 50/- suits left. All we have left in the Man's Shop now are utility suits at 28/5. We don't think they are very good value—too cheap—but if you would like a suit on appro, we can send one on to you."'*
British: (Pub. Photochrom) View of Winchester Cathedral. Posted 8 January 1944. Value A

401 *'We'll be seeing you somehow.'* Bicycling was actively encouraged to save fuel. Slogan on reverse reads: *'"We shall never stop, never weary and never give in." The Prime Minister.'*
British: (Pub. Regent Publishing Co.) Artist Kit Forres. 1945. Value A

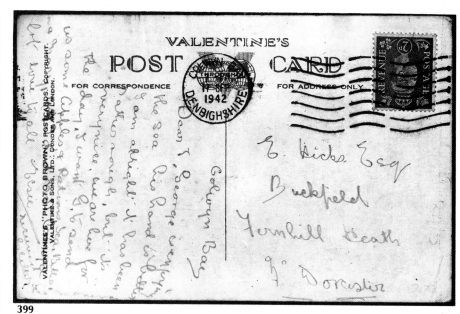

399

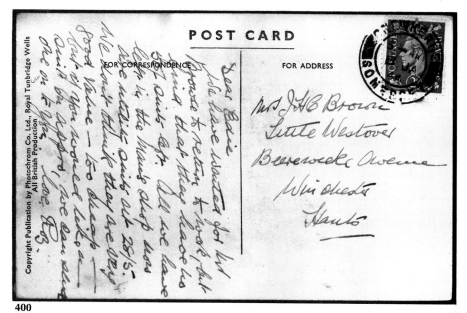

400

"WE'LL BE SEEING YOU SOMEHOW"

401

—NON MAIS... CROIS TU QUE J'SUIS
MOCHE AVEC C'TRUC-LÀ?
—OH! TU SAIS... ÇA NE TE CHANGE
PAS TELLEMENT....

402

"EVACUATED ?
"NO, JUST BUSTIN' TO GO"

403

How's your coal holding out?

SIX
OAKS

404

STILL "IN THE PINK"
THANK YOU, EVEN IF
THERE IS A WAR ON!

"TOUT SUITE"
NUDIST CLUB
STRICTLY
PRIVATE

405

"THE NEW REFRIGERATOR HAS JUST
ARRIVED, DEAR! JUST FANCY BEING
ABLE TO KEEP *EVERYTHING ICY COLD.*"

Save
Coal!

406

"Has your missus been evacuated?"
"Not yet, but she's takin' all sorts
of pills!"

407

I'D LOVE YOU TO SHARE MY SHELTER
WITH ME.

408

IS MY JOURNEY REALLY NECESSARY

409

SOMETHING ACCOMPLISHED,
SOMETHING DONE, HAS EARNED
A NIGHT'S REPOSE!

W

410

402 *'Don't you think I look weird with this contraption?'* *'Well you know it doesn't change you much.'* Message on reverse reads: *'I see that the Delauné family have no chance of re-establishing themselves. Fate is unjust to such brave folk who have helped us so much. I hope the future will be more favourable to the rebirth of their business.'* Many families on the continent were left completely destitute as a result of the war.
French: (Pub. Guy) Artist Joseph Hémard. 1945. Value A

403 *'Evacuated?'* *'No, just bustin' to go.'* Message on reverse reads: *'Percy was home and we had a jolly good laugh at the breakfast table, he had four days leave to make up for Xmas.'* As the war progressed leave became rarer and some unfortunate soldiers, especially those who went out to the Far East early on, never had a leave period.
British: (Pub. Regent Publishing Co.) Artist 'A.E.C.' Circa 1939. Value A

404 *'How's your coal holding out?'* The output of coal fell each year as more miners were called up. By 1942 there was severe shortage of fuel and only opencast mining saved the day.
British: (Pub. H & K) Artist 'J.N.' Circa 1942. Value A

405 *'Still "In the Pink" thank you, even if there is a war on!'* A fear of mass gas attacks was great. Gas masks were issued and gas mask drill taught from the very beginning. There were even Mickey Mouse gas masks for children.
British: (Pub. W.B.) Artist Stocker Shaw. Circa 1940. Value A

406 *'The new refrigerator has just arrived, dear! Just fancy being able to keep everything icy cold!'* It was most unpatriotic to buy such a luxury as a refrigerator.
British: (Pub. H.B. Ltd.) Circa 1942. Value A

407 *'Has your Missus been evacuated?'* *'Not yet, but she's taking all sorts of pills!'* The message on the reverse reads: *'Hope nothing like this happens to you. Any chance of having a shove-ha'penny board to while away the dark and dreary hours!?'*
British: 'Cheerful' series. 12 November 1939. Value A

408 *'I'd love you to share my shelter with me.'* Nights spent in crowded, smelly shelters became the norm and engendered a camaraderie that people almost looked forward to. There were singsongs and music, card games and chat, and some 'dreadful' goings on—young girls were advised not to go into the shelters without their parents. Anderson shelters were built in gardens, and Morrison shelters were constructed under dining room tables.
British: 'Humoresque' series. Artist Vera Paterson. Circa 1940. Value A

409 *'Is My Journey Really Necessary?'* This was one of the most successful slogans of the war. One version of it was drawn by Bert Thomas for the Railway Executive Committee showing a pointing Tommy asking the question. Fougasse also drew some memorable posters.
British: (Pub. Tuck) Artist Dinah. 1944. Value A

410 *'Something accomplished, something done, has earned a night's repose.'* The 'W' stands for Warden.
British: (Pub. Bamforth) Artist D. Tempest. September 1942. Value A

411 *'Who Goes There?' 'Friend with Girl.' 'Pass, Friend; HALT, Girl!' (Oh Boy, Oh Boy!)* The Home Guard (which started the war under the title 'Local Defence Volunteers' and was renamed by Churchill) were prepared to protect Britain from the generally expected Invasion. Their enthusiasm and vigilance were a source of both amusement and admiration. The writer of this card comments, 'These L.D.V. men take a bit of watching.'
British: (Pub. Bamforth) Artist D. Tempest. September 1940. Value A

412 *'Hey Missus! Yer down the wrong A.R.P. Shelter!'* The A.R.P. (Air Raid Precautions) Wardens did gallant and sterling work— on lookout duty, fire fighting duty and, after the raid, in the grim and gruesome work of clearing the rubble and recovering bodies. Throughout most people remained cheerful and philosophical, buoyed up by the indomitable British sense of humour.
British: (Pub. Bamforth) Circa 1940. Value A

411

412

413

414

415

416

417

418

419

420

421

413 *'It's what I shay. . . .
TOO MUCH TALK about Air
Raids! They've already scared
the pants off this poor feller!'*
Government propaganda
during the early days of the
war prepared the populace
to expect an all out bombing
campaign by the Germans.
In fact, by the end of 1941,
190,000 bombs had been
dropped on Britain and
43,667 civilians had been
killed, including 5,460
children under 16.
*British: (Pub. Bamforth)
No. 663. Artist D. Tempest.
Circa 1939. Value A*

414 *'Who Cares a Darn?'*
Clothes were rationed from
June 1941 by the issue of
coupons supposedly suf-
ficient to provide one new
outfit a year. Message on

reverse reads: *'My dear Pal,
Here we go again. I had
rather a strenuous day
yesterday walking miles over
wild country. The demon-
stration was wonderful. A
nice kind piece of shell fell
about 10 yards away from this
Tommy and it was red hot.'*
*British: (Pub. Tuck) Artist
Dinah. Circa 1942. Value A*

415 *'Sew What?'*
*British: (Pub. Tuck) Artist
Dinah. Circa 1942. Value A*

416 *'Hi! You mustn't do
that—that's "a fluctuating or
warbling signal of varying
pitch!"'* The vigilant A.R.P.
Warden has recognized the
note of the siren. There were
several different signals: one
to indicate the beginning of
an air raid, a double warning
to indicate shelling, a
'cuckoo' signal to warn of
enemy aircraft overhead and
the comforting sound of the
'All Clear.' G. L. Stampa, the
artist, was a regular
contributor to *Punch.*
*British: (Pub. Fine Arts
Publishing Co.) 'By
permission of the Proprietors
of Punch.' Artist G. L.
Stampa. 1939. Value B*

417. 417A *'Official Air Raid
Casualty Card.'* This stark
printed postcard, addressed
to the Admiralty, the War
Office or the Air Ministry as
appropriate, was to inform
servicemen that a member of
their family had been killed
or injured in an air raid.
During the worst periods of
the Blitz in 1940, there was
more likelihood of the
civilian members of the
family becoming casualties if
they lived in London or one
of the major cities, than their
serving members.
*British: (Pub. H.M. Stationery
Office) Official Postcard.
Circa 1940/1941. Value B*

WITH THE HOME GUARD
This amusing series by
G. Fyffe Christie, who had
been designing postcards
since the First World War,
owes much to Bruce
Bairnsfather's immortal First
World War character, 'Old
Bill.' The much loved,
walrus-moustachio-ed,
archetypal soldier of the
Great War, was revived in
poster and postcard form
with disappointing results at
the outbreak of World War
II. Bairnsfather was
eventually given the
recognition he deserved by
the Americans when he was
appointed official cartoonist
to the U.S.A.F.

418 *'Up Guards! And At 'Em.'* This famous phrase was attributed to the Duke of Wellington at the Battle of Waterloo. In a letter to J. W. Croker, Wellington admitted, 'What I must have said and possibly did say was, stand up Guards! and then gave the commanding officers the order to attack.'
British: (Pub. Photochrom) No. 4. Home Guard Silhouettes series. Artist G. Fyffe Christie. Circa 1940. Value B

419 *'Old Bill: "Did I ever tell you boys how I saved the guns at Mons?"'* The assumption that the methods of the First World War would work for World War II, coloured the thinking of the Allied military forces and left them susceptible to the rapid warfare of the German Blitzkrieg.
British: (Pub. Photochrom) No. 5. Home Guard Silhouettes series. Artist G. Fyffe Christie. Circa 1940. Value B

420 *'Hullo! Sonny.'* *'Grandsonny to you.'* Perhaps the most useful function of the Home Guard was to make old-timers feel they were fulfilling a useful function and 'doing their bit.' Its main official purpose was to counter the universally expected invasion by Hitler, 'Operation Sea Lion.'
British: (Pub. Photochrom) No. 6. Home Guard Silhouettes series. Artist G. Fyffe Christie. Circa 1940. Value B

421 *'Pardon me I saw it first.'* The name 'Home Guard' was first used during the American Civil War. It was revived by Churchill, whose mother was American, on 14 July 1940.
British: (Pub. Photochrom) No. 2. Home Guard Silhouettes series. Artist G. Fyffe Christie. Circa 1940. Value B

422 *'Sugar's rationed, but you don't need coupons for this sweet stuff!'* Even sweets were rationed in July 1942.
British: 'Humoresque' series. Value A

423 *'Home Grown.'* Every available piece of cultivatable ground was utilized. Allotments were even cleared from bombsites.
British: (Pub. Tuck) No. 9D. Artist Dinah. Circa 1942. Value A

422

Home Grown

423

424

Inside Information

425

WE DON'T MIND

PRE WAR

IF WE DO!
WITH APOLOGIES TO ITMA

426

" I'm afraid I don't know the title, but I left my ration book in page 92."

427

NEVER BEFORE IN THE HISTORY OF **HATS** HAVE WE WOMEN HAD TO PAY **SO MUCH** FOR **SO LITTLE!**

428

I'VE COUPONS ENOUGH I'M GLAD TO SEE, TO BUY A NEW DRESS FOR LITTLE ME!

429

'WELL, WE SHALL HAVE TO COME TO IT.'

430

431

432

433

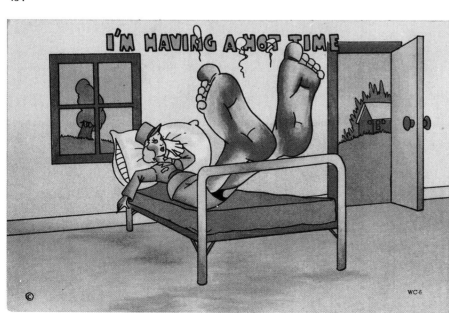

434

435

424 'I'm much "olderer" than you. I can almost remember when orange juice had skin on.' Free orange juice was issued to children in concentrated form and as 'orange juice jelly'—which they loved in jam tarts. Real oranges, bananas, pine-apples, coconuts and other exotic imports totally disappeared and the occasional lemon was so rare that it was often auctioned.
British: (Pub. H.B. Ltd.) Value A

425 'Inside Information.' 'Sold Out.' Food rationing was imposed in January 1940 and food, or the lack of it, became one of the main topics of conversation. Written just before Christmas 1944 this postcard reads: 'Tell Nellie (I) have a piece of pork so far for meat.' There was no turkey or goose on most Christmas tables that year.
British: (Pub. Tuck) Artist Dinah. 1944. Value A

426 'We don't mind if we do! With apologies to ITMA.' The Colonel's favourite catch phrase applied to a sight that was all too rare in many pubs. 'The pub with no beer' was a common phenomenon, in wartime Britain.
British: (Pub. Bamforth) Value A

427 'I'm afraid I don't know the title, but I left my ration book in page 92.'
British: (Pub. Tuck) Circa 1941. Value B

428 'Never before in the history of HATS have we women had to pay SO MUCH for SO LITTLE!' Churchill had made his world-famous and enduring tribute to the heroes of the Battle of Britain on 20 August 1940. The phrase, 'Never in the field of human endeavour was so much owed by so many to so few,' immediately went into English legend to be quoted, mis-quoted and parodied as no other sentence before or since has been.
British: (Pub. Bamforth) No. K165. 'Taylor Tots' series. Artist Arnold Taylor. Circa 1940. Value A

429 'I've coupons enough I'm glad to see
  To buy a new dress for little me.'
British: (Pub. Valentine's) Artist Mabel Lucie Attwell. 1943. Value B

430 'Well, we shall have to come to it.' Cosmetics were officially regarded as extremely non-essential items but many were made on the black market to satisfy the continuing demand from women.
British: (Pub. Regent Publishing Co.) Artist Kit Forres. Circa 1944. Value A .

WITH THE W.A.A.F. (WOMEN'S AUXILIARY AIR FORCE)

431 'A W.A.A.F. Helps A Pilot With His Kit.' After the Battle of Britain, R.A.F. pilots were certainly the most hero-worshipped section of the fighting forces and serving in the W.A.A.F. became very popular!
British: (Pub. Tuck) No. 25. 1939—40. Value B

432 'A Balloon Operator.' The R.A.F. Balloon Command was formed in November 1938. Its 47 Auxiliary Squadrons included W.A.A.F. personnel and deployed 1,450 balloons in September 1939.
British: (Pub. Tuck) No. 4. 1939—40. Value B

433 'Mounting And Loading Guns.' The W.A.A.F. was awarded full military status in 1941 and was allowed to wear uniforms similar in style and colour to the R.A.F.
British: (Pub. Tuck) No. 5. 1939—40. Value B

U.S. WOMEN'S SERVICES

434 'I'm Getting A Big Bang Out Of This Army Life.'
American: (Pub. Beals, Desmoines, Iowa) WC-23. 'Art-Tone "GLO-VAR" Finished.' 1943. Value B

435 'I'm Having A Hot Time.'
American: (Pub. Beals, Desmoines, Iowa) WC-6. 'Art Tone "GLO-VAR" Finished.' 1943. Value B

BRITISH WOMEN'S SERVICES

436 'W.A.T. A Naughty Girl You Are.' The A.T.S. (Auxiliary Territorial Service) reached its peak strength of 213,000 in August 1943. Its Royal Patron was the Princess Royal, whose elder son, Lieutenant Viscount Lascelles of the Grenadier Guards, was taken prisoner by the Germans. He was released just in time to join in the Royal V.E. Day celebration dinner at Buckingham Palace.
British: (Pub. Photochrom) No. 501. 'Celesque' series. 1942. Value A

437 'Every Nice Boy Loves A Sailor.' 'Up with the lark and to bed with a WREN' was a current war-time joke. The women's services in general were regarded with suspicion—from the moral point of view. This was usually an undeserved slur on some fine, brave girls. They did sterling work and generally encouraged and comforted wherever and however seemed most appropriate. When serving abroad, they were often the only girls the lads could communicate with.
British: (Pub. Valentine's) Artist Mabel Lucie Attwell. Circa 1943. Value B

438 'You Know What Men Are.' Of the three women's services, the Women's Royal Naval Service was considered the most glamorous. It reached its peak in June 1944 with a strength of 74,000. Message on reverse reads: '. . . Mummy, I have had a lovely leave. Ever Yours, Rhona.'
British: (Pub. Valentine's) Artist Mabel Lucie Attwell. 1944. Value B

439 'W.A.T.'s Doing.' Originally known as the 'W.A.T.S.' (Women's Auxiliary Territorial Service), the 'W' was later dropped from common usage and they became known as the A.T.S.
British: (Pub. Valentine's) Artist Mabel Lucie Attwell. Circa 1940. Value B

440 'Y.W.C.A. Canteen Folkestone.' A good sprinkling of women in uniform on both sides of the counter can be seen in this photograph taken in January 1940.
British: Value B

FREE FRENCH 'CORPS FEMININ'
441 'Captain Terré and her Staff.' The enthusiasm of the French girls is evident— as is their affection for their Chief.
Card printed in Britain for the Free French: Red and Blue 'France Libre' on Cross of Lorraine on reverse. 1940. Value B

442 'The "Corps Feminin" on Parade.' As the caption explains, the Women's Corps of the Free French Army was a purely voluntary force.
Card printed in Britain for the Free French. 1940. Value B

436

437

438

439

440

441

Les Volontaires du Corps Féminin des F.F.L.
The "Corps Féminin" on Parade.

442

443

444

CHAPTER EIGHT

Imprisonment, Resistance & Allies

445

446

PRISONERS OF WAR
443 *'Group in Battledress.'*
This picture was taken at
Stalag (Stammlager—strictly
translated this means a
P.O.W. camp for other ranks
but the term Stalag is often
used to describe any P.O.W.

At the height of their success, the Germans occupied or controlled most of Europe. There were therefore two sorts of prisoners: fighting men captured in battle and the enslaved populations trying to carry on their lives under Nazi rule. Both groups had their own picture postcards.

On the whole, servicemen in German Prisoner of War camps were treated reasonably well, although wherever there was a strong Nazi presence in an area, the frequency of beatings and torture increased.

It has been estimated that towards the end of the war there were some four million prisoners of war held by both sides. In Germany there were over one and a half million Allied prisoners, but because the figures relating to the Soviet Union are so uncertain all other estimates are at best approximate. The Italians managed to have their men held captive by both sides, since they had changed their allegiance from the Axis to the Allies in 1943.

Throughout hostilities in all theatres, the International Red Cross made determined efforts to provide food parcels and medical supplies to prisoners as well as to help them to maintain their links with their homes. It may be surprising to some to see the sequence of cards showing the life of the British P.O.W.s at Fort Rauch. It does not seem too bad — Red Cross parcels, boxing matches, inter-camp rugby matches, amateur theatricals and an apparent general air of ease. The cards we produced during 1942-43 before Germany had had time to assess the defeats at Alamein and Stalingrad. Conditions probably worsened after 1943 and, since the camp was in Poland, where many concentration camps were located, the Fort Rauch P.O.W.s may have had a much harder time later. Nevertheless the postcards somehow survived.

Resistance by the people of the occupied countries continued at home and overseas. Underground printers produced leaflets and newspapers rather than postcards. But Resistance organisations set up by expatriates in Britain did use postcards to gain publicity and to raise funds for their causes. The most prominent of all such organisations was that set up by General de Gaulle — the Free French.

On 18 June 1940, the day after he had escaped from France, de Gaulle broadcast to the French people via the BBC. He told all Frenchmen that they should join him in London in order to continue the fight against the Nazis. The French Government, which had capitulated to the Germans, ordered the General to return to France and when he refused they sentenced him to death. The French North African Colonies were where de Gaulle planned to set up the Headquarters of Free France, and between 8 October and 17 November 1940 he toured them, forming the 'Defence Council of the Empire' to administer the territories.

Despite the moral and administrative support of the Allies, de Gaulle had an uphill struggle to build the Free French movement. His forces received little credit for the contributions they made towards the struggle against the Axis. In 1940 and 1941, led by General Leclerc), they launched a series of attacks against the Axis in North Africa. They were involved in the Sidi Barrani fighting, helped the British to defeat the Vichy forces in Syria and made a gallant contribution to the delay of Erwin Rommel at Bir Hacheim in 1942. During that same year the small Free French Air Force in North Africa claimed 300 enemy kills, but ultimately what sustained the movement and enabled it to grow to represent the whole French nation was the strength of character of Charles de Gaulle.

There are cards mocking the Occupiers – and cards exhorting the Occupied to conform in some way. The Germans' Allies, the Italians, were briefly the Occupiers of Eritrea, while for a time Britain's future Allies, the Americans, were energetically occupying themselves with a World's Fair in New York, hoping that the war would go away. It did not.

447

448

449

camp) XXID in 1942. The reverse of the card has the official camp mark on it—*Gepruft* (passed). In World War II as in the First World War the Germans seemed to encourage the production and use of picture postcards to show how well their captives were treated. A handwritten note on the card reads: *'Detachment of R.A., Fort Rauch, Posen, 1942.'*
German: Value B

444 *'Group in Greatcoats.'* These prisoners were luckier than many. They had warm winter clothing. As the war progressed the Germans commandeered the belongings of their captives in order to supply their own needs. The card has been given the official mark of Stalag 344 and has a rubber stamped reminder in German which reads: *'Picture only authorized. No words allowed!'*
German: Value B

445, 446 In some camps the facilities afforded the prisoners were very good indeed and men learned new skills, including foreign languages. The artist who drew 'Ted' has certainly produced a good likeness. Both cards were made at the end of 1942 in Stalag XXID, each has the camp rubber-stamped censor clearance.
German: Each card value B

447, 448, 449 *'Theatricals.'* If a P.O.W. was lucky he found himself in a 'good' camp, where his major problem, aside from the fact that he was a captive of the enemy, was boredom. Of course, prisoners were subject to the indignities of searches, hard labour and, when food was scarce, short rations, but for many men to be in captivity was a way to survive. One of the ways to relieve boredom was to put on entertainments. It is said that many of the Goon Show ideas originated from German P.O.W. camps —'Goon' was the prisoners' name for the German camp guard. This series of cards records the show of 'Aladdin' that the inmates of Fort Rauch Stalag XXID put on at Christmas 1942. On the reverse is written: *'Cast of Aladdin and Stage and Theatrical Hands Tea party after pantomime had run for 2 weeks. Xmas 1942. Fort Rauch. Posen.'* The Aladdin story certainly seems very flexible, and while the P.O.W.'s were enthralling the Goons with their magic lamp, 100,000 Germans were being throttled to death in the noose tightening around Stalingrad.
German: Stalag XXID, with the camp censor mark. Each card value B

450

451

450, 451 The striking thing about these cards is how cheerful most of the prisoners look. The pictures were taken between October 1942 and early 1943, by which time the tide of the war had turned from the high-water marks of Alamein and Stalingrad, and was now running against the Axis. News from the outside world was precious to a P.O.W. and new arrivals were carefully questioned for the latest developments. Friendly German guards sometimes brought in newspapers and, in some camps, prisoners managed to construct home-made radio sets and listen to the B.B.C.
German: Stamped with the camp mark. Each card value B

452 *'Official P.O.W. Post.'* This card was posted in Australia on 8 June 1945, to an Australian P.O.W. in Thailand. The Japanese landed in South East Asia (Thailand) in December 1941 and forced the Thais to allow the use of their country during the Japanese assault on Burma and Malaya. Most of the Thai people were against the Japanese and the resistance movement, which operated throughout the war, was so strong that Thailand was not treated as an enemy when hostilities ceased. The Japanese, however, were not signatories to the Geneva Convention and conditions in their P.O.W. camps were often horrific.
Australian: (Official P.O.W. Post) Value A

453 *'Church Service.'* This is one of the few cards from Stalag XXID on which no one is smiling. Perhaps the group is actually taking part in a religious service. However, close examination of the card reveals that the window and curtains are *trompe d'oeil* paintings on stage scenery. The establishment of fixed routines, including roll calls, kit inspection, drill and religious services for prisoners by prisoners, helped many men to retain their self-respect.
German: Stalag XXID. Value B

454 Stalag XXID seems to have been a pretty good place. Perhaps the postcards were purely propaganda. If so, their message was plainly carried. It seems extra-ordinary that sports teams could travel from camp to

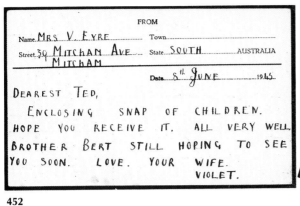

452

456

453

457

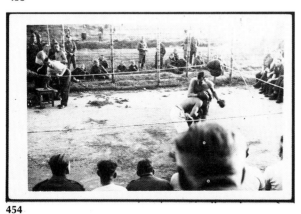

454

458

455

459

460

461
Adolf Hitlers Landhaus am Obersalzberg bei Berchtesgaden.

462
LEURS GUEULES : 1. La vie était belle en 1940!

463
LEURS GUEULES : 2. Retour au Heimat après le pillage (19..

464
LEURS GUEULES : 3. Nous ne connaîtrons plus les « Wehrmacht's kontrolle ».

465
LEURS GUEULES : 4. Un « as » des... bureaux de la Luftwaffe.

466
5. Ceux qui singèrent... LEURS GUEULES... en pire.

467
LEURS GUEULES : 6. The Siegfried Line Sisters.

468
LEURS GUEULES : 7. Les piliers du régime nazi.

469
LEURS GUEULES : 8. La belle jeunesse du Grand Reich...

470
LEURS GUEULES : 9. Beautés allemandes d'exportation.

471
LEURS GUEULES : 10. Le fond du panier.'

472
LEURS GUEULES : 11. Les désespérés.

473
LEURS GUEULES : 12. Ce qu'on a souhaité voir leurs talons...

camp. But no guard would have ventured into the boxing ring. However, examination of the card shows the Germans watching the contest from behind the safety of the wire fence. An apocryphal story is told of one of a group of P.O.W.'s who, upon being forced to write home in praise of the Germans, wrote as follows: *'We are well looked after and given plenty of food. I want everyone to know that the Germans are considerate and thoughtful so tell it to the family, tell it to the Army, tell it to the Navy, tell it to the Air Force and tell it to the Marines.'* The last phrase meant 'don't believe a word.'
German: Stalag XXI with camp censor mark. Value B

455 *'War Graves.'* The headstones are those erected by the Imperial War Graves Commission (now Commonwealth War Graves Commission—C.W.G.C.) to commemorate the British and Commonwealth fallen of both wars. Many First World War graves were destroyed during the Second World War, but Posen in 1942, which is the area this card records, seems intact if untidy. Posen, or Poznan, is roughly half way on line between Berlin and Warsaw and was part of Poland incorporated by the Nazis into the Third Reich. Concentration camps were set up in which thousands of Poles were tortured and murdered. Roughly 200 miles south of Posen lay Oswiecim, one of the most notorious of all death camps, where almost three million Polish Jews perished. Its more common name is Auschwitz.
German: Value B

456 *'Red Cross Parcels.'* These two prisoners identified on the reverse as 'Albert and Ted' are carrying Red Cross parcels. The Red Cross maintained a card index on the location of millions of prisoners of war and carried out thousands of visits to camps in order to see that their detention conditions conformed to international agreements drawn up in The Hague at the turn of the century and later extended in 1929 in Geneva.
German: Stalag XXID.
23 October 1942.
Value B

457 'Rotterdam.' The Phoney War ended on 10 May 1940 when the German attack began across the Dutch and Belgian borders. Paratroop forces landed in the Rotterdam area and, by 14 May, negotiations were under way for surrender. Because of a confusion in Luftwaffe communications, on the afternoon of the 14th more than 50 He111's bombed the city. The act was represented by Allied propaganda as one of wanton destruction and casualties were exaggerated at twenty times the real figure of less than 1,000 killed. Later in the war, when the British and Americans began their raids against German cities, the Rotterdam incident was resurrected in justification. This card is said to have been produced by resistance forces in Rotterdam soon after the bombing.
Dutch: 1940. Value B

458 'Paris in Deutscher Hand.' German forces entered Paris on 14 June 1940 and took the city virtually intact. Eight days later France accepted the German terms of surrender, so in just six weeks France had been conquered. It was an achievement that Von Schlieffen, who had planned to do precisely that in 1914, would have applauded. Paris remained in German hands until August 1944.
German: (Pub. The 'Western Front Illustrated' magazine) Series 1. Value B

459 'The Generals' Hall, Munich. Feeding the Pigeons.' While the rest of Europe was in turmoil, and much of it being destroyed, things in Germany seemed very normal—on September 1940, anyway. The message reads: 'Dear Lu, I received a letter from you today and am sending you another pretty viewcard. . . . Yours, Denise.' The postal slogan on the reverse reads: 'Don't forget to use your street and number.' However, things were not exactly as they seemed to be on the surface. Hitler did not have the full support of the *Wehrmacht* Generals and it is an odd coincidence that the Nazi flags in front of the Feldherrnhalle have been painted on the postcard.
German: (Pub. A. Lengauer, Munich) No. 222. Value B

460 'Burning Oil Installations.' The lightning war was carried out by co-ordinated groups of tanks, mobile artillery, mechanized infantry and the Luftwaffe. Of all the aeroplanes used in the air war the Junkers Ju87—the Stuka—struck the most terror into the hearts of those fleeing the German onslaught. This picture is captioned on the reverse: 'A Stuka attack.'
German: (Pub. Heinrich Hoffman, Munich) Artist Prof. A. Janesch. The painting is dated 16.8.40. Value C

461 'The Berghof.' In direct contrast to the concrete bunker in which Hitler ended his life is the house at Obersalzburg above Berchtesgaden where he established his headquarters in the 1930's.
German: Value C

THEIR MUGS
This set of 12 cards is mysterious. The drawings are mostly dated 1943 and the publisher is clearly acknowledged on the reverse as 'L.E.L. Brussels.' In 1943 Underground papers and radio stations operated despite all the invaders' attempts to silence them, but it seems most unlikely that an underground postcard publisher would put his name on the product—and even claim copyright. The pictures are amusing and under some circumstances might have been tolerated by the Germans—but not by 1943. The most likely explanation is that the cards were published between September 1944, when Belgium was liberated, and the end of the war in 1945.
Belgian: (Pub. 'L.E.L. Brussel') Artist 'Bizuth.' Each card value B

462 'What A Life in 1940.'
463 'It Was A Great Victory.' (1940)
464 'No More Wehrmacht's Kontrolle For Us.'
465 'A Tough One Of The Luftwaffe's . . . Officers.'
466 'Monkeying The Real Ones . . . But Worse.'
467 'The Siegfried Line Sisters.'
468 'Pillars of The Nazi Party.'
469 'The Reich's Beautiful Manhood.'
470 'The Merry Wives of . . . Berlin.'
471 'The Nazi's Last Hope.'
472 'Desperadoes.'
473 'The Back of A Foe is Better Than His Face.'

474

475

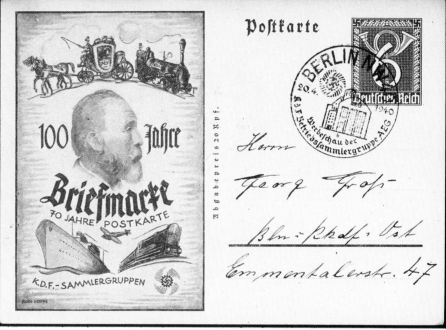

476

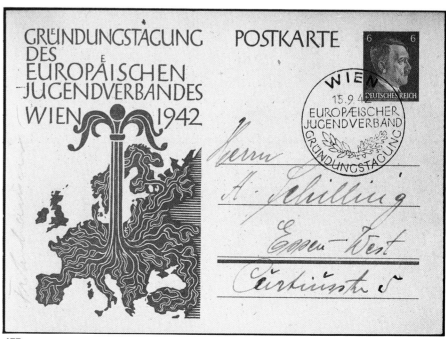

477

478

479

common anti-communist purpose. This card commemorates a conference held in Vienna to discuss the formation of a league of European Youth.
German: (Official card) Posted Vienna 15 September 1942. Value C

478, 479 *'The Old Gang.'* While conscription in most countries was selective, taking the individual's age and occupation into account, the United States, with a population so much larger than the size of the Army it required, could consider other factors. The Old Gang would be at home and the authorities encouraged them to remember their fellows at war.
American: (Pub. Asheville Post Card Co.) Each card value B

480 *'New York World's Fair 1940.'* The theme of the 1939–40 New York World's Fair, in which 63 nations participated, was 'The World of Tomorrow.' Not all of the countries who participated in the first year of the Fair continued on to the second. The war had involved them.
American: (Advertising give-

474 *'The Dustbin.'* Scarcity of most consumer items forced all nations to make the most of what they had. The Governments then had to persuade the people to co-operate. In particular, food had to be made to stretch as far as possible. In Britain anti-waste campaigns were launched against the 'Squander Bug,' a nasty little insect who encouraged people to spend money on non-essential items and to resist the frugality required for the War Effort. The German equivalent of the 'Squander Bug' was the 'Dust Bin,' here seen inviting

a housewife to throw away something which she could actually use. On the reverse is the slogan (translated): 'Fight Waste.' The card may have been issued in Holland during the Nazi occupation.
German: Value C

475 *'Metal Parade.'* As the war progressed, shortages of materials forced both sides to explore any possible source for vital war commodities. One supremely important material was metal. In Britain old saucepans and iron railings were turned into Spitfires. Here the German War Comrades Association

parade to hand over their standards and medals as part of the German People's Metal Collection.
German: (Pub. Kyffhauser) Value C

476 *'100 Years of Postage Stamps.'* The Germans used the postcard as part of their normal propaganda machine. Some of the issues were so low key in their intent that the publishers probably did not consider them to be propaganda. The Nazi Party continued to hold its rallies and a wide range of 'Events' designed to encourage Workers, or Farmers, or Youth, or

Fishermen, or Soldiers. Very often the occasions were partly supported by the sale of postcards. This one commemorates 100 years of the postage stamp (invented by the Englishman, Rowland Hill, in 1840) and 70 years of postcards.
German: (Official postcard) Posted 20 April 1940. Value D

477 *'Vienna 1942.'* The Third Reich was planned to last a thousand years, and the youth of the country was the future. Through the Hitler Youth Organization he promoted his ideals of Aryan superiority and sought to bring Europe together in a

480

481

483

482

away for the U.S. Railway Post Office) Posted 27 October 1940, the last day of the Fair and 24 hours before Italy invaded Greece. *Value B*

481 *'An American Postcard to England.'* World War II ended with unconditional surrender on 7 May 1945 at Rheims. This card was sent to England just one month later. The message reads: *'Dear Sir, When you will again be able to export kindly let us hear from you. . . .'* The true spirit of enterprise, but privation, rationing and Government controls on commerce were to continue for some time. *American: (Official card) Value B*

FREE POLES
482 *'Anniversary of the New Polish Postal Service.'* The Commander-in-Chief of the Free Poles was Wladyslaw Sikorski, who had gathered together the Polish Army in France to resist the Germans. He was killed in a 'plane crash in Gibraltar on 4 July 1943. *Free Polish: Cancelled by the Polish Field Post Office No. 1. 17 December 1942. Value C*

483 *'Polish Army in France.'* This card carries an extraordinary range of cancellations. It was apparently posted in France in the Deux-Sevres area on 27 May 1940, the day after the Dunkirk evacuation began. It has 'm/s' BATORY' on it, which is perhaps the ship on which some of the Poles were evacuated, plus the slogan mark of the Polish 2nd Division in France. On the reverse are the ink stamps of the 'GOC POLISH MOTORISED TROOPS HAYDOCK PARK' and 'THE COMMANDER OF POLISH CAMP NO. 5.' *French: (Pub. M.D., Paris) 1940. Value D*

THE FREE FRENCH
484 *'The Free French Forces in North Africa Salute the Flag.'* *French: (Pub. Friends of Free France (A.V.F.)) Value B*

485 *'Free French Sailors Present Arms to General de Gaulle.'* *French: (Pub. Friends of Free France (A.V.F.)) Value B*

486 *'Free French Navy. The Triomphant.'* When the Germans invaded Vichy France in 1942 the French scuttled their ships—77 in all,

including three battleships, seven cruisers and 32 destroyers. The Free French Navy helped by the Allies maintenance resources and refits in the United States, grew to a strength of more than 50 combat and 200 merchant vessels. It played a major part in the Battle of the Atlantic. *French: (Pub. Friends of Free France (A.V.F.)) Raphael Tuck trademark. Value B*

487 *'Sailors of the Free French Navy.'* *French: (Pub. Friends of Free France (A.V.F.)) Value B*

488 *'Free French Aircraft.'* De Gaulle's troops numbered half a million by 1944 when, under his declared Provisional Government, all resistance forces were united, but because they were so widely scattered the largest strength was still centred in Africa—in Algiers. *French: No. 51-2141 Value B*

489 *'General de Gaulle's First Manifesto to Frenchmen.'* *French: No. 51-2141 Value B*

490 *'Free French Forces in Eritrea.'* Eritrea was part of Italian East Africa and, under General Leclerc, Free French troops took part in actions there in 1940–41. *French: No. 51-2141 Value B*

491 *Arrival in London of the 183 Frenchmen Escaped*

from Germany.' The Free French were steadily strengthened as more Frenchmen became disenchanted with the Vichy regime and their number rose from about 10,000 in 1940 to 100,000 in 1942. *French: No. 51-2141 Value B*

484

485

486

487

L'aviation française libre en Afrique.
Aircraft of the Free French Forces in Africa.

488

Tirailleurs des F.F.L. en Erythrée.
Free French Forces in Eritrea.

490

Le premier appel du Général de Gaulle.
General de Gaulle's first manifesto to Frenchmen.

489

Arrivée à Londres des 183 évadés d'Allemagne.
Arrival in London of the 183 Frenchmen escaped from Germany.

491

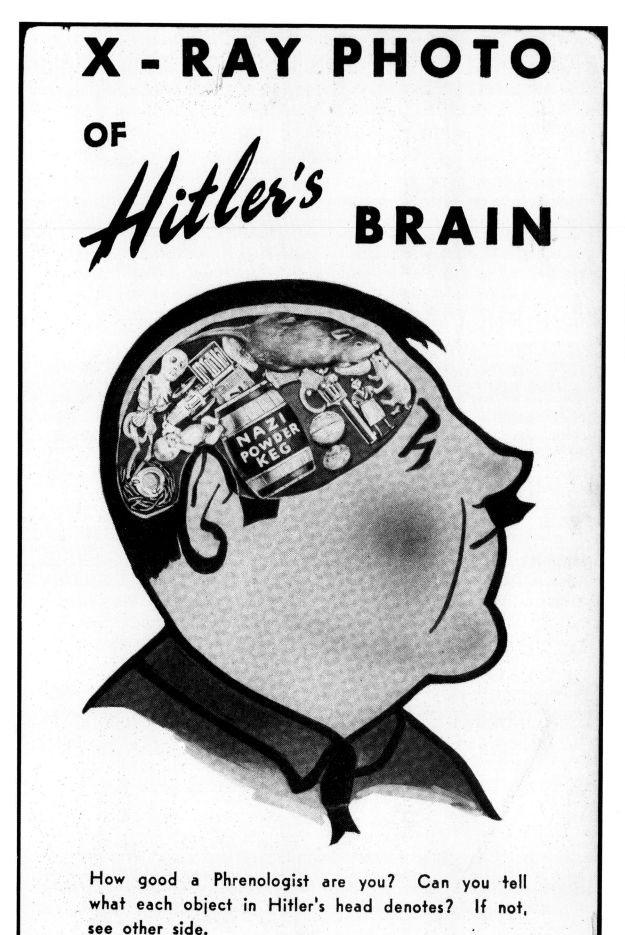

X - RAY PHOTO
OF
Hitler's BRAIN

NAZI POWDER KEG

How good a Phrenologist are you? Can you tell what each object in Hitler's head denotes? If not, see other side.

© 1942 B. F. LONG

492

493

494

492 'X-Ray Photo of Hitler's Brain.' Printed caption on the reverse reads: 'RAT—Has invaded and betrayed every country with which he had a peace pact. MATCHES—Has burned art and literature. POWDER KEG—Has tried to blow civilization to pieces. BABY—Wants more babies for cannon fodder. GUN—Has a gun at the head of everyone in Europe. PIG—Wants to hog the world. BUTCHER—Wants to carve to pieces everyone who will not yield to him. SKELETON—Brings death and destruction. CANNON—Has slain innocent women and children. "HAYWIRE" and "CRACKPOT." NUT—Fit subject for the bughouse.' American: Artist B. F. Long. 1942. Value B

493 'Look! Uncle Sam made monkeys of 'em.' The subjects are Tojo, Hitler and Mussolini. The printed slogan on the reverse reads: 'For Victory Buy United States War Bonds and Stamps.' American: (Pub. D.R. & Co.) 'Slam the Axis' Postcard. 1943. Value B

CHAPTER NINE

Humour

"We Nazis should all hang together."

495

496

494 *'If this were Hitler what would* You *do Chums?'* Arnold Taylor, famous for his seaside pictures of fat ladies' bottoms, draws Hitler in typical vulgar postcard style. *British: (Pub. Bamforth) Artist Taylor. Circa 1940. Value B*

Humour and morale in wartime are closely related. If a soldier can laugh at a situation, the chances are that he can endure it. The same applies to civilians fighting to survive on the Home Front. The value of humour as a useful tool was recognised by the Establishment during World War I with the appointment of Captain Bruce Bairnsfather (the creator of Old Bill, *Fragments from France* and *The Better Ole*) as the first ever 'Officer Cartoonist'.

During World War II, Bairnsfather was appointed official cartoonist to the U.S. Air Forces in Europe and together with other successful soldier/airmen artists like Bill Mauldin, Dave Breger, 'Jon' and 'Chad', continued his morale-raising work through World War II.

Regular Service magazines, such as the American *Stars & Stripes* and *Yank*, the British newspapers *SEAC*, and *Union Jack*, were published side by side with localised publications like *Victory*, a magazine for the India Command published in Calcutta; *Ceylon Review*; *Jambo* (published in Nairobi for the troops in East Africa) and the desert newspapers like *Tobruk Truth*, *Crusader* and *Eighth Army News*.

Service newspapers of all the nations were liberally sprinkled with cartoons. The French and Germans seem obsessed with the standard and variety of army cooking, the Americans seem to find their newly joined recruits and the rigours of fatigues and other unpleasant duties amusing, while the British see the funny side of the behaviour of Tommy in the role of innocent abroad. They printed their own postcard comments, or eagerly bought locally produced versions, showing them being fleeced by wily Cairenese or seduced by dark eyed Italian Signoritas.

Airforce humour is liberally sprinkled with current airmen's slang, army humour often makes the Sergeant the funny guy, while naval humour frequently plays on the 'girl in every port' theme.

Many of the postcard's stock pre-war artists had a new lease of life during the war. Designs by the undisputed king of seaside innuendo, Donald McGill, and his heirs to the throne, Dan Tempest and Arnold Taylor, Harry Parlett (better known as 'Comicus') and even Bert Thomas, the Welsh artist who gained fame during the First World War, found their way on to postcards once again. Current well-known newspaper and magazine cartoonists turned to wartime topics for inspiration and the works of Grimes and Gilbert Wilkinson, for example, were reproduced in postcard form.

The German 'Big Three' — Hitler, Goebbels and Goering — all had distinctive enough features to make them a caricaturist's dream. Hitler's toothbrush moustache and dark side-swept fringe, Goebbels' knobbly head on a skinny neck and Goering's florid girth were exaggerated into easily drawn, easily recognisable symbols of ridicule. The same applied to Mussolini's flamboyant personality and Tojo's oriental features.

With hopeful wishful thinking, they were pictured in all manner of humiliating situations — being kicked up the backside, locked up, strung up . . . in fact, just as the Kaiser and the Crown Prince had been during the First World War.

Current catch phrases from comedy shows, like the phenomenally popular ITMA, and Ministry of Information propaganda slogans were also parodied on the postcard — all helping to spread the message of laughter or of wartime wisdom.

Wartime inventions and paraphenalia like prefabs, Anderson shelters, air raid warnings, gas masks and barrage balloons all came in for comic treatment. The very act of ridiculing some of the more dangerous and unpleasant aspects wartime made them immediately more familiar and less frightening. The simple, therapeutic value of 'a good laugh' has always been regarded as an effective tonic in Britain. As 'Mona Lott,' one of ITMA's regular characters used to say, 'It's being so cheerful as keeps me going.'

495   'We Nazis should all hang together.' Goering, Hitler and Goebbels swing together.
British: Value B

496   'Won't you get a spanking.'
French: Artist Cass. Circa 1940. Value B

497   'It will be a far, far better world soon dear!' The famous Bonzo dog rids the world of Arch Enemy No. 1.
British: (Pub. Valentine's) Artist George Studdy. 1939. Value B

498   'Hitler in the Corridor. Message on reverse reads: 'I know you will be pleased to hear that I have got my old Rank again having been promoted Sergeant; quite a nice New Year's honour.'
British: 'Humoresque' series. Artist J. Turner. Circa 1939. Value B

499   'I'm dreaming of a White Christmas.'
*British: (Pub. Tuck) Artist **Laurie Tayler, Christmas** 1943. Value B*

500   'I've been dreaming, Herbert . . . I'm sure there's one of them JERRIES under the bed!'
   'Well that's nowt fresh, is it?' The colloquialism for chamber pot gave rise to many jokes of this kind.
British (Pub. Bamforth) Circa 1939. Value A

501   'Sunk without warning, Conshtable,—you'd better report to Winshton!' The overfull bath was certainly a matter for censure. To conserve fuel, 5in was the permitted depth.
British: (Pub. Bamforth) Artist D. Tempest. 1941. Value A

IT WILL BE A FAR FAR BETTER WORLD SOON DEAR !

497

HITLER IN THE CORRIDOR (Official).

W.C.

498

"I'M DREAMING OF A WHITE CHRISTMAS"

With acknowledgments to the Paramount Picture "HOLIDAY INN"

499

"I'VE BEEN DREAMING, HERBERT---I'M SURE THERE'S ONE
O' THEM **JERRIES** UNDER THE BED!"
"WELL, THAT'S NOWT FRESH, IS IT?"

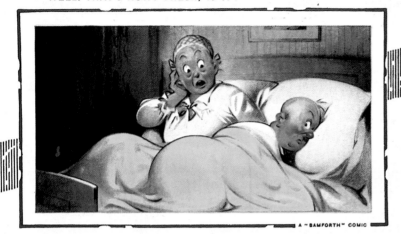

500

501

ONE THING ABOUT IT, JOE! THESE PEOPLE "DIGGING FOR VICTORY"
ARE SHOWING UP IN THEIR TRUE COLOURS!

502

503

504

IT'S ALTERED THINGS, YER KNOW, WITH BOTH
MI KIDS EVAPORATED AND MI 'USBAND BUSY
IN ONE O' THEM DETERMINATION SQUADS!

505

"No, sir, 'is father ain't here.
You see he's what you might
call one of the 'prefabricated
babies'!"

506

"MY SON'S IN THE BALLOON BARRAGE
SECTION!"
"IS THAT SO?"

507

ALL MY OWN WORK BY GRIMES   *With acknowledgments To "THE STAR"*

"Garn'! 'Op it—we was playing 'ere first."

508

ALL MY OWN WORK BY GRIMES   *With acknowledgments To "THE STAR"*

"If you ask me, this war is going to last for the
duration, if not longer."

509

ALL MY OWN WORK BY GRIMES.   *With acknowledgements To "THE STAR"*

"Lovely rain—think of my lettuces."
"Think of my utility suit!"

510

"TOTAL WAR!"
By Gilbert Wilkinson
With Acknowledgments to the "Illustrated"

"But, what the heck has this
to do with typing?"

511

"WHAT A WAR!"
By Gilbert Wilkinson
With Acknowledgments to the "Daily Herald"

"I wish you'd wait till I come in! Now
you've eaten the Smiths' dinner,
I'm cooking for them!"

512

"TOTAL WAR!"
By Gilbert Wilkinson
With Acknowledgments to "Illustrated"

"Next time you're on Light Duty,
Private Smith, you must give me
another lesson"

513

502 *'One thing about it, Joe! These people "Digging for Victory" are showing up in their true colours.'* As imported foodstuffs became rarer and vegetables assumed a more important role in the nation's diet, 'Digging for Victory' became a way of life and many lawns were sacrificed for carrots. Ironically this postcard was sent from Downpatrick, Co. Down, Ireland, and the message reads: *'Having a very nice time—perfect weather and gorgeous food!'* British: (Pub. Bamforth) 1941. Value A

503 The general vicissitudes and hardships of the war were all the more easily borne with a laugh. *'I'm telling you! If Hitler wants any more territory HE CAN HAVE MINE!'* This card was posted exactly one month before the outbreak of war. British: (Pub. Bamforth) Artist D. Tempest. August 1939. Value A

504 *'Your shopping today COSTS YOU A LOT And when you get home, WHAT HAVE YOU GOT?'* Rising prices were the inevitable result of shortages. British: (Pub. Bamforth) No. K77. 'Tempest Kiddy' series. Value A

505 *'It's altered things, yer know, with both my kids evaporated and mi 'usband busy in one o' them determination squads.'* By 1940 most of the kids had come back from being evacuated and, towards the end of the war when the Nazi camps were discovered, extermination squads were no longer the subject of jokes. British: (Pub. Bamforth) Artist D. Tempest. 1939. Value A

506 *'No Sir, 'is father 'aint here. You see he's what you might call one of the "prefabricated babies!"'* Prefabricated was a word that came into use during the war, particularly in relation to houses. Known as prefabs, the cheap buildings were used to rehouse homeless families on a temporary basis. The last of them are just now disappearing. British: (Pub. D. Constance) No. 1511. Artist Donald McGill. Value A

507 *'My son's in the Balloon Barrage Section!' 'IS THAT SO?'* The balloon barrage was designed 'to force attacking aircraft to heights at

which accurate bombing is impossible and where the use of machine guns upon a civilian population is impracticable.' The balloons were generally regarded with affection and toy barrage balloons were on sale for Christmas 1939.
British: (Pub. Bamforth) Artist D. Tempest. 1939. Value A

ALL MY OWN WORK

This popular series, drawn by Leslie Grimes, appeared daily in the newspaper, *The Star.* Grimes, who had joined up in the First World War at the age of 16, transferring to the R.A.F. when it was formed and crashing twice, found a job on the staff of *The Star* when he was demobilised. He had a reputation for working with incredible speed, squatting on the floor like a pavement artist and working in chalk. 'My way of finding jokes,' he said, 'is first to find a subject that is in everyone's mind and fit an "angle" to it. Sometimes it simmers for days and then clicks into place like a jigsaw puzzle. But don't wait; get on with a sketch, and hope a joke will suggest itself. What the hell! The worst joke will please somebody, and the best is often too clever to get over.' Grimes' gift for finding 'a subject that is in everyone's mind' was particularly evident in his wartime cartoons. The postcard series were published by Raphael Tuck and each card bore a stirring slogan on the back—such as *'Express your thanks by building tanks,' 'Your L.S.D. will make men free'* etc.

508 *'Garn! 'Op it—we was playing here first.'* This cartoon has a very strong kinship to Poulbot's First World War drawings of *'Les Gosses dans les Ruines'* (Urchins in the Ruins). Many of the London children who were evacuated in the first wave of panic in September 1939 had returned home by the spring of 1940. The C.O.R.B. (Children's Overseas Reception Board) scheme to send children of all backgrounds and classes abroad met with limited enthusiasm—'I would rather be bombed to fragments than leave England'—was the attitude of one typical youngster. When the *City of Benares* carrying many children to supposed safety across the Atlantic was

torpedoed in October 1940, the 'seavacuation' halted.
British: (Pub. Tuck) Artist Leslie Grimes. Value B

509 *'If you ask me, this war is going to last for the duration, if not longer.'* 'The duration' was the stock phrase to describe 'as long as the war shall last' and came to be regarded as a calculable length of time, like a 'week,' 'a decade,' or 'a century.' When the Phoney War period erupted into menacing action by the Germans, it was soon recognized that 'the duration' was a long, rather than a short, measure of time.
British: (Pub. Tuck) Artist Leslie Grimes. Value B

510 *'Lovely rain—think of my lettuces.' 'Think of my utility suit!'* The two wartime comments on this picture refer to both the 'Dig for Victory' campaign to raise more homegrown vegetables and to the fact that clothing was not only scarce but of very inferior quality—the suit was liable to shrink if wet!
British: (Pub. Tuck) Artist Leslie Grimes. Value B

WHAT A WAR/TOTAL WAR SERIES

Gilbert Wilkinson drew a weekly series called 'Total War' in the picture magazine *Illustrated,* and 'What a War,' which appeared every morning in the newspaper the *Daily Herald.* He was born in Liverpool where he trained for a year at Art School. The family then moved to London and Gilbert continued his studies at the Bolt Court and Camberwell Art Schools. He won a free scholarship offered by a firm of colour printers and served seven years apprenticeship with the firm. During the First World War he fought with the London Scottish and between the wars established a reputation as being one of the finest pen draughtsmen in Britain. His covers for *The Passing Show,* for which he drew for 20 years, also proved him to be a brilliant colour artist. His work appeared in a host of publications—*Strand, London Opinion, Good Housekeeping* and on the other side of the Atlantic, *Judge, Life,* and *Cosmopolitan.* The *Saturday Evening Post* offered him regular work, but his British commitments were too great. The postcards of the

"COR! PARATROOPS!!"

514

Wilkinson cartoons were published by Raphael Tuck, with a quotation from the Prime Minister on the reverse.

511 *'But, what the heck has this to do with typing?'* Even in the services, women were mainly restricted to what was regarded as suitable female occupation, such as cooking, cleaning and secretarial work. Whatever the job, fitness was seen as an important requirement.
British: (Pub. Tuck) Artist Gilbert Wilkinson. Value B

512 *'I wish you'd wait till I come in! Now you've eaten the Smiths' dinner, I'm cooking for them.'* Normal British reserve was severely encroached upon during the war. Neighbours became more helpful and 'pulling together' was a way of life.
British: (Pub. Tuck) Artist Gilbert Wilkinson. Value B

513 *'Next time you're on Light Duty, Private Smith, you must give me another lesson.'* Lack of fuel made many take to the pedal bike—which seems a particularly unsuitable vehicle for our hefty lady sergeant.
British: (Pub. Tuck) Artist Gilbert Wilkinson. Value B

LAURIE TAYLER

Another competent and pleasing wartime artist was Laurie Tayler. His well drawn, gently humorous comments were published by Raphael Tuck in postcard form, with the standard slogan or Prime Minister's message on the reverse.

514 *'Cor! Paratroops!!'* It was firmly believed at the beginning of the war that the Germans would make massive use of parachute

BLIMEY! I'VE GAINED THREE STONE!

515

ARRIVAL PLATFORM

ENCIRCLEMENT!

516

517

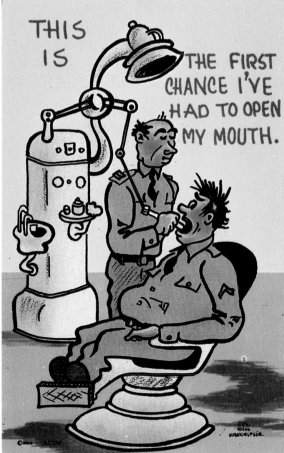

518

519

520

landings to invade Britain. During the Phoney War period the equivalent of 'Reds under the bed' was rather 'Paras in the marrers.' *British: (Pub. Tuck) Artist Laurie Tayler. Value B*

515 *'Blimey! I've gained three stone.'* If World War II Tommy's pack weighed 42lbs he could consider himself better off than his First World War counterpart who often went into battle with twice that weight. *British: (Pub. Tuck) Artist Laurie Tayler. Value B*

516 *'Encirclement.'* No wonder the whole family is so delighted to see Dad again. In a virtually man-less world families had to cope alone and exist on the miserable allowance granted to servicemen's families. Slogan on reverse reads: *'Express your thanks by building tanks.' British: (Pub. Tuck) Artist Laurie Tayler, Value B*

AMERICAN SERVICE HUMOUR

517 *'Blackout of the Rising Sun.'* Just four months after the surprise assault on Pearl Harbour by aircraft of the Japanese Navy, 15 B25 bombers took off from the U.S. Carrier *Hornet* on 18 April 1942 and attacked Tokyo. Although none of the planes returned, the morale of the Allies and the U.S. in particular was greatly strengthened by the action. *American: (Pub. MWM Minnesota) No. AV210. Value B*

518 *'This is the first chance I've had to open my mouth.'* The U.S. Army dealt with 18 million cavities a year throughout the war. Many serving soldiers in the U.S. Army were talented cartoonists—notably Bill Mauldin and Dave Breger. Their skills were employed in raising morale by laughter-making through their drawings, which were published in a variety of Service magazines and newspapers. *American: (Pub. MWM) Artist Cpl. Bill Havenstein. Value B*

519 *'Landing in Occupied Territory.'* The most flexible method of putting an airborne army on the ground is by parachute and the Americans claim that the concept of airborne forces was originated by Benjamin Franklin, in 1784.

American: (Pub. MWM Minnesota) No. AV202. Value B

520 'Things are Sure Looking Up for Me.' U.S. airborne units had their nicknames. The 82nd and the 101st Parachute Divisions were known as the 'All Americans' and the 'Screaming Eagles' respectively. The 11th Airborne Division was called 'The Angels.'
American: (Pub. MWM Minnesota) No. AV206. Value B

521 'Hi-Yah!' The U.S. troops first came into the war after Pearl Harbour.
American: (Pub. Curt Teich & Co.) Circa 1942. Value B

522 'Perfect Three Point Landing, Buddy!' The reference to 'Three Points' originates from the three wheels of the early aeroplanes—one on each wing and one on the fuselage—which were supposed ideally to contact the ground simultaneously during landing. The horse has a symbolic meaning, for the Americans referred to their air mobile forces as 'sky cavalry.'
American: No. AC-9. Value B

523 'I just joined up,—who do I see about a girl in every port?' The United States Marine Corps swelled to 500,000 to wage war in the Pacific.
American: (Pub. Tichner Bros.) Value B

524 'We won't be able to submerge yet—the laundry isn't dry.' The Depression of the 'Thirties had curtailed the U.S. Defense Budget and the U.S. Navy lagged behind its Japanese opponents, especially in submarine capacity. In 1940 the 'Two Ocean Navy Bill' allowed the building of 1,325,000 tons of new warships.
American: (Pub. Tichnor Bros.) Value B

525 'Boy!—We get more darn subs this way.' Hitting the periscopes of submarines with a hammer was a ruse first proposed by the British in the First World War. Their plan required a three man team—one to row out to the raised periscope, one to place a black bag over it to obscure the view and the third to hit it with the hammer.
American: (Pub. MWM) Value B

523

521

522

524

525

526

527

528

529

530

531

French Maginot Line and it was completed in 1940.

530 'Excuse me Sir, the girls want the Siegfried Line.' Belgian: (Pub. S.A. Intertrade, Brussels) Artist Bob Bondart. 1944. Value B

531 'It'll Soon Be Hanging On The Siegfried Line!' British: (Pub. Tuck) No. 3064. 'Give 'em Socks' Postcard. Artist Bert Thomas. Circa 1940. Value B

532, 532A 'Latest View of the Italian Fleet.' Message on reverse reads: 'How's this for a joke. All Churchill's fault eh?' British: 1941. Value A

ITMA WISECRACKS
Each card in this series is captioned 'An ITMA Wisecrack.' They were published by Raphael Tuck and carried a message of encouragement from Mr Churchill on the reverse. They were drawn by Bert Thomas, a Welshman, whose famous First World War picture, 'Arf a Mo, Kaiser,' raised £250,000 for the *Weekly Dispatch* Tobacco Fund for the troops. Thomas drew the large propaganda posters for outside the National Gallery and the Royal Exchange. After the war he drew for the *Evening News*, the *Sketch*, *Punch* and other humorous journals. He was also successful as a commercial artist. Unlike Bruce Bairnsfather, his First World War contemporary, he managed to adapt his style and outlook to catch the public's mood and spirit again in World War II.

533 'It's That Man Again.' This was the title of radio's most popular wartime show, coined from the current 1939 catch phrase used to describe Hitler as he annexed yet another territory, 'It's that man again!' The idea for the programme, which was to reach peaks of surrealist humour and pave the way for The Goons and *Monty Python* in future generations, was hatched at the old Langham Hotel (later part of the B.B.C.). The original meeting was between Tommy Handley, the comic genius who was the star and piyot of the show, Ted Kavanagh, the inspired scriptwriter and Francis Worsley, the resilient producer. Michael North, a schoolmate of Worsley's, wrote the catchy signature

526 'This Production Line's Gettin' too fast for me!' The joke is not far fetched. One engine fitter was actually carried into the air on a tailplane from the deck of an aircraft carrier. He got back safely. The artist's interpretation of the aircraft's ability to defend itself is accurate. British machines were more vulnerable. *American: (Pub. MWM. Minnesota) No. AV211. Value B*

527 'Shove Off.' 'I haven't got a handkerchief. What else could I drop?' Stamped on reverse: 'Passed by censor for transmission through the post.' *American: (Pub. Ex. Sup. Co., Chicago) 1941. Value A*

528 'P.S.—Met An Old Friend Here.' The U.S. War Department took the decision to enlist four million men for the War Effort, with proportionate strength in infantry, armour and airborne divisions. *American (Colorite Publishing Co., N.Y.C.) Value A*

529 'Ship Ahoy! Here's Jackie Tarr. . . .' *American: (Pub. Ex. Sup. Co., Chgicago) Value A*

THE SIEGFRIED LINE
We're gonna hang out the washing on the Siegfried Line was one of the most popular songs of the early years of the war. The strong line of fortifications made up of steel and concrete ran the whole length of Germany's western frontier. Its construction had been started in 1936 as an answer to the

532A

532

tune that introduced the show from its first broadcast on 12 July 1939. It was avidly listened to by Resistance fighters on the continent under German occupation. In Holland there were even stories of local Gauleiters who also listened with amusement and the Polish Resistance, knowing no English, listened for the infectious feeling of the laughter of the studio audience. For listeners in Jersey, the cast incorporated hidden coded messages to indicate that escapees had survived.
British: (Pub. Tuck) Artist Bert Thomas. Value B

534 *'Don't forget the Diver!'* became one of ITMA's most oft-repeated catch phrases. It originates from one of Tommy Handley's boyhood memories of a diver on New Brighton Pier who, wearing his bathing suit and demonstrating a helmet he was never seen to wear, used the words to solicit people coming off the ferryboat. In the show he was played by Horace Pervical and his parting words were, 'I'm going down now, Sir.'
British: (Pub. Tuck) Artist Bert Thomas. Value B

535 *'I don't mind if I do'* was Colonel Chinstrap's inevitable riposte to any of Tommy Handley's phrases that could be misinterpreted as an invitation to a drink. One of ITMA's favourite characters, the Colonel was another of Jack Train's brilliant creations. Train, a seasoned and talented performer, was one of the original members of the cast and toured in the 1940 Jack Hylton ITMA Stage Show. Jack's health kept him out of the show for a year from

"It's that man again!"

533

"Don't forget the Diver!"

534

"I don't mind if I do"

535

"Can I do yer now—Sir?"

536

"Nothing at all—Nothing at all!"

537

"Gee Boss—Sumpin terrible's happened"

538

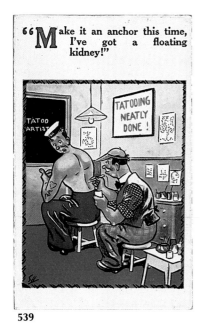

539

"ake it an anchor this time, I've got a floating kidney!"

540

"But you told me to 'Pack up my troubles' in my old kit bag, Sergeant!"

541

"HOW DO YOU LIKE MY PENDANT?— A PRESENT FROM THE R.A.F." "OH BOY, AND **WHAT A LANDING GROUND!**"

542

I WILL BE DROPPING IN ON YOU SOMETIME

NA POO, NA POO! I'M FEELING BLUE; AIN'T I GONNA HAVE NO MORE NEWS FROM YOU?

543

544

Refresher Course

545

"Don't panic, it's my sister's."

"BUT, COLONEL ... THAT'S 'TWO-GUN' McCOY FROM TEXAS—THE BEST MAN WE'VE GOT!!"

546

DON'T LOOK NOW, OLD GIRL, BUT YOUR UNDER-CARRIAGE IS COMING DOWN

547

September 1943 during which the Colonel was sorely missed. *British: (Pub. Tuck) Artist Bert Thomas. Value B*

536 *'Can I do yer now, Sir?'* was, without doubt, the most famous of all the ITMA catch phrases. It was the opening gambit of Mrs Mopp, alias Dorothy Summers, Tommy Handley's cockney charlady who made her first appearance on 10 October 1941. Mrs. Mopp's other regular sayings were: 'I've brought this for you, Sir,' as she gave Tommy a ridiculous gift, and 'T.T.F.N.'—'Tata for now'—which he would answer with a string of obscure initials like 'N.L.Y.G.D.I.T.B.'—'Never let your garters dangle in the bath.' The ITMA team were moved to hear that a little boy, trapped in the rubble after one of the Baedeker raids in Bath (on cities of outstanding beauty or historical value, named after the German Guide book) was heard by a Warden shouting, 'Can you do me now, Sir!' *British: (Pub. Tuck) Artist Bert Thomas. Value B*

537 *'Nothing at all—Nothing at all!'*—or 'Notting at all,' as the slogan was pronounced by Dino Galvani, the actor who played Signor So-So. He was master of the mispronunciation, or malapropism. So-So had been intended as an Italian counterpart for Jack Train's sinister German spy 'Funf,' but turned out to be far too lovable and friendly to sustain a sinister air. Funf's special sepulchral tone was achieved by Train talking into a tumbler to simulate a menacing long distance phone call. *British: (Pub. Tuck) Artist Bert Thomas. Value B*

538 *'Gee Boss—Sumpin terrible's happened.'* This was the opening line for Sam Scram, Tommy Handley's American henchman, played by Sydney Keith. Sam had a sidekick called Lefty, who was an ex-gangster. They made their appearance in ITMA or ITSA ('It's that sand again') as the first series from Bangor, North Wales, was called in the spring of 1941. Set in the mythical resort of 'Foaming at the Mouth' it guyed the Government's 'Holidays at Home' campaign. The catch phrase was changed on a historic

548

occasion during the summer of 1943 to 'Boss, boss, something wonderful's happened!'—it was the fall of Mussolini.
British: (Pub. Tuck) Artist Bert Thomas. Value B

BRITISH SERVICE HUMOUR

539 *'Make it an anchor this time, I've got a floating kidney.'* Tattooing, the art of puncturing the skin in patterns and rubbing in colouring material to fix the design indelibly, was prevalent from pre-Christian times in certain Eastern civilizations. The practice was brought to Europe by sailors, who have always favoured this brand of personal adornment.
British: (Pub. H.B. Ltd.) Artist 'S.H.' Circa 1944. Value A

540 *'But you told me to "Pack up my troubles" in my old kit bag, Sergeant.'* As the songs of the Boer War, like *Soldiers of the Queen* and *Goodbye Dolly Gray* were sung during the First World War before it developed its own songs, so the songs of the First World War were sung at the beginning of World War II.

'Comicus' was the pseudonym of Harry Parlett, who had been designing comic postcards since before the First World War.
British: (Pub. H.B. Ltd.) Artist 'Comicus.' 1943. Value A

541 *'How do you like my pendant?—A present from the R.A.F.' 'Oh boy, and WHAT A LANDING GROUND!'* Badges and brooches of service insignia were proudly worn by the girls who were left behind.
British: (Pub. Bamforth) Artist D. Tempest. Value A

542 *'I will be dropping in on you sometime.'* Agnes Richardson was drawing 'cute kids' in wartime situations during the First World War. Message on

reverse reads: *'Is it possible to get odorono or something of that kind? I can't get any.'* Deodorants were regarded as non-essential (although the masses of people sleeping closely together in the shelters each night during the Blitz would have implied otherwise) and were therefore hard to get.
British (Pub. Photochrom Co.) Artist Agnes Richardson. 1942. Value A

543 *'Na Poo. Na Poo! I'm feeling blue; ain't I gonna have no more news from you?'* The First World War slang phrase 'Napoo', from the French *'Il n'y en a plus'* ('There's no more'), was still used by the old breed of professional soldier at the outbreak of World War II.
British: The 'Vera Paterson' Postcard. Circa 1940. Value A

544 *'Refresher Course. Message on reverse reads: 'So this is why you enjoy a Refresher Course! They've some very nice refreshments here at the "Barley Mow"—I've sampled it.'*
British: (Pub. Tuck) Artist Dinah. 1943. Value A

545 *'Don't panic, it's my sister's.'* There were many war babies born who would never know their fathers. Relationships were accelerated, standards of morality dropped in hurried leave-time liaisons. The Frenzied, Fearful Forties were certainly a prelude to the Swinging Sixties.
British: (Pub. D. Eisner & Son) Artist Bob Wilkin. Value A

546 *'But, Colonel . . . That's "Two-Gun" McCoy from Texas—the best man we've got.'* This Colonel owes much to the immortal creation of David Low, Colonel Blimp, the Diehard Reactionary.
British: 'Humoresque' series. Artist Cecil T. Rigby. Value A

549

550

551

552

553

554

EXPLOITS

—J'étais en sentinelle avancée, soudain surgit une patrouille ennemie... Pan! pan! pan! pan! j'en abats cinq!...

- Alors ??...

- Alors, je ne sais plus, je me suis réveillé à ce moment là!

555

LE PREMIER VOL DE NUIT

- Tiens-toi bien, j'amorce une "chandelle".

- T'es pas fou, tu vas nous faire repérer avec ta lumière!...

556

Si vous préferez ... j'ai des copains qui en ont des roses!...

557

CORVÉE Prenez-moi le balai et nettoyez-moi ça, en vitesse et qu'ça saute !
— Mais ! sergent, c'est "Lid're" qui l'emporte pour balayer la table du réfectoire !

558

— Dans le civil, je suis homme-sandwich...
— Ne vous laissez jamais faire prisonnier : les boches vous boufferaient !

559

La chasse au œufs
Op eierenjacht

560

547 'Don't look now, old girl, but your under-carriage is coming down.' The R.A.F. version of 'Madam, your slip is showing.'
British: (Pub. William Foster) Circa 1940. Value A

548 'Pilot: "Only just managed to pull out of that dive. We might have had an accident."
'Observer: "Might! . . . I'VE HAD ONE!"' This is a favourite postcard joke, applied to nervous people forced to speed in all manner of vehicles over the years. The card was posted from the Isle of Man and talks of a '5 hrs. delay' in telephoning the mainland.
British: (Pub. Bamforth) Artist D. Tempest. 1941. Value A

FRENCH SERVICE HUMOUR
549 'You ought to take me for a cruise on your cruiser.' At the outbreak of war, France had two battle cruisers, seven heavy cruisers and 12 light cruisers.
French: Artist Cass. Circa 1939. Value B

550 'My Conqueror!' 'My Victory!' The womanizing capabilities of the French sailor were legendary.
French: Artist Cass. Circa 1939. Value B

551 'Mastery of Navy on sea and shore!' A certain number of women's Forces came to Britain and served with the Free French.
French: Artist Cass. Circa 1939. Value B

COME TO THE COOKHOUSE DOOR
552 'Gentlemen, lunch is ready.'
French: Artist Cass. Circa 1939. Value B

553 'I have again surpassed myself.'
French: Artist Cass. Circa 1939. Value B

554 'Next time bring me fork and spoon.' (Literal translation, 'Service is badly neglected.')
French: Artist Cass. Circa 1939. Value B

555 'Exploits' 'I was on forward observation post duty when an enemy patrol rushed at me. Bang! Bang! Bang!—I got five of them.' 'Then? . . . 'Then I don't know any more—I woke up!'
French: (Pub. A. Noyer, Paris) Circa 1939. Value A

556 'First Night Flight.' 'Hold tight, I'm going to let off a burst.'
'Don't be a fool, you'll

make a target of us with your light.'
French: (Pub. A. Noyer, Paris) 'Collection Comique Militaire 157.' Circa 1939. Value A

557 'If you prefer, I've got friends with pink ones.' Parachute silk was universally greeted with delight to make feminine underwear and blouses—even wedding dresses. French: Artist Jacques Faizant. Value A

558 'FATIGUES.' 'Take a broom and sweep that clean, and jump to it.'
'But Sergeant, Lidoire has taken the broom to sweep the dining room table.'
French: (Pub. G. Artaud, Nantes) 'Editions Gaby.' Circa 1939. Value A

559 'In Civilian life I'm a sandwich board man.'
'Don't let yourself get taken prisoner: the hun would gobble you up.'
French fear and hatred for the Germans was ingrained and almost sacred in its singlemindedness. The punishments inflicted during the Franco-Prussian War of 1870–71 and the First World War still hurt.

561

562

563

564

565

567

568

566

THE SECOND GREAT WAR

— No, no, NOT on it's NECK!!

ON ACTIVE SERVICE IN EGYPT Serie 7-10

569

No. 519. --- AND THEY CALL THIS A BLACKOUT.!

570

HOTEL

No. 517. "THE GOOD-VIEW HOTEL."

571

No. 522. THE ETERNAL FEMININE.

572

No. 518. WRITING HOME.

573

No. 504. THE SERVICES HANDICAP.

574

I'm too short, George. Is her
face as nice as her legs?

575

Gee, what a ride! Hitler should have
to do this for three hours a day!

576

We only serve milk and cocoa. —
Do you like milk, George?

577

French: (Pub. P.C., Paris)
Circa 1939. Value A

560 'The Hunt for eggs.'
Belgian: (Pub. R.C. Brussels)
1945. Value B

561 'Our Menu Card.
What we eat today:
1. Breakfast: Porridge
2. Jellied sausage, bread,
   coffee
Lunch: Dried fruit with
   dumplings
Supper: Bread, tea,
   butter. . . .'
The sender adds the words:
'. . . it's different to 'Our
Menu Card' add 'hot pot' to
the list. The message on the
reverse reads: 'We would
like to have so much to eat.'
German: (Pub. Erich
Kaunghammer, Berlin) 1942.
With Field Postmark 1942.
Value B

562 'Our Modern Army:
Sergt. ''Here you are boys,
thought you'd like breakfast
in bed this morning as it's
rather cold!'''
British: 'Humoresque' series.
Artist Reg Carter. Value A

563 'I asked for a nice
clean job—and I got it.'
American: (Pub. Colour-
picture, Mass.) Series L Army
Comics. Circa 1941. Value B

THE SOLDIER ABROAD
564 'To your health,
Darling . . . and to final
victory.'
Belgian: 1944. Value B

565 'For Evermore!' Slogan
on reverse reads: '''We shall
continue steadfast in faith
and duty till our task is
done,'' the Prime Minister.'
British: (Pub. Tuck) Artist
Dinah. Value A

566 'Join the Army and See
the World.'
American: No. 375. Circa
1941. Value B

567 'Stomach Timetable.'
Mud with straw
Foot rags with fleas
Calves sweetbread with
sparrow.
Message on reverse reads:
'I am now in Augsburg. The
food is better here than in
Landsberg.'
German: Artist Barlog. Field
Postmark 1943. Value C

568 'After the War: Eggs
and Bacon? I've forgotten
how to cook them.'
Belgian: (Pub. S.A.
Intertrade, Brussels) Artist
Cheveral. Value B

569 'The Second Great
War: On Active Service in
Egypt.' Camel rides were one
of the traditional tourist

attractions for soldiers.
*Egyptian: (Pub. Eastern
Publishing Co. Cairo)
Series 7. No. 10. Artist
Saroukhan. Circa 1944.
Value B*

570 *'And they call this a
Blackout!'* In Cairo soldiers
caroused and relaxed in the
many bars with names like
'The Spitfire,' 'The Anzac,'
'Churchills,' and night clubs
like 'Bardia's,' where they
enjoyed the exuberant
cabaret. Liaisons were
formed and as easily broken
in the heightened emotional
encounters that wartime
precipitated.
*Egyptian: (Pub. Eastern
Publishing Co. Cairo)
No. 519. Artist Saroukhan.
Circa 1944. Value B*

571 *'The Good-View
Hotel.'* The most famous
hotel in Cairo was
Shepheards, where the Staff
of General Headquarters
Middle East was based.
*Egyptian: (Pub. Eastern
Publishing Co. Cairo)
No. 17. Artist Saroukhan.
Circa 1944. Value B*

572 *'The Eternal Feminine.'*
Cairo shops were full of the
luxuries which could no
longer be found in most
Allied countries. Members of
the Women's Services in
Egypt and North Africa could
hardly believe the coupon-
less display of frivolous
undies available.
*Egyptian: (Pub. Eastern
Publishing Co. Cairo)
No. 22. Artist Saroukhan.
Circa 1944. Value B*

573 *'Writing Home.'*
Saroukhan uses the eternal
'French teacher' joke in this
picture.
*Egyptian: (Pub. Eastern
Publishing Co. Cairo)
No. 18. Artist Saroukhan.
Circa 1944. Value B*

574 *'The Services
Handicap.'* Quick to exploit
the commercial potential of
soldiers out to enjoy their
leave at almost any price, the
Cairenese swallowed their
objection to war and
explored every avenue of
imaginative recreation.
*Egyptian: (Pub. Eastern
Publishing Co. Cairo)
No. 04. Artist Saroukhan.
Circa 1944. Value B*

PALESTINE

575 *'I'm too short, George.
Is her face as nice as her legs?'*
*Palestine: (Pub. Martin
Feuchtwanger, Tel Aviv)
Artist Rivo Blass. Circa 1940.
Value B*

576 *'Gee what a ride!
Hitler should have to do this
for three hours a day.'*
*Palestine: (Pub. Martin
Feuchtwanger, Tel Aviv)
Artist Rivo Blass. Circa 1940.
Value B*

577 *'We only Serve milk
and cocoa—Do you like
milk, George?'*
*Palestine: (Pub. Martin
Feuchtwanger, Tel Aviv)
Artist Rivo Blass. Circa 1940.
Value B*

ITALIAN

The British and
Commonwealth forces
basking in the luxury of
victory were the subject of a
series of postcards by a witty
but, unfortunately, anonymous artist, whose only
signature was a discreet sun
symbol.

578 *'Canada Club. Tactful
methods of approach.'* The
Canadians of General
Frederick's force were
amongst the first to penetrate
Rome. By 11 o'clock on
4 June 1944 they had
captured almost half of the
City's bridges.
*Italian: (Pub. Capriotti,
Roma) Authorized by P.W.B.
Rome. 'The English in
Rome.' Series 28.7.1944.
Value B*

579 *'The Roman Forum.
The Red Cross at Work.'* The
Roman female population
welcomed the Allies with
flowers, tears and cheers.
*Italian: (Pub. Capriotti,
Roma) Authorized by P.W.B.
Rome. 'The English in
Rome.' Series 28.7.1944.
Value B*

580 *'Saint Peter's Square.
All Roads Lead to Rome.'*
These New Zealanders had
been part of the eager race
to Rome under their
colourful commander, Sir
Bernard Freyburg V.C.
*Italian: (Pub. Capriotti,
Roma) Authorized by P.W.B.
Rome. 'The English in
Rome.' Series 28.7.1944.
Value B*

581 *'Piazza di Spagna. Look
out for the shops.'* The
invasion was for the most
part peaceable and orderly
in relation to the civilian
population. There had been
some cases of drunkenness
and rape in the first euphoria
of triumph and the M.P.'s
were on the alert to quell
further violence.
*Italian: (Pub. Capriotti,
Roma) Authorized by P.W.B.
Rome. 'The English in
Rome.' Series 28.7.1944. Value B*

578

579

580

581

CHAPTER TEN

Patriotism, Propaganda & Sentiment

583

584

BEFORE 1939
582 *'Czechoslovakian Mobilization.'* The German propaganda campaign against the supposed oppression of the Sudetenland began as early as 1936. In March 1938 after Hitler annexed Austria, the Czechs began a partial mobilization, followed by the French in September. This card encourages the population to support the Armed Forces and on the

orld War II postcard patriotism differed little in style and sentiment from that of World War I. There are similar pictures of powerfully evocative symbols like flags, with national emblems such as the Rising Sun of Japan, the Maple Leaf of Canada, and British bulldogs and lions galore.

Passionate localised issues, like the winning back by France of Alsace-Lorraine, and the revenge of Pearl Harbor by the Americans, were well expressed on the simple postcard, and the joining together of different nations against the common enemy was a favourite theme.

The Germans and the Italians made the most effective use of the postcard for propaganda and morale-raising purposes. Both countries had organised propaganda machines allied to their one-party, one-leader structure. Mussolini encouraged a school of competent artists who transferred his Fascist aims to colourful, emotion-catching designs for the poster and the postcard. They appealed to the basic desires of the populace for a strong, proud and victorious nation. The glorious designs, the élan and ambitions, were belied by Italy's pathetic performance on the field of battle in North Africa.

Goebbels, who ran Hitler's Ministry of Propaganda, learned much from the Italian Fascists. His original contribution to the sphere of disseminating propaganda, however, lay in his imaginative use of the radio. He instituted the idea of 'Black' radio stations – stations which purported to be that which they were not. From the outbreak of war until the Fall of France, for instance, Germany operated a station which broadcast from within France. It pretended to be a 'freedom' station, its main broadcaster, a Frenchman called Ferdonnet, exhorted his countrymen to save France (by casting in their lot with the Germans). Ferdonnet was listened to in France with the same mixture of amused tolerance and irritation with

which William Joyce ('Lord Haw Haw') was listened to in Britain.

Britain responded with her own 'Black' radio broadcasts. 'Soldatensender Calais,' which purported to be broadcast from German-occupied Europe to German occupation forces, was one of the most effective stations in sapping German morale. Mostly, however, the BBC concentrated on broadcasting the bald truth — quickly and accurately, and they scored heavily against German radio in terms of credibility, as Goebbels' claims became more and more extravagent and further divorced from reality.

Neutral Portugal, which nevertheless supported her traditional ally Britain, produced a striking and prolific series of postcards contrasting the lying claims of Nazi radio with the British facts.

One of the most effective British propaganda tools, often portrayed on the postcard, was the 'V for Victory' sign. Launched from London in the Spring of 1941, it employed a symbol which could be interpreted both audibly and visibly. The V sign was simple to scribble on walls and pavements, it was transmitted easily in morse (· · —) and even in music (the first three notes of Beethoven's Fifth Symphony). It spread like a virus throughout occupied Europe and was a major source of embarrassment and irritation to the Germans. It became linked with Churchill — a powerful combination — and for the first time had Germany seriously worried in the war of nerves.

As well as being a cheap, easily propagated and immediate medium for propaganda, the postcard was also the best means of conveying the serviceman's love for the family he was fighting for — and their's for him. Loving and sentimental messages were succinctly and simply expressed by a printed picture – by flowers and hearts, lovers and pretty verses. They united families, reassuring the troops away from home that their girls were being faithful, and the folks at home that their lads were safe.

585

586

587

588

reverse it has a stamp symbolizing the fraternity of the Czech and French forces. *Czech: (Official Card). Posted 29 May 1938, four months before Munich. Value C*

583 *'IV Adunata Nazionale.'* Mussolini had developed his technique of mass persuasion through pomp and ceremony well before Hitler, and the Führer learned much from Il Duce. This card celebrates the 4th National Rally of the Army Engineers held on 23-25 May 1936 in Florence, but the event of the year was the Olympic Games in Berlin. *Italian: (Pub. A.N.A.G. The National Army League). Artist Virgilio Retrosi. Posted 10 December 1936. Value C*

584 *'Asch is Free. Heil Hitler.'* In the build-up to the German occupation of the Sudetenland, Neville Chamberlain, the British Prime Minister, persuaded the French and other interested nations to agree to Hitler's territorial demands on Czech territory. Chamberlain, believing that he had averted war, met the Führer at Bad Godesberg, on 21 September 1938. At the meeting he learned that German forces had crossed the Czech frontier and that 12 German hostages had been shot. Hitler, having opened the meeting by turning down Chamberlain's proposal, stated that he would intervene militarily if any more hostages were shot and in effect demanded the complete capitulation of the Czechs. It was this meeting which led directly to the Munich Agreement eight days later. This card shows in black the Asch area of Western Czechoslovakia, which was 'liberated' by German troops on 21 September 1938. The slogan reads: *'We've done it! Asch is free! Heil Hitler!'* The card was posted on 21 September so it must have been prepared in advance. *German/Czech: Value D*

SOLIDARITY AGAINST BOLSHEVISM
The Nazis' fear of communism was second only to their anti-Semitism, and with Fascist Italy they saw their role as defenders of Europe. As the war progressed Hitler hoped to unite all the Western nations, including England, against Russia.

585 *'Germany and Italy Strike the Russian Hydra.' Italian: Official Armed Forces postcard). Value D*

586 *'Europe Against Anti-Europe.'* On the reverse is a printed message from Mussolini: *'The future is ours and is safe in our hands, since it will be the product of our courage and our inexhaustible desire for life and victory.' Italian: (Official Armed Forces postcard). Posted 4 December 1942, three months after Monty trounced the Axis at Alamein. Value D*

587 *'Europe Marches Against Bolshevism.'* In July 1942, de Gaulle broadened the appeal of his Free French resistance organization by changing its name to *France Combattante* (Fighting France). This prompted the U.S.S.R. to recognize de Gaulle as France's resistance leader and they encouraged the French Communists to join the organization. Thus with solidarity under one leader, the French resistance forces became immediately more effective The assortment of nations supposedly marching with Germany begin on the right with France — perhaps a reaction to de Gaulle, whose African activities were beginning to rouse French patriotism — and continue with Hitler's staunch, if weak ally, Italy. *German/French: (Pub. International Exhibition of Bolshevism against Europe. Paris). 9 June 1942. Value D*

GERMAN SENTIMENT
The Allied image of Nazi Germany was of a heartless state machine operated by homicidal fanatics. Hitler's actions made that propagandist representation also one of reality in many ways, but the German soldier had his own love of home, pride in his calling and belief in his future.

588 *'The Iron Cross 1939.'* In 1939 Hitler upgraded the Iron Cross to an Order. The highest award was known as the Grand Cross, and then there were five variants of the Knights Cross plus the Iron Cross 1st and 2nd Class. This is the new Knight's Cross and ribbon, which was black on the reverse and had '1813' (the inauguration year of the Prussian Iron Cross) on the lower arm. *German: (Official card). Value C*

Gezeichnet für das FELDBLATT POSEN

589

590

591

592

594

Churchill, der moderne Heinrich VIII.

595

593

596

589 '1914.'
German: (Pub. Fieldservice Magazine 'Posen.' Commemorating Army Day 17 March 1940. Titled on reverse: German Infantry 1914 and 1939.' Value C

590 'Don't You Worry.'
The first verse (translated) reads:
'When some weeks
I don't send you a letter
You must understand, darling
The Fieldpost is not easy.
A thousand transports roll here
Over the railway lines.
They are all more important than my words
Do not be worried at home.'
German: (Pub. G & S) No. 405. Value C

591 'The Woods Are Beautiful.' The first verse (translated) reads:
'Yesterday evening I stopped in the beautiful green woods
A soldier was sitting on the moss
Holding his sweetheart on his lap.
Yes the woods are beautiful in the country
And sweet is passion when one is in love.'
German: (Pub. G & S) No. 403. Value C

592 'A Medic Helps A Wounded Comrade.'
German: (Pub. Army propaganda unit) No. 5. Artist Ernst Eigener. Sketches from the Eastern Front. Value D

593 'Coming Home.' The caption on the reverse reads:
'Cheerful, at the Front — at home'.
German: No. 4017. Value C

DUTCH AND NON-GERMAN NAZIS
Many people in the countries occupied by Hitler's forces were enthusiastically pro-Nazi and S.S. Regiments were raised to fight alongside the Germans. Anti-British propaganda in languages other than German was not exclusively German produced but often a product of foreign Nazi sympathisers.

594 'Yes, Daladier, That's The Way It Goes!' Daladier, the French Prime Minister, was one of the signatories to the Munich Agreement, and adopted a *laisser faire* attitude to General Gamelin's mobilization of French forces in response to the German attack on Poland. He was forced to

„American Journal" op 19. 8. 1942 over Dieppe:

„Wij en de Britten rukken Frankrijk binnen

597

598

599

resign in March 1940 by
those who wanted a more
positive approach to the war
and was arrested by the
Vichy Government in
September of that year.
*German (probably): Circa
1940. Value B*

595 *'Churchill, The
Modern Henry VIII.'* Henry
VIII had six wives. The
bleeding hearts here
represent British withdrawal
from France and Norway,
and her inactivity over
Poland. Who else will
Churchill let down? He has
the axe ready.
*German (probably): Circa
1940. Value B*

596 *'De Gaulle, Where Are
Your French Brothers?'* On
3 July 1940 the British

attacked and sank units of
the French fleet at Mers-el-
Kebir in Algeria. This
hardened Vichy French
attitudes towards de Gaulle
and strengthened the
position of Marshal Pétain.
*German (probably): Circa
1940. Value B*

597 *'Dieppe. We and the
British Have Invaded France.'*
The Americans believed,
from the early days of the
war, that an Allied landing
should be made in France as
soon as possible. This was
resisted by Winston
Churchill, who, perhaps in
the hope of showing good
faith, sponsored a raid on the
French Channel port of
Dieppe. On the morning of
19 August 1942, 5,000
Canadians, 1,000 British

Commandos and 50
American Rangers went
ashore. The operation
was a disaster. The
Germans had
spotted the naval force
before it reached its
objective and the assault
troops were without heavy
gunfire support from the sea
(the largest Allied ships were
destroyers). Over half of the
Allied force was killed or
captured and the whole
episode made marvellous
propaganda for the Nazis.
The British later maintained
that lessons learned from the
Dieppe Raid were invaluable
in guaranteeing the success
of D-Day, but luckily within
three months the victory at El
Alamein enabled Dieppe to
be quietly forgotten. The
quotation in the caption is

WORDS THAT DON'T RING TRUE!

"*Danger from British air attacks,
according to experience so far, does
not make any action necessary.*"

D.N.B. (German Official News Agency),
16th October, 1940.

600

WORDS THAT DON'T RING TRUE!

"*The relations between the Führer and
the Duce are as cordial as those between
two brothers.*"

"*Asahi Shimbun*" on Matsuoka's
impression of his journey, quoted in
a German broadcast to England,
23rd April, 1941.

601

602

supposedly from a magazine
called *The American Journal.*
Dutch (probably): Artist E. H.
Value C

COMPIÈGNE
At the end of the First World
War the defeated Germans
signed the Armistice in

Marshal Ferdinand Foch's
private railway coach in the
forest near Compiègne in
France. The coach was
preserved in the forest as a
symbol of French triumph,
and 22 years later on 22 June
1940, Adolf Hitler made the
French surrender to the

603

604

605

Nazis in the same coach,
which was then moved to
Berlin for display and finally
destroyed in an Allied air
raid in 1943.

598 '*Around The Table.*'
The French delegation, led
by General Charles
Huntziger, consisted of a
former ambassador, an air
force general and an
admiral. They faced the
Germans across the table
and discussions continued
for two days until the French
were warned that if they did
not agree to German
demands in one hour the
negotiations would be
broken off. They agreed.
*German: (Pub. Hoffmann)
Posted at Wiesbaden 28
August 1940. No. C5. Value
D.*

599 '*In Commemoration of
The Armistice.*' The date and
time of the Armistice are
given as 1.25 a.m. on
25 June 1940. It is generally
accepted that General
Huntziger signed the
document at 6.50 p.m. on
22 June and that it was due
to go into effect at 1.25 a.m.
on 25 June. When that
moment came, Hitler had
completed his tour of Paris
and the *Wehrmacht* were
toasting him with
champagne.
*German: (Pub. Garloff
Magdeburg) No.
E/0195/L/1011. Value D.*

**WORDS THAT DON'T
RING TRUE!**
'Divide and Conquer' is the
theme of these cards
designed for circulation in a
neutral country. The propaganda is aimed at increasing
friction within the ranks of
the Axis, between Goering's
Luftwaffe and the Führer,
and between Italy and
Germany. The drawings are
caricatures on phrases used
by Axis announcements.

600 '*Danger From British
Air Attacks, According to
Experience so Far, Does Not
Make Any Action Necessary.*'
*British (probably): No. 51-
2185 (probably a series
number). Value B*

601 '*The Relations
Between the Führer and the
Duce Are As Cordial As Those
Between Two Brothers.*'
*British (probably): No. 51-
2185 (probably a series
number). Value B*

602 '*United States Navy.*'
America initially determined
to keep out of the European
war, but its government took

606

607

608

609

610

precautions to increase the Armed Forces. In July 1940 the 'Two-Ocean Navy Act' authorized a 70% increase in naval tonnage so that, by Pearl Harbour, the personnel strength of the Naval Coast Guard and Marines had doubled in 18 months to almost half a million. By the end of the war there were more than four million. *American: (Offical navy card) Value B*

603 *'Artist Noah Bee.' Jerusalem: (Pub. M. J. & B. Miller) Passed for circulation by the Deputy Chief Field Censor. Value B*

604 *'Weather Report Hot.'* The Japanese began their war in December 1941 with simultaneous attacks on Pearl Harbour, Malaya, Thailand and Bataan. Within a few days they were in control of Guam, had invaded Burma, landed in Borneo and virtually destroyed the American air forces in the Philippines. After the Battle of Midway, in 1942, the balance shifted and the Americans began to push the Japanese back. This

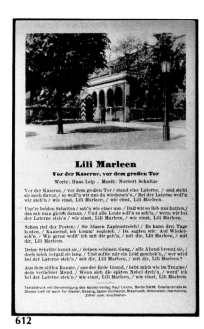

611

612

613

614

614A

card certainly shows a Japanese on the run, but the reference to 'REIGN' remains obscure. Perhaps it was an American nickname for an offensive operation or maybe just bad spelling!
American: (Pub. E. C. Kropp, Milwaukee) No. C134. Value B

605 'Keep 'Em Flying.' This card was posted by an air cadet at S.A.A.A.B. (Santa Ana Army Air Base) California in August 1942 when the situation in the Pacific was improving for America. He comments on his course and the exams which he has to do:
'... Physics coming Sat and am going to study it after this card. Hardest part of course coming yet ... Maxwell Field send our service records here and will get paid FULLY in few days. Love Steve.' Maxwell Field air base in Montgomery, Alabama, was headquarters of the Air Training system. Steve probably began his training there, and with the massive increase in the numbers of personnel to be adminis-tered, systems like 'Pay' sometimes went awry. Junior officers were taught to make certain that the men under their command were being paid correctly and promptly.
American: (Pub. Curteich-Chicago) No. AC-6. Value B

AN IRANIAN ALLEGORY
Iran assumed strategic importance to the Allies when Russia entered the war in June 1942. Upon Iran's refusal to expel German Nationals, a joint British-Soviet force entered the country, meeting a short-lived resistance. A treaty was signed guaranteeing Iran neutrality and the Persian corridor became an impor-tant supply route from the West to Russia.
This anti-German series of exquisite cards parallels Hitler's Nazism and crimes against humanity with the Iranian folk story of the cruel and wicked reign of Sultan

Zahat, who was overthrown by his good Minister Kaveh. (The Iranian captions are translated literally.)

606 'Full of anger I came against you, the King, that you may know I am Judg-ment. There is a limit to cruelty and reason tells me that I must take action.' (Kaveh, the reasonable and just Minister represents the Allies, and attempts to stop the reign of terror.)
Persian: Circa 1942. Value D

607 'The goodness is gone, leaving foolishness to re-capture the scene. The devil's badness was endless and there was no word of love.' (Goebbels in the shape of a horned devil helps his cruel master, Hitler.)
Persian: Circa 1942. Value D

608 'From his shoulders two snakes grew, which brought him power, but which brought harm to the people.' (The snakes are Mussolini and Tojo.)
Persian: Circa 1942. Value D

609 'The way he saw it from the Palace. Three warriors appeared suddenly.' (Roosevelt, Stalin and Churchill, each puffing his favourite form of tobacco, ride on, resembling the Three Wise Men.)
Persian: Circa 1942. Value D

610 'Tie him so well that only the ultimate power is able to untie him.' (Kaveh, with the help of the three Allied Warriors, has Zahat-Hitler in captivity and drags Goebbels behind him.)
Persian: Circa 1942. Value D

611 'Bombs On England.' A favourite song of the Luftwaffe taken from their film, *Feuertaufe* (Baptism of Fire) which told the story of the Blitzkrieg. The music was written by Norbert Schultze.
German: (Pub. Ross-Verlag, Berlin) No. R107. Value B

612 'Lili Marleen.' Also written by Norbert Schultze, this song became as popular as *Tipperary.*
German: (Pub. Robert Franke, Hamburg) No. 88. Value B

613 'Pinelands.' Australia and New Zealand immediately joined Britain when war was declared, giving their allegiance to 'one King, one cause, one flag.' Canada made her own declaration six days later, while in South Africa, Prime Minister Hertzog declared

BY GYULA ZILZER

FASCISM·MEANS WAR!
FASCHISMUS IST KRIEG!
LE FASCISME - C'EST LA GUERRE!
EL FASCISMO - ESTA LA GUERRA!

615

L'EXTRÊME ONCTION   2   LETTE OELUNG
EXTREME UNCTION   OSTATNIE NAMASZCZENIE

617

ARRÊTEZ-VOUS!   I   HALT!.
HALT!   ZATRZYMAĆ SIĘ!

618

"DREI JAHRE!
FÜNF JAHRE!!
ACHT
JAHRE!! !"

"BITTE, HERR FÜHRER,
WIE LANGE
DAUERT
NOCH IHR
BLITZKRIEG?"

616

LA LETTRE   6   DIE TODESNACHRICHT
THE DEATH-NOTICE   OSTATNI LIST

619

CROIX D'HONNEUR   5   DIE « EHRENKREUZE »
THE FIELD OF HONOUR   KRZYŻE ZASŁUGI

620

S.O.S. (DÉSARMEMENT OU DÉSASTRE)   II   S.O.S. (ABRÜSTUNG ODER UNTERGANG)
S.O.S. (DISARMAMENT OR DISASTER)   S.O.S. (ROZBROJENIE LUB KRES)

621

OUVREZ VOS CŒURS   12   ŒFFNET EURE HERZEN!
OPEN YOUR HEARTS   OTWÓRZCIE SERCA!

622

623

624

625

626

627

628

629

630

631

that South Africa should stay out. Jan Christiaan Smuts, then Minister of Justice, insisted that the country should stand alongside its Commonwealth partners, and, in a close vote, the House of Assembly supported Smuts. He became Prime Minister and formed a War Cabinet on 6 September.
South African: (Pub. National War Fund) Posted 5 December 1940. 'Pinelands' official cancellation on reverse. Value C

614, 614A *'We Shall Get 'Em!'* This postcard is a 'hold-to-light,' a genre popular in the classic collecting period before the First World War. When held to a light, four prisoners appear in the card's cage — Goering, Goebbels, Hitler and Mussolini.
British: (Pub. Cockayne & Co., London) Value C

615 *'Fascism Means War.'* Prior to America's precipitate entry into the war, prompted by the Japanese attack on Pearl Harbour, the European nations vied for her favours much as they had during a similar period in the First World War.
French: (Pub. Edition du Carrefour, New York City) Artist Gyula Zilzer. Value C

616 *'Three Years.'* This is 'black' propaganda, in which the finder is led to believe that the message originated within Germany. Thus a disgruntled German would be more inclined to feed and develop his dissatisfaction if he felt that others shared his views. The reverse of this card reads: 'Postcard', in German script and the children are asking their leader, *'Please Führer, how much longer will your lightning war last?'* The answer is: *'Three years! Five years!! Eight years!!'* The card, which is French, was dropped on Rhine and Moselle towns in March and April 1940.
French: (Official card) Value D

617, 618, 619, 620, 621, 622 *'Anti-War.'* The policy of appeasement sought to avoid war. Amongst the many voices raised against plunging the world into another period of suffering and destruction was, 'Vox Mortuum' — the 'Voice of the Dead.' This was the title of a series of 12 designs by B. Nowak-Varsovie, which

etched in black and white the realities of any new war. The 12 pictures had the sub-title 'Lest we Forget' and were sponsored and published by 'The International Association of Propaganda by Picture' under the auspices of the 'World Union of Women for International Concord' based in Geneva, Switzerland.
Swiss: Each card value C

FRENCH SENTIMENT

The French capitulated so quickly in World War II that there was little opportunity for their postcard publishers to resurrect the huge market they had enjoyed during the First World War.

Nevertheless, during the Phoney War of 1939 and 1940, the French did produce cards for their own market and for the occasional British soldier who might want one.

The cards shown here were purchased from a stationer's roadside carousel in Verdun in 1979! They had recently been discovered in a cellar. The examples here are captioned with their English translations.

623 'Military Post.' 'A parcel for him. Some sweets and . . . a loving heart.' *French: (Pub. SSS. Paris) No. 205 (probably a series number). Value B*

624 'Military Post.' 'News from the Front or Cupid's indiscretions.' *French: (Pub. SSS. Paris) No. 205 (probably a series number). Value B*

625 'Military Post.' 'Waiting for the Postman.' *French: (Pub. SSS. Paris) No. 205 (probably a series number). Value B*

626, 627 'Message To A Friend.' 'I cannot find the words and my clearest language fades away at the memory of your charming face.' *French: (Pub. MD. Paris) Value B*

628 'Confidences.' 'Your confidences enchant and intoxicate me but for myself I can only say, "I love you."' *French: (Pub. MD. Paris) Value B*

629 'Birthday Wishes.' This French card, embroidered on silk, was made for the occupying German forces. Life had to go on, after all. *French: (Pub. CEK. Paris) Value C*

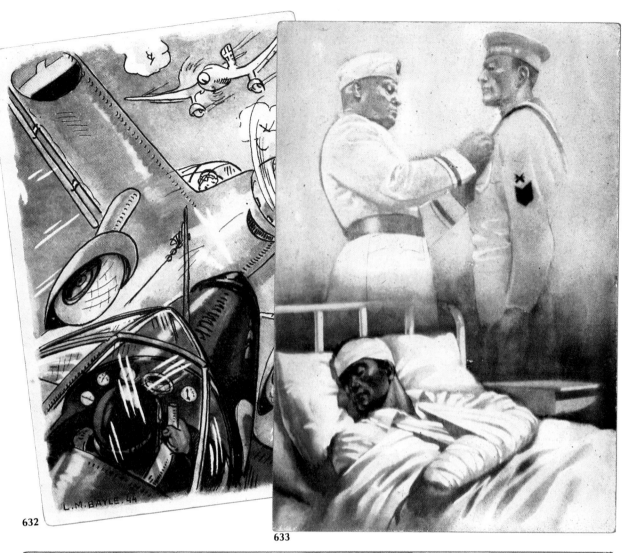

632

633

634

SANTE PATUSSI

Tenente osservatore, da Tricesimo (Friuli), alla memoria.

« Ufficiale osservatore dall'aeroplano, capace, attivissimo, entusiasta, chiesta ed ottenuta l'assegnazione in zona d'operazioni, svolgeva attività intelligente e coraggiosa in numerose azioni in zona desertica. Durante una missione di ricerca di camerati dispersi in mare, attaccato da cinque velivoli da caccia, con calma esemplare rispondeva ai furiosi assalti nemici che già avevano danneggiato il velivolo e ferito il resto dell'equipaggio. Vista l'arma abbandonata dall'armiere ferito ed accortosi di un nuovo attacco avversario proveniente dal basso, si precipitava per reagire in quella direzione. Colpito una prima volta a una gamba, continuava a sparare, finché una seconda raffica lo abbatteva sull'arma. Avvenuto l'ammaraggio in mare aperto, benché con le carni straziate e lacerate e col corpo immerso in gran parte nell'acqua entrata nel velivolo, insisteva perché il pilota unico illeso, deponesse sul battellino, di salvataggio, prima gli altri feriti. Durante 17 ore di permanenza sul mare, senza alcun conforto di medicinali nè di viveri nè d'acqua, sorretto soltanto dalla sublime forza d'animo e dal senso del dovere, incitava i compagni feriti alla sopportazione del dolore e alla speranza della salvezza, esaltando il camerata pilota e lo aiutava, pur morente, nell'orientamento del canotto verso la riva amica. Consco della fine imminente, dava l'ultima parola di sollievo ai camerati, ammirati per tanto stoicismo e rivolgeva un augurio alle sorti della Patria ed espressioni di saluto alla madre. Chiudeva così nell'angusto spazio del battello, ancora in pienomare, la giovane esistenza, dando, fino all'ultimo anelito, insuperabile esempio di forza d'animo, senso del dovere, sublime cameratismo. »

(Cielo del Mediterraneo orientale, 25 giugno 1941-XIX)

Heroic Deeds of the War—V.C. Series

LEADING SEAMAN JACK MANTLE, V.C.
H.M.S. "Foylebank"   Photo: U.P.U.

Here is a moving story typical of the heroism of the men in England's "little ships." On H.M.S. "Foylebank," LEADING SEAMAN JACK MANTLE was in charge of the starboard gun. When his ship was attacked by enemy aircraft, his left leg was shattered by a bomb, but he stood fast by his gun and went on firing with his hand-gear only, for the ship's electric power had failed. Almost at once he was again wounded in many places; but he carried on and his great courage sustained him until the end of the fight when he fell by the gun he had so valiantly served.

635

Heroic Deeds of the War—V.C. Series

SERGEANT ALFRED HULME, V.C., New Zealand Exp. Force
Photo: Official, Crown Copyright Reserved

A farmer until he volunteered for the N. Z. Army, SERGEANT HULME had learnt how to walk without snapping twigs and how to stalk game without disturbing it. So, in Greece and in Crete, he took on the role of stalker and sniper. Adopting the same form of camouflage as the Germans, and acquiring a German rifle and automatic pistols, he actually joined up with a German party of snipers, hid himself under cover of a parachute, and picked them off one by one. He was almost killed by his own comrades when a party of Maoris attacked a further batch of Germans with whom Sergeant Hulme had mingled. Later, he was severely wounded in the shoulder—but he had personally accounted for 33 snipers.

636

FRANK LEEDALE, 17 year old Lancashire "Deck Boy," for 12 days a captive on the "Graf Spee" and twice wounded.
PHOTO "WELGRIFF" 101 GROSVENOR ST. MANCHESTER

637

Germans issued postcards of Knight's Cross winners and the Italians published grand artistic representations of daring deeds. Higher awards for conspicuous gallantry, such as the Victoria Cross, were much reduced, though there was a proliferation of minor medals: over six million Iron Cross 2nd Class and three quarters of a million Iron Cross 1st Class were awarded.

632 *'Aerial Combat.'* The printed text on the reverse reads: *'On 15 June 1940 during a dog-fight, pilot Lieutenant Marcal Bihan seeing his adversary getting away, deliberately collided with him and dragged him with him in his descent thus finding a glorious death.'* French: (Pub. Moullet-Marseille) Artist L. M. Bayle. 1944. Value B

633 *'A Dream.'* The simple caption on the reverse reads: *'A hero's dream.'* Il Duce is pinning something on the sailor's chest, but it is difficult to guess what it might be because Italy had such a variety of awards. Campaign medals were issued for Abyssinia, Spain, Africa, Greece, Yugoslavia, France and Russia. Perhaps the sailor was dreaming of being awarded the Gold Medal for Military Valour — the most highly coveted. Italian: (Pub. V. E. Boeri Rome) Artist Averardo Circello. Value C

634 *'Sante Patussi.'* This card is to the memory of Observer Lieutenant Sante Patussi, who with three comrades, was shot down into the sea after a fierce dog fight, on 25 June 1941. For 17 hours Patussi encouraged his companions and then died. His award was the Gold Medal for Military Valour, Italy's most distinguished recognition of gallantry. Italian: (Pub. Tecnico-Editoriale Italiano Rome) Artist Giulio Bertoletti. Value C

635 *'Leading Seaman Jack Mantle, V.C.'* Jack Mantle stayed at his gun on *H.M.S. Foylebank* throughout an enemy attack, despite being mortally wounded and having to operate the weapon by hand when the electric power failed. V.C. cards were included in tobacco parcels, paid for by school-children's

(7) El Acorazado Alemán «GRAF SPEE» antes de ser velado.
(7) The German Pocket Battleship «GRAF SPEE» before blown up.

638

630 *'Memory.'* French: (Pub. MD. Paris) Value B

631 *'Happy Birthday.'* During the First World War, sentimental embroidered silk cards had been hand-made by seamstresses close to the front lines and they had proved very popular with the Tommies. This card was

made for the occupied French. French: Value B

HEROES

In a war of machine versus machine there was less room for acts of individual heroism than there had been 20 years earlier. In Britain, the first heroes were the pilots in the Battle of Britain. The

(1) Acorazado Alemán «GRAF SPEE» después de la 1ra. explosión.
(1) German Pocket Battleship «GRAF SPEE» after the 1st explosion.

639

(3) El entierro de los marinos del «GRAF SPEE»
(3) The funeral of the sailors of the «GRAF SPEE» who were killed in the action

640

(2) El Capitán del Acorazado «GRAF SPEE»
(2) The Captain of the German Pocket Battleship «GRAF SPEE»

641

subscriptions made on Empire Day.
British: (Pub. Overseas League) Value A

636 *'Sergeant Alfred Hulme, V.C., New Zealand Expeditionary Force.'* Alfred Hulme pretended to be a German during the fighting in Greece and Crete, and, using a captured telescopic rifle, he picked off 33 Nazi snipers. He narrowly avoided being killed by his own side.
This V.C. card and the one above were returned by the grateful recipient to 'The Pupils of Wyke Regis Mixed School, Weymouth, Dorset,' who had raised the funds for the tobacco parcel in which the card was included.
British: (Pub. Overseas League) Value A

637 *'Frank Leedale.'* During the First World War, the boy hero, Jack Cornwall, caught the public's imagination and postcards of him helped to raise funds for the Star and Garter Homes. This card of Frank Leedale seems to have been a piece of private enterprise. The caption reads: *'Frank Leedale, 17 year old Lancashire 'Deck Boy,' for 12 days a captive on the Graf Spee and twice wounded.'* Frank has put his autograph, the name of his new ship and the date in pencil on the back — *S.S. Taeroa 24-3-1940.'*
British: (Pub. Melgriff Manchester) Value C

THE GRAF SPEE INCIDENT
Potentially one of the biggest British morale-boosting propaganda stories of the war, 'The *Graf Spee* Incident' perversely added to the respect accorded to the Germans. The *Admiral Graf Spee* had been preying on Allied shipping in the South Atlantic since the beginning of the war. The British cruisers *Ajax*, *Achilles* and *Exeter* met the *Graf Spee* in the Battle of the River Plate on 13 December 1939 and forced her into Montevideo for repairs. Captain Hans Langsdorff and his crew were tricked by the British into believing that a large naval force was on its way to attack them. Langsdorff took his ship out to sea, blew it up and then shot himself.

638 *'The Graf Spee Before Being Blown Up.'*
South American (probably): (Pub. Herman) No. 7. Value C

642

643

644

645

646

647

THE MAKOVSKI PICTURE CARDS SALE TOWARDS
MRS. CHURCHILL'S "AID TO RUSSIA" FUND

PRICE   ONE   SHILLING

648

649

639 *'The Graf Spee After The First Explosion.'*
South American (probably): (Pub. Herman) No. 1. Value C

640 *'The Sailor's Funeral.'*
South American (probably): (Pub. Herman) No. 3. Value C

641 *'The Captain of The Graf Spee.'*
South American (probably): (Pub. Herman) No. 2. Value C

PC OF PARIS
The publishers PC of Paris produced a series of cards during the Phoney War period in which they used the artist Paul Barbier to chronicle the acts of Nazi Germany. Unlike Barbier's idealistic coloured drawings, these black and white sketches are clear interpretations of the present, and forebodings of the future.

642 *'I've Nothing More To Ask.'* As Hitler obtained each new concession from the nations of Europe he would promise, 'I've nothing more to ask.' His territorial gains appear in order — Austria, Czechoslovakia, Poland. Next? Barbier must have suspected that it would be France.
French: (Pub. PC, Paris) No. G.20 Signed Paul Barbier 1939. Value C

643 *'Hitler's Dream.'* Barbier's view of Hitler's ambition includes the moon. The dream depicted here is of a German dominated world and moon both dripping with blood.
French: (Pub. PC, Paris) No. G.22 Signed Paul Barbier. 1939. Value C

644 *'Calamity! What Have You Done To Germany.'* Beethoven and Goethe are resurrected by Barbier to lament the torn up treaties, and the death and destruction caused by the Nazis.
French: (Pub. PC, Paris) No. G.5 Signed Paul Barbier. 1939. Value C

645 *'Hitler, Goering, Poland, Stalin.'* Hitler attacked Poland from the West and shortly afterwards Stalin attacked from the East.
French: (Pub. PC, Paris) No. G.23. Unsigned. Value C

FUND RAISERS
In wartime government fund raising becomes a major activity. The Germans used official postcards to raise Party funds while, at the opposite end of the scale

650

651

were the British, unofficially
raising money through
county ladies, well versed in
collecting monies for charity;
National savings, which
could be made directly by
buying stamps or bonds, or
by simply donating money.
In addition to the National
fund raising organizations,
there was the Red Cross
which sought help from all
countries. These cards
record a few variations on
the theme.

646 *'Made In Germany —
Finished In England.'*
Appeals were frequently
made to local loyalties. This
one asks for donations to
'our local Spitfire Fund', and
the exhibition of items of
equipment, both Allied and
Axis, as a spur to generosity
parallels a similar use of
'tank banks' and 'submarine
banks' in the First World
War.
*British: (Pub. CT Photo)
Value C*

647 *£1. 18s. 0d.* Saying
'thank you' was a most
important part of fund raising
because the process of
collecting money became
ever more pressing as the
war went on.
*British: (Pub. 'Aid to Russia'
Fund) Value A*

648 *'Makovski Picture
Cards.'* Mrs Churchill's 'Aid
to Russia' Flag Day Fund was
founded in October 1941
and raised £2 million in just
over a year. Oddly she was
in Moscow on Fund business
on VE Day.
On the reverse of this card,
which sold for the high price
of one shilling, is the printed
message: *
*Valiant Russia, we who love
    thy song,
Thy people and the magic of
    thy land
ENDURE until we reach thy
    side and stand
AT ONE with thee.
    ENDURE, hold fast, be
    strong.'*
It is signed, 'Jessica
Borthwick.'
*British: (Pub. 'Aid to Russia'
Fund) Value B*

649 *'Buy More War
Bonds.'* War bonds were
government issues providing
long term funds to aid the
war. Unlike 'donations',
such as those raised by Mrs
Churchill, monies paid for
War Bonds were due for
repayment plus a fixed
amount of interest. The
interest rate was low in order
to keep the government debt
down and the loan period

652

653

Vanga e medaglia

656

657

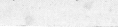

658

659

655

was usually a matter of years.
*American: (Pub. U.S.
Treasury Department, War
Savings Staff) Value B*

650   'Buoni Del Tesoro
Novennali.' This invitation to
subscribe to 5% Nine Year
Treasury Bonds was issued
by the National Bank of
Lavaro. The issue of such
bonds was authorised by the
government. The slogan
'Vince Remo' apparently
written on the carriage door,
means literally 'conquer
difficulty.'
*Italian: (Pub. Bank of Lavoro)
Value B*

651   'Quick Help.' The
written message on the
reverse (translated) reads:
'... To send money to
prisoners you must fill in a
form at the National Bank
making 5 copies — it's the
only place you can send it. If
you like I'll bring you one on
Sunday ...' The card was
posted in occupied Belgium
to an address in Turnhout,
Belgium. Could the prisoners
referred to be soldiers — or
Jewish relatives? By 1942
there were 15 major con-
centration camps.
*Belgian: (Pub. Belgian Red
Cross) Artist Massonet. Circa
1942. Value B*

FASCIST PROPAGANDA &
MILITARISM

The Encyclopaedia
Britannica defines Fascism as
'a political attitude which
puts the nation-state or the
race, its power and growth
in the centre of life and
history.' It has become
synonymous with the name
and career of Benito
Mussolini in Italy, but Hitler
and his National Socialism
and Franco and his Falangists
were also exponents of this
fanatical political ideology.

652   '150th Battalion
CCNN.' The Italian
Regiments used mottos,
emblems, insignia and

symbols to instil pride and
loyalty. The 150th's motto –
'Annihilate as they Pass!'
*Italian: (Pub. V. E. Boeri)
Value C*

653   '4th Alpine Regiment.'
The Italians had a long
tradition of Alpine troops to
safeguard their northern
border.
*Italian: (Pub. F. Duval,
Milan) Posted after the war.
Value C*

654   'Three Fascist Leaders.'
'Heil Hitler,' 'Viva Espana'
(Franco); 'Viva l'Italia'
(Mussolini). Posted in Cadiz
on 30 October 1937 by a
student at the German
College to his uncle in
Austria.
*Spanish: (Pub. L & A Placer)
1937 Value D*

655   'Order and Spirit.'
Fascism preaches courage
and audacity within the
framework of a tightly
disciplined authoritarian
state.
*Italian: (Pub. Arti Grafiche
Favia) Artist G. Filoginno.
Circa 1938. Value C*

656   'Spade and Medal.' All
the efforts of the workers
were channelled into striving
for the rebirth of a new
Roman Empire — by military
might.
*Italian: (Pub. Acta, Milan)
Artist Boccasile. Mid-1930's.
Value C*

657   'The day of Armed
Force. 4 Nov.' The Defence
of the Fatherland is the
sacred duty of the Citizen.
Card promulgated by the
Minister of Defence.
*Italian: Artist Soldatini
(which, incidentally, means
'soldier boy'). Value C*

658   'The recreation centre
is the Bridge between the
Party and the People who
fight and work.' The
Dopolavoro (Recreation
Centre) was a Fascist

660

663

661

664

665

662

666

667

institution for providing leisure activities after work hours. This card is dedicated by the Directors and Workers of the Carlo Erba Co., Milan, to their fighting comrades. Slogan and symbol of the PNF (National Fascist Party) on reverse.
Italian: Circa 1940. Value C

659 *'Official Fascist party Propaganda.'* The main tenets of Mussolini's Fascism are set out on the symbolic eagle: patriotism, faith, obedience and belief in the infallibility of Il Duce dominate.
Italian: (Pub. Acta, Milan) Artist Boccasile (1901-1952) was the movement's greatest artist. Mid-1930's. Value C

660 *'Omnes Difficultates Perpetior'* The motto of the 7th Artillery Regiment.
Italian: (Pub. V. E. Boeri) Artist Ferrari. Value C

661 *'301st and 311th Mountain Sections of The 1st Division.'* Nicknamed 'The Implacables.' Battle honours were achieved by these sections in the East African campaigns of 1935 and 1936 in Calamino, Amba Aradam, Amba Tzellere and Abbi Addi.
Italian: (Pub. V. E. Boeri) Circa 1939. Value C

662 *'On the Amba and Beyond.'* The XII Colonial Artillery, Baggage Animals. (The Amba was an Ethiopian mountain where the drivers of the baggage animals distinguished themselves.)
Italian: (Pub. V. E. Boeri) Artist D'Ercoli. Circa 1939. Value C

663 *'24th Legion Reconnaissance Troops.'* These special stamps (the brown 10 Lire, orange 20 Lire and green 25 Lire) commemorate Hitler and Mussolini's Alliance. *'Two Peoples: One War.'*
Italian: (Pub. V. E. Boeri) 1941. Value C

668

664 *'Accustomed to Conquer.'* Members of the 9th Infantry Regiment won medals for their bravery in Eritrea in 1895-6, in the First World War and in the Campaigns of 1940. *Italian: (Pub. V. E. Boeri) Artist D'Ercoli. Circa 1941. Value C*

665 *'Like a hawk after its prey.'* The 25th Colonial Battalion. One of the main results of the Ethiopian Campaign (in which the Colonials fought with panache and success) was to give Mussolini, and the nation he had led to expect a second Roman Empire, an inflated opinion of the ability of their Armed Forces. *Italian: (Pub. V. E. Boeri) Artist D'Ercoli. Circa 1939. Value C*

666 *'70th Infantry Regiment — Ancona — East Africa.'* On the memorial, *'The Defeat at Adua on 1 March 1896 has been revenged by the Victory of 6.X.1935.'* The defeat was at the Battle of Adua, when an Italian force of 20,000 under General Oreste Baratieri rashly attacked 90,000 of Emperor Mevelek's warriors. The victory was the Italian Invasion of Ethiopia. *Italian: (Pub. V. E. Boeri) Artist La Monaca. Value C*

667 *'Angels Watch Over The Seaborne Patrol.'* *Italian: (Pub. V. E. Boeri) Artist Cesare Stefanini. Value D*

668 *'Brotherhood of the German and Italian Armies.'* *Italian: (Pub. F. Duval, Milan) Artist S. Bartoli. 1941. Value D*

669 *'Two have fallen, the others will soon join them.'* Italian forces conquer. *Italian: (Pub. Acta, Milan) Artist Boccasile. Official PNF postcard. Dedicated by the Directors and Workers of the Carlo Erba Company, Milan, to their fighting comrades. Circa 1940. Value D*

670 *1941* Several versions of this powerful propaganda postcard were printed. Some have official PNF (National Fascist Party) backs and were dedicated to members of the fighting forces by the Carlo Erba Company in Milan; others are official military Field Postcards with PNF slogans. *Italian: (Pub. Acta, Milan) Artist Boccasile. Official PNF postcard for the Armed Forces. 1941. Value D*

669

670

671

672

673

674

675

676

CAPITAL E TRABALHO!

677

PODERES POLICIAIS DE ESTALINE SÔBRE A EUROPA.
NÃO SEJAS MOLE, CARO ESTALINE, TU VÊS QUE NÓS FAZEMOS O QUE PO-
DEMOS, TU ÉS O ÚNICO QUE PODE DESTRUIR COMPLETAMENTE A CULTU-
RA SECULAR DA EUROPA.'

678

PESADELOS.

679

„ — Come on, Franklin!"

680

Tem de se contentar com isto, não temos outra coisa!

681

671 *'To fight! The Word of the Black Shirts.'* The Blackshirts were Mussolini's uniformed Fascist followers and paramilitary force, similar to Hitler's 'Brown-shirts' — the S.A. of the early 1930s.
Italian: (Pub. 'E.P.O.C.A.,' Milan/Rome) Official PNF card for the Armed Forces. Value C

672 *'Death choosing its victims.'* On the reverse a quotation from Mussolini reads: *'And we, oh Mother Italy, we offer you without fear, without regret, our life and our death.'*
Italian: (Pub. V. E. Boeri) Artist Berthelet. Value D

ITALIAN SENTIMENT
Italian sentiment was as heartfelt as its patriotism. Partings and thoughts of the loved one gave rise to strong emotion.

673 *'Farewell.'* Message on the reverse reads: *'I will wait for you to the Day of Victory when your chest wil be adorned with the medal of Military Valour.'*
Italian: (Pub. V. E. Boeri) Artist Floriano Pepe. Circa 9141. Value C.

674 *'Blessing!'* On the reverse is an extract from a letter from Luigi Zanow to *'La Mamma Cairoli Veronese,'* asking her not to forget the soldier who was fighting her war, and assuring her that when they meet again he will be able to tell her of a fantastic victory. *Italian: (Pub. V. E. Boeri) Artist Manilo D'Ercoli. 1942. Value C.*

LILI MARLEN [sic]
This is the Italian version of the popular World War II song. On the reverse of each card is printed: *'Exclusive concession to EDISIONI SUVINI ZERBONI, Milano, owner of the words and music of Lili Marlen in Italy.'*

675 *'Give me a rose to hold on the heart.'*
Italian: Value B

676 *'Every evening underneath the lamplight.'*
Italian: Value B

THE FREE SWISS PRESS
A series of powerful anti-Allies propaganda postcards were published in neutral Switzerland. Printed in black on cream board, they are the work of several, unfortunately un-credited, artists, each with his own distinctive style. Most of them have captions in Portuguese. Portugal, another neutral country, disseminated propaganda for both sides.

677 *'Capitalism and Labouring!'* Stalin, the worker, exhausts himself pedalling the capitalists, Roosevelt and Churchill. *Swiss: (Pub. 'Freiheitsverlag Schweiz.') Value B*

678 *'Stalin's powers over Europe.'* 'We're not soft, dear Stalin, you see we're doing what we can. You're the only one who can completely destroy the secular culture of Europe,' say Roosevelt and Churchill. *Swiss: (Pub. 'Freiheitsverlag Schweiz.') Value B*

679 *'Nightmares.'* The nightmare which terrifies Churchill and Stalin is the German U-boat threat to Atlantic shipping. Allied shipping losses in the winter of 1942/43 from U-boats hunting in 'Wolfpacks' were very heavy, but the use of carrier borne anti-submarine 'planes and more effective radars had put the Germans on the defensive by 1944. *Swiss: (Pub. 'Freiheitsverlag Schweiz.') Signed 'Hetto.' 1942. Value B*

680 *'Come On Franklin.* Death beckons Franklin (Roosevelt) to bring America into the war. *Swiss: (Pub. 'Freiheitsverlag Schweiz.') Value B*

681 *'You'll have to be content with this, we don't have anything else.'* Churchill is not satisfied with the amount of naval help Roosevelt is offering him. *Swiss: (Pub. 'Freiheitsverlag Schweiz.') Value B*

PORTUGUESE PROPAGANDA
Portugal was officially neutral during World War II, but as traditionally, 'Britain's **oldest ally**, she aided the Allies by granting bases in the Azores and finally broke diplomatic relations with Germany in May 1945.

Many of these Portuguese cards take items of German propaganda, as disseminated by Goebbels from his Ministry of Propaganda and Public Enlightenment (often by radio), and contrast them with the British version of the same fact. The cards were produced in English and Portuguese versions.

682 *'How The R.A.F. Is Sinking Axis Shipping.'* 110 ships were sunk or damaged in May-September 1940, 610 in the same period in 1941. *Portuguese: No. 51-2276. Value B*

683 *'This Bomb Weighs 2,000 Pounds.'* Later in the war, 4,000 lb 'Blockbusters' were used by the R.A.F. and some bombs were dropped that weighed over 10 tons. *Portuguese: No. 51-2026. Value B*

684 *'England Is Already Under The Control of our Air Army.'* (A German broadcast on 22 September 1940) Terrible damage was indeed wreaked on civilians and buildings during the heavy attacks of August and September. The cost, however, was high: 1900 German planes to 600 British according to this postcard. *Portuguese: No. 51-9504. Value B*

685 *'1st July 1940 Germany cried "In a few weeks England will be on the ground broken, as France is now."'* (German Home Broadcast) The essential preliminary to Hitler's invasion of Britain set out in Directive No. 16, dated July 1940, was the control of the air space over the Channel

682

686

690

683

687

691

684

688

692

685

689

693

694

695

696

and the southern coast of England. The Luftwaffe was unable to win the Battle of Britain and 'Operation Sea Lion' remained a figment of Hitler's imagination.
Portuguese: No. 51-2276.
Value B

686   'A German Journal Boasts: ''the effect of U-boat warfare is becoming more deadly.'' Sept. 1941.* Commander Kell, confessed at a conference in Berlin on 4 September 1941 that 'British convoys are greatly strengthened and British 'planes and warships chase German submarines away.' There was truth in both statements.
Portuguese: No. 51-2228.
Value B

687   'I will personally guarantee that not a single bomb will be dropped on* **the Ruhr.' Goering, August** *1939.* Situations were very much reversed in Britain and Germany during the first year of the war. The Germans were assured they would not be bombed, the British were warned they would be. In fact, the Blitz on Britain didn't start until August 1940.
Portuguese: No. 51-9504.
Value B

688   'The German Airforce Has Smashed The Important Aeroplane Factories in the British Isles.'* (German Radio, March 1941) In fact, the production of aeroplanes in Great Britain in March 1941 had doubled in a year.
Portuguese: No 51-761.
Value B

689   'Losses of the Italian Army in Africa' (on 30 June 1941).* From an original force of 550,000 Italian soldiers, the British and Allied forces had captured or killed, 457,000 men. (Each block represents 27,000 men.) The Italians also lost 100,000 men in Albania and Greece.
Portuguese: (Pub. 'Litografia de Portugal,' Lisbon) Value B

690   'In Liberty — Strength.'* AUSTRALIA: In the freedom of the British Common-wealth, the Continent of Australia grew strong, her power great, her industries flourishing. It is for this reason that today Australia is in the front line of the battle against Nazi tyranny which would destroy the freedom of the whole world.
Portuguese: No. 51-530.
Value B

691   'In Liberty — Strength.'* INDIA: No other country in the British Commonwealth is taking a more energetic part in the struggle against the Nazi aggressor than India. So many Indians and their sons work and struggle to destroy the tryanny which, it is well-known, would mean the end of all free progress and peace.
Number of factories 1914 — 2,874. 1936 — 9,323.
Portuguese: No. 51-761.
Value B

692   'In Liberty — Strength.'* CANADA: To defend the freedom, which makes her so powerful and happy, Canada has put into the struggle all her vast resources of war. She helped to protect the world from German tyranny in the last war. And today she is doing it again.
Production of copper 1914 — 34,258 tons. 1939 — 271,474 tons.
Portuguese: No. 51-1094
Value B

693   'In Liberty — Strength.'* NEW ZEALAND: It was through the freedom of the British Empire that prosperity and contentment came to New Zealand. Today the strength of New Zealand is employed, both in man-power and its great resources, in the fight against the evil forces of Nazi brutality.
Exports of Frozen Meat 1914 — 3,229,973 hundred-weights. 1933 — 5,373,601 hundredweights.
Portuguese: No. 51-1064
Value B

694   'English:'* Resistance workers all over occupied Europe listened avidly to the BBC news, with its opening 'Victory' sign of the three first notes of Beethoven's Fifth Symphony. Many were shot for doing so.
Portuguese: No. 2123. Value B

695   'No Enemy, However Strong, Will Be Able to Carry The War Into Germany In The Air,'* maintains Goebbels, to the satisfaction of Goering and Hitler. They are shown green with fright as 'Up to 20 July 1941, the R.A.F. bombed Germany alone 1,800 times.'
Portuguese: No. 51-1046.
Value B

696   'German Broadcast: ''The R.A.F. have to drop their bombs from 30,000 feet up because of the efficiency of the German defences.''*

'THE TRUTH! An actual photograph of a raid on a German power station, **(Knapsack, Rhineland)**,taken from another British bomber engaged in the same raid . . . The R.A.F. have made over 4,000 attacks on German military objectives.' The strategic bombing of R.A.F. Bomber Command, once they changed from costly day-time raiding to effective night-time bombing, was crippling in its effect and the industrial Ruhr was virtually put out of action by the beginning of 1944. *Portuguese: No. 51-2123. Value B*

PIN-UPS

The 'Pin-up' had been created in the First World War — literally the picture of a glamorous girl that was pinned up in the dugouts and trenches. The term came into its own during World War II, when the girls shed more clothes and camiknickers and bikinis (or 'twopieces' as they were then called) replaced the seductive lingerie of the First World War period.

697 *'Black And White Two-Piece.'* The wedge heels worn by this pin-up came in at the end of the war, foreshadowing the 'platform soles' of the '70s. *French: Artist André Hermond. Value B*

698 *'Striped Two-Piece.'* Erogenous zones shift! During the First World War legs and ankles — encased in titillating black stockings and high heels — were in. In World War II interest changed to the bosom! *French: Artist Andre Hermond. Value B*

699 *'Green Lovely On A Magenta Background.'* The turban was converted into a glamorous head covering by the fiery Latin American star, Carmen Miranda. *Belgian: Probably produced after the Liberation. Value B*

700 *'Siren Calling.'* The artist, Barribal, successfully bridged the gap between the two wars. His red-headed 'sirens' were provocative and exciting in the First World War but his World War II seductress still has the distinctive pouting lips of his wife, Babs, — the only model he was allowed to paint. *British: (Pub. Valentine's 'Barribal' Postcards) No. 40-2. 1940. Value C*

697

699

698

700

701

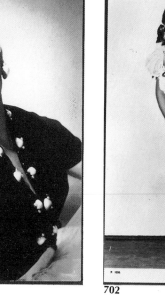

702

703

704

705

706

707

708

709

THE FILM STARS

The great therapeutic leisure activity of the war years was 'going to the pictures' — or 'the movies.' 'Sex Appeal' replaced 'IT' as the desirable attribute for female stars, and stories were mostly escapist or romantic. The 'war stories' came AFTER the war!

701 'Lana Turner.' The original 'Sweater Girl.' *British: (Pub. 'L.D.' London) 'Film Stars' Autograph Portrait Series.' No. 32. Value B*

702 'June Haver.' With Betty Grable, June Haver restored interest in legs! *British: (Pub. 'The People Show Parade Picture Service.') No. P.1050. Value B*

703 'Bette Davis.' With Joan Crawford, Bette Davis shared top billing in 'dramatic roles.' *British: 'Picturegoer' Series No. 1342. Value B*

704 'Errol Flynn.' Flynn's swashbuckling roles were great escapist material. *British: (Pub. 'Celebrity Autographs.') No. 187. Value B*

705 'Mickey Rooney.' *British: (Pub. 'Celebrity Autographs.') No. 182. Value B*

706 'James Mason.' The villain everyone loved to hate. *British: Value B*

PROPAGANDA

A series of carefully chosen quotations by influential German officers, which have an anti-Nazi ring about them.

707 'Rear Admiral Lützow.' Statement by the Rear Admiral on German Radio in February 1942 to the effect that the German Navy was not strong enough at the outbreak of war and in spite of efforts since, it still was not strong enough to gain mastery of the sea. Comment below, 'How right the Admiral was!' *Portuguese: No. 51-2394. Value B*

708 'Field Marshal von Rundstedt.' 'For a continental power desirous of destroying England, to have any probability of achieving victory, he must necessarily ally himself with Russia or with the United States.' From a lecture by Rundstedt on a staff course. *Portuguese: No. 51-2378. Value B*

709 *'Field Marshal von Leeb.'* '' 'Whoever achieves great success in the field of politics must not consider himself as possessing any knowledge of military science simply by having read the works of Clausewitz or von Moltke — or, because once in the past he served in the ranks with the position of corporal.'' — Leeb. 1937. 'Hitler, a corporal in the First World War, assumed supreme command of the German Army on 19 December 1941.' *Portuguese: No. 51-2378. Value B*

BRITISH PROPAGANDA

710 *'The Die is Cast.'* Poet Allan Junior comments with commendable British pluck and grit on the outbreak of war. *British: (Pub. Valentine's) No. 392. 1939. Value A*

711 *'Big Ben Silent Minute Observance.'* The chimes of Big Ben, which prefaced the BBC News Bulletins, were a re-assuring sound — to secret listeners of the Resistance throughout Europe, as well as to those in the British Isles. *British: 1944. Value A*

712 *'As Sure As The Morning Sunrise.'* The ruins of Coventry Cathedral. *British: 1940. Value A*

713 *'Heavy Artillery: Please Write Frequently.'* *British: (Pub. Photo-Multo Ltd., Elland) Value B*

714 *'Victory'* Churchill's famous 'V' sign adopted from the V for Victory campaign initiated from London by the Belgian broadcaster, Victor de Laveleye. The Germans tried to counter this effective campaign by saying that the V stood for Viktoria -German victory. *Portuguese: Value C*

715 *'The Symbol of Victory.'* *British: (Pub. Valentine's) ''Helpful Thoughts'' Postcards. No. 665. Circa 1940. Value A.*

SET OF ''PATIENCE STRONG'' POSTCARDS

British: (Pub. Valentine's) Embosse Series. No. 39. 2. Circa 1939 value A

716 *'Nothing To Fear.'*

717 *'Keep Calm.'*

718 *'Might and Right.'*

719 *'When Duty Calls.'*

710

712

713

714

715

716

717

718

719

720

720 *'V France.'* The cockerel is the traditional symbol of French pride and courage and is often found on First World War memorials. Here it combines the 'V for Victory' symbol which became associated with Churchill. The colours in the word 'France' represent the blue, white and red of the National flag, the *Tricolore. French: 1945. Value B*

721 *'Invasion Craft Go Into Action.'* The Invasion of France, known as D-Day, took place on 6 June 1944. Officially codenamed 'Overlord,' it was planned to take place on the stretch of Normandy coastline, known as the Cotentin Coast, extending to the west from the mouth of the Orne near Caen, to Cherbourg. The Allied Supreme Commander was General Dwight Eisenhower, Air Chief Marshal Tedder was Deputy Supreme Commander, General Montgomery was Allied Ground Commander, and General Bradley, U.S. Ground Commander. In this joint Allied exercise the Americans landed on two beaches codenamed 'Utah' and 'Omaha,' the British landed on 'Gold' and 'Sword,' and on 'Juno' an international force of Canadians and Free French landed. The Americans were to parachute behind 'Utah' and the British airborne was to land to the east of the Orne. The actual landing operations were codenamed 'Neptune' and the element of surprise was well maintained. The Germans were

CHAPTER ELEVEN

Liberation & Victory

721

expecting the Invasion in the Pas de Calais area and Rommel was even on his way back to Germany on leave when it happened. It is an interesting parallel that Kesselring had also been confident enough that no big allied activity could be expected to go on leave, prior to the bombing of Monte Cassino in 1943. Through Churchill's imaginative portable 'Mulberry' harbour set up at Arromanches, the Invasion force was supplied for its path of liberation through France towards Berlin. The small town of Ste.Mère Eglise, where the U.S. 82nd Airborne, the 'Screaming Eagles' landed on the surprised Germans, was the first French town to be liberated. A bright pink milestone outside its Town Hall marks Kilometer Zero on 'Liberation Highway' towards Germany.
British Pub. G.P.D. No. 445/2/5 Value B

World War II was an adventure, a taste of danger and new experiences, of travel abroad, of meeting new people, of tasting new foods and drinks, and of a heightened sense of comradeship. It was a particularly big step for U.S. troops coming to Europe to train and fight.

After her late, but positive, contribution to the Allied effort in the First World War, America reverted to a policy of isolationism. During the 1930's she kept out of foreign quarrels while she put her own economy in order after the Depression. In 1935 the Neutrality Act was passed, prohibiting the shipment of goods from the U.S.A. to any nations involved in war. This was amended in 1939 to a 'cash and carry' policy which required countries at war to 'pay up front' for their supplies. Even when America was attacked at Pearl Harbor by the Japanese, some bankers and financial men did not consider it provocation enough to enter the war against Germany.

However, once involved, the G.I.'s threw themselves into the fray with verve and enthusiasm. Their brashness and occasionally insensitive exhibition of their prosperity sometimes irritated the deprived European Allies in whose countries they were based. Their genuine desire to do the job well, however, their gum and chocolate, nylons and strong liquor melted much opposition as they forced their way towards the goal of Berlin. For many G.I.'s it was their first ever visit to the home of their emigrating ancestors – from Britain, Holland, Italy, Poland and, of course, Germany. At their peak, the U.S. armed forces approached some 12½ million (about one in eleven of the 1940 total population) and their commitment was strong, continuing in the Pacific for several months after the war in Europe ground to a halt in May 1945.

By and large the friendly invaders, British as well as American, were welcomed with rapture as they successively released the countries of occupied Europe from Nazi rule. The renewed freedom of the press gave vent to a glorious outbreak of celebratory postcards in France, Belgium, Holland and Denmark. Although the card on which they were printed was often of poor quality, the ink fluctuating from garish to weak, the message was universal and joyous, 'We are Free!'; 'Thank you, Allies'; 'Welcome!'. Montgomery was one of the great heroes of these celebratory cards.

One grim task for the many allied soldiers was to open the S.S.-run concentration camps and reveal the undreamt of atrocities that had been perpetrated in them. Pictures of the walking skeletons at Belsen, the mass graves at Auschwitz and countless other abuses almost too terrible to comprehend, flashed around an astounded world. The impact of discovering these unspeakable horrors was a memory that many impressionable servicemen would never be able to erase. When victory in Europe was formally proclaimed on 8 May 1945, following Hitler's ignominious suicide in the Berlin bunker on Tuesday 1 May and the signature of the surrender documents by Dönitz, his successor, at Luneberg and by General Jodl at Reims, almost hysterical rapture erupted.

Civilians and service personnel in the motley uniforms of scores of branches and nationalities mingled in the great city centres and in the hamlets. The Royal Family, together with everyone's number one hero, Winston Churchill, appeared again and again on the balcony of Buckingham Palace. But the war was not yet over. The horrors of Hiroshima and Nagasaki and the difficult mopping up operations in the Pacific were yet to come.

So great was the impact on the civilised world of the fearsome atomic bombs dropped on Japan on 6 and 9 August 1945, that the fear of ever seeing their like used again has, until the day of writing this sentence, been sufficient to deter the Great Powers from entering into a Third World War.

May it always be that way.

722

723

724

725

726

727

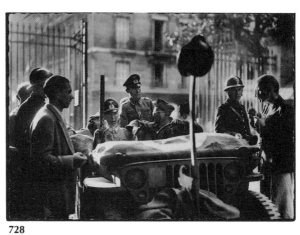

728

729

LIBERATION DE PARIS
A remarkable series of news photographs which capture the drama, joy and excitement of the Americans as they fight their way into Paris. The capture of Paris, with all its artistic and architectural treasures intact, had been one of Hitler's most triumphant coups. Its liberation on 25th August 1944, when the American 4th Infantry Division broke through, was cause for jubilations. The Americans were followed a day later by General de Gaulle who, with his Generals Leclerc and Koenig, marched through the streets in triumph.

722 *'A Barricade.'* Barricades are the traditional form of street fighting by the Parisians. On 19 August the Communist Resistance, under Colonel Henry Tanguy, threw up barricades and attacked the German garrison. As General von Choltitz had not received the reinforcements Hitler had promised him, and as he did not wish to see Paris reduced to a ruin, he negotiated a truce with the Resistance through the neutral Swedish Consul General, Raoul Nordling. When this broke down, Choltitz brought out his tanks against the Partisans. *French: (Pub. 'C.A.P.' Paris. 'Real Photo') No. 51 Series No. 44. 1944. Value C*

723 *'Leclerc's Armoured Tanks in the Place de la Concorde.'* On de Gaulle's insistence, General Eisenhower ordered General Leclerc's 2nd Armoured Division to join the Americans and enter Paris on 25 August 1944. *French: (Pub. 'C.A.P.' Paris. 'Real Photo') No. 69 Series No. 44. 1944. Value C*

724 *'One of Leclerc's tanks in action.'* The German resistance was token. General von Choltitz had too great a respect for the history and tradition of the beautiful city to risk damaging it. *French: (Pub. 'C.A.P.' Paris. 'Real Photo') No. 53 Series No. 44. 1944. Value C*

725 *'American anti-aircraft gun in the Place du Châtelet.'* The strain is evident on the Parisians' faces as they watch their American liberators set up an anti-aircraft gun. *French: (Pub. 'C.A.P.' Paris. 'Real Photo') Series No. 44. 1944. Value C*

726 'Tanks and the Free French outside the Senate House after the Surrender.' General von Choltitz surrendered Paris, much against Hitler's wishes, without a fight to the death. The young partisans, proud of their weapons and American helmet, can hardly believe their good fortune. The motto of the French Revolution, 'Liberté, Égalité, Fraternité, stands proudly above the gateway to the Senate House.
French: (Pub. 'C.A.P.' Paris. 'Real Photo') No. 60 Series No. 44. 1944. Value C

727 'Armoured car parked outside the defences of the Senate.' (German Headquarters)
French: (Pub. 'C.A.P.' Paris. 'Real Photo') No. 56 Series No. 44. 1944. Value C

728 'The Surrender Order is brought from the Senate House.' A moment of sweet triumph for the Parisians and one of bitter disappointment for the Germans. The driver seems to be trying to offer some comfort to his officer.
French: (Pub. 'C.A.P.' Paris. 'Real Photo') No. 58 Series No. 44. 1944. Value C

729 'German prisoners outside the Palais de Luxembourg.' The ultimate moment of vindication. The Germans seem resigned to their lot.
French: (Pub. 'C.A.P.' Paris. 'Real Photo') No. 44 Series No. 44. 1944. Value C

730 Reconstruction.' Man on left, 'For goodness sake — are we going to reconstruct, yes or no?' Boss of the office, 'Impossible, the Liberation Committee has decided our material isn't 'resistant' enough.
French: Artist Marc Ely. 1944. Value B

731 'Foreseen and Organised Withdrawl [sic].' Goering, in particular, was notorious for pillaging art treasures, vintage wine and other booty from France by the train load. These soldiers would not enjoy their booty for long.
French: Artist Jean Schnebelen 1944. Value C

732 'What about your pride now, Fraulein?' The heartless German women Gauleiters were particularly hated by the French.
French: Artist Jean Schnebelen 1944. Value C

730

731

733

732

734

735

736

737

738

739

733 *'Strategic Withdrawl [sic].'* This fleeing German soldier tries to protect himself with emblem of the Red Cross.
French: Artist Jean Schnebelen 1944. Value C

734 *'Strategic Withdrawl [sic].'* The once all-mighty Germans are shown as fleeing with humble hand-carts, salvaging anything they can.
French: Artist Jean Schnebelen 1944. value C

LIBERATION SERIES
Part of a set of eight cards which were published to mark the beginning of the Liberation of France. Produced in Cannes they bear a censor's number and are printed in vibrant colours on board that is so thin as to be almost paper. It is an extremely rare set.

735 *'What do you think of the boss?'* Goebbels asks Goering, while holding a microphone. *'Like you, my dear,'* Goering answers. *'Good, then I arrest you,'* is the reply.
French: (Pub. Editions Lenoir, Cannes) Censor's No. 26. A.M.10. 1945. Value D

736 *'Beloved Liberty.'* The ball and chain of Nazi occupation is broken by the combined might of the United States, Britain, Russia and Free French.
French: (Pub. Editions Lenoir, Cannes) Censor's No. 26. A.M.10. 1945. Value D

737 *'United to reconstruct a more beautiful France.'* The French factory worker, student and peasant work together to re-unite the occupied parts of France. A week after the Allied Invasion of Normandy, de Gaulle returned to France to visit the newly liberated parts of Normandy and many Frenchmen rallied to support him.
French: (Pub. Editions Lenoir, Cannes) Censor's No. 26. A.M.10. 1945. Value D

738 *'De Gaulle and the Cross of Lorraine.'* De Gaulle took the double-barred Cross of Lorraine as the symbol of the Free French, which he led from his headquarters in Britain and Algeria with dogged courage against tremendous odds. The symbolism was two-fold. Lorraine, with Alsace, represented the struggle to throw off the yoke of German occupation. Ceded to the Germans after

the 1870-71 Franco-Prussian War, it had reverted to France under the Treaty of Versailles in 1919, was retaken by the Germans in 1940 and reverted to France in 1945. De Gaulle may have adopted the ancient Cross as a counter to the swastika, which was also an ancient form of the cross.
French: (Pub. Editions Lenoir, Cannes) Censor's No. 26. A.M.10. 1945. Value D

739 *'Honour to the Resistance.'* The term Maquis comes from the Corsican undergrowth which gave cover to bandits. The complex underground organisation that was the French Resistance was headed by Georges Bidault, whose forces co-operated with de Gaulle's Free French. During the Nazi occupation agents did much valuable espionage and sabotage work for the Allies. If caught they were tortured, sent to concentration camps or shot by the Germans if their membership (which reached about 300,000) was discovered. They helped in smuggling British pilots shot down over France back to Britain, organized groups of Partisan Freedom Fighters, and were frequently helped by coded messages broadcast over the BBC News. Warning of the impending Invasion of Normandy was communicated to the Resistance by broadcasting the first line of a poem by Verlaine. The second line was broadcast 48 hours before the Invasion.
French: (Pub. Editions Lenoir, Cannes) Censor's No. 26. A.M.10. 1945. Value D

FRENCH SATIRICAL SERIES OF THE ALLIED INVASION

740 *'The Coloured G.I. Boots The Germans Out Of France, Watched With Approval By The Russian Bear.'*
French: Artist Adli. 1944. Value D

741 *'Hitler, Goering and Goebbels Are Pushed Out Of Paris By The French Resistance.'*
French: Artist Adli. 1944. Value D

742 *'Churchill Sinks The German Mädchen With His Cigars.'* The Invasion of the Normandy beaches in June 1944 catches the Germans unprepared.
French: Artist Adli. 1944. Value D

740

741

742

. . . ON LES A EUS, LES BOCHES !
EN TOCH HEBBEN WE ZE GEHAD, DE MOFFEN !
TOMMY, OUR BEST PAL !

743

FINIES LES VACANCES !
OH, RATTEN EN MUIZEN, WIJ MOETEN VERHUIZEN !
GOOD TIMES ARE OVER !

745

. . . ENFIN !
. . . TOCH !
. . . AT LAST !

747

TU Y CROIS ENCORE AU DÉBARQUEMENT, TOI ?
. GELOOF GIJ NOG AAN EEN LANDING . . ?
YOU STILL BELIEVE THEY WILL.
. . . LAND OVER HERE ?

748

LA ROUTE DE BERLIN, S. V. P. ?
DE WEG NAAR BERLIJN, A. U. B. ?
THE ROAD TO BERLIN, PLEASE ?

744

CONQUÊTES !
EEN HARTVEROVERAAR !
CONQUESTS !

746

N'INSISTONE PAS !
LAAT ONS MAAR HET HAZENPAD KIEZEN !
NO USE INSISTING !

749

PARADE A BERLIN . . .
WELDRA BERLIJN . . .
SOON TO BERLIN . . .

750

SERIES CELEBRATING THE LIBERATION OF BELGIUM

743 *'Tommy, Our Best Pal.'* The message is obvious. 'Tommy' has been singled out because, to a first approximation, the British under Montgomery liberated the Channel coast area and the Low Countries while the Americans headed across France towards Paris and Germany.
Belgian. Circa 1944. Value B

744 *'The Road To Berlin, Please?'*
Belgian. Circa 1944. Value B

745 *'Good Times Are Over!'*
Belgian: Circa 1944. Value B

746 *'Conquests.'* Not all soldiers were front line fighting men. In fact the vast majority of soldiers were supporting troops, whose task was to operate the supply systems that provided the ammunition, petrol, food, equipment and general material needed to sustain an army at war. As Europe was liberated, the support, or rear echelon forces, had more time to fraternise with the grateful locals than the Front-end men did.
Belgian: Circa 1944. Value B

747 *'At Last!'*
Belgian: Circa 1944. Value B

748 *'You Still Believe They Will . . . Land Over Here?'* By 1943 the Germans knew that an Allied cross-Channel invasion attempt was inevitable and took steps to strengthen their coastal defences along what they called the Atlantic Wall. The Allies created an extremely thorough and complex deception plan which set out to convince the Germans that the invasion, when it came, would be in the area of Pas de Calais and not along the Normandy coastline. During the build-up hours to the assault there were deception plans called 'Taxable,' and 'Glimmer' and 'Titanic,' which were airborne diversions using dummy paratroopers and Window (metal foil dropped by aeroplanes to confuse enemy radar signals). These Germans seem to have been taken in.
Belgian: Circa 1944. Value B

749 *'No Use Insisting!'* Discretion is clearly the better part of valour when faced by Russia, America, Britain, Belgium, Free France and the Netherlands.
Belgian: Circa 1944. Value B

750 *'Soon To Berlin.'* Berlin capitulated to the Russians in May 1945 so the card and its companions in this set is firmly dated between June 1944 and May 1945.
Belgian: Circa 1944. Value B

751 *'Long Live the Allies and Long Live my Soldier Boy.'* Message (in English dated 1945) on reverse reads: 'To my darling Valerie from Daddy.'
Belgian: (Pub. Coloprint) No. 298. Circa 1944. Value B

752 *'Well then Tommy, tell them at home how you were received in Belgium.'*
Belgian: (Pub. Coloprint) Circa 1944. Value B

753 *'La Zeelandaise.'* Zeeland is in Southern Holland, bordering Belgium, and this card makes a pun of the phrase, *'Des Élans D'Aise'* and the words *'Des Hollandaise'* — the Dutch. The caption reads: 'The Zeelanders have, you see, a wealth of comforts for the Allies.'
Belgian: (Pub. Coloprint) Circa 1944. Value B

754 *'As I Am Motorised, Am I Authorized To Kiss You?'* It is said that an individual in uniform is able to go anywhere at any time by walking fast and carrying a piece of paper. 'Liberation' brought with it a legion of controls designed to make maximum use of the limited resources available. Permits or 'Authorizations' were required for practically everything.
Belgian: (Pub. Coloprint) No. 312. Circa 1944. Value B

751

752

753

754

755

LA PAIX IMPOSÉE... LES RAPACES ENCHAINÉS

756

SALUT À LA BELGIQUE LIBÉRÉE

757

BRITANNIA RULES THE WAVES

758

DERNIER COUP DE MASSUE DE L'ONCLE SAM.

759

A L'EST

L'URSS INDOMPTABLE, SERRE LES KAMERADS.

760

755 'What Can Hitler Do Against Three?' The 'Three' here are France, Britain and Belgium.
Belgian: (Pub. Coloprint) No. 313. Circa 1944. Value B

756 'Peace has been imposed: the rapacious birds of prey have been chained up.' The victorious allies, Free France, Britain, America and Russia chain up the Nazi eagles.
Belgian: (Pub. anonymous) 1944. Value D

757 'Salute to Free Belgium.' Roosevelt raises his hat to the Liberated Belgium. Before his untimely death on 12 April 1945 he was able to see much of Europe freed.
Belgian: (Pub. anonymous) 1944. Value D

758 'Britannia Rules The Waves.' A slim, youthful Churchill, sporting the continental idea of an English gentleman's dress, but smoking his habitual cigar, surveys Britain's fleet, watched with approval by Britannia and surrounded by the emblems of the British Empire.
Belgian: (Pub. anonymous) 1944. Value D

759 'Uncle Sam's last blow with the club.' America prepares her weapons to deal Hitler, his hands red with the blood of the 'Fortress of Europe,' a final *coup de grace*. Note the crosses marking the graves in Russia. Russian losses during World War II were three times those of Germany.
Belgian: (Pub. anonymous) 1944. Value D

760 'The indomitable Russian bear squeezes the Kamerads.' Hitler made the classic mistake of engaging in war on two fronts and, like Napoleon, he was beaten by the Russian winter.
Belgian: (Pub. anonymous) 1944. Value D

761 'The steam roller has passed.' The Russian Army has traditionally been likened to a crushing steamroller because of its vast manpower resources. The German Commander, Manteuffel, commented in 1944, 'The advance of a Russian Army is something that Westerners can't imagine. Behind the tank spearheads rolls on a vast horde, largely mounted on horses.'
Belgian: (Pub. anonymous) 1944. Value D

761

762

763

764

765

Laat de kurken knallen!!
Vrij Holland viert feest!

766

HEY BILL, THAT DUTCH GIRL SMILED AT ME
PERHAPS SHE'LL ASK ME HOME TO TEA.
THE FIRST TIME THAT I SAW YOU SID,
I SMILED, JUST LIKE THAT DUTCH GIRL DID.

SIKKO VAN DER WOUDE

768

Vuurwerk!!!
Vrij Holland viert feest!

767

LIBERATED HOLLAND

1945

HAPPY DAYS ARE HERE AGAIN
LET'S SING A SONG OF CHEER AGAIN

769

770

771

772

773

774

775

776

777

762 'They're gone.' The Brussels street cleaner sweeps away all traces of Nazi occupation. In his dust cart are the German street signs and the German flag is on the ground. The play bills advertise *They've had it!*, *Twilight of the Two*, 'Adolf and Musso-Comedy. *Belgian: (Pub. anonymous) 1944. Value D*

763, 764, 765 'Greetings From Liberated Holland.' *Dutch: Series number 4 K1392 Artist Piet Broos. Each card Value B*

766 'Bring out the wine, Holland is free.' *Dutch: Artist Steen. 1945. Value B*

767 'Fireworks. Holland is free.' *Dutch: Artist Steen. 1945. Value B*

768 'The Tank Commander.' 'Hey Bill, that Dutch girl smiled at me, Perhaps she'll ask me home to tea.' 'The first time that I saw you Sid, I smiled just like that Dutch girl did.' Message on the reverse (in English) reads: 'The Dutch girl looks like Strube's (Express) little man. Lots of love, Dad. XXX' *Dutch: (Pub. Sima) Artist Sikko van der Woude. Posted 10 June 1945. Value B*

769 'Happy Days Are Here Again.' The Dutch had hard times ahead although the euphoria of relief doubtless sustained them for some time — relief from both Nazi occupation and from bombing by the Allies. *Dutch: (Pub. Sima) Artist Sikko van der Woude. 1945. Value B*

770 'A Dutch Welcome. Holland waves her flag on high.' *Dutch: (Pub. Vlaggekaarten) Artist Smeele. 1945. Value B*

771 'A Jeep For Two.' On the back is a message from a Corporal in the Royal Electrical and Mechanical Engineers to his Dutch girl friend in Enschede. The card is from the British Army of the Rhine where the soldier was stationed with No.3 Armoured Fighting Vehicle Servicing Unit and was posted on 9 September 1945. 'Darling, Just a p.c. to tell you that I am back in Antwerp. I am so happy to receive your letter dated 1 Sept 45. Thanks a million darling. I will write you a long letter this afternoon. I am true to you and love you very much. Your letter has made me feel 100%. There is nothing I wanted more. Love Ken. XXXXXXXXXXXXXXXXX' *Belgian: (Pub. Coloprint) No. 329 Artist 'Henry'. Value B*

SMITS
All these cards were published in Eindhoven, Holland and drawn by Smits. The town was liberated soon after D-Day and thus Smits' drawings were done between June 1944 and war's end in May 1945.

772 'Be clever Adolf, ask by an announcement in the papers, if someone wants a good Führer with staff: otherwise we'll become unemployed . . .' *Dutch: (Pub. Einhovensch Dagblad) Circa 1944. Value C*

773 'Goebbels.' 'Goebbels last journalistic looping-the-loop . . . ''. . . so that we at last succeeded in shortening our communication lines so much that we can hand-over our materials now.'''' *Dutch: (Pub. Einhovensch Dagblad) Circa 1944. Value C*

774 'Have a look Adolf . . . Greater Germany.' *Dutch: (Pub. Einhovensch Dagblad) Circa 1944. Value C*

778

Hurra!

779

Fra Ungpigeværelset —

780

— I love you!

781

— Hvor mange Autografer har du faaet?
— Otte Brown og fjorten Smith!

782

Hurra!

783

Hurra for Montgomery!

775 *'The new quisling uniform.' Vidkun Quisling, a Norwegian politician, who collaborated with the German occupation forces, led a pro-Nazi anti-British government under the Reichskomissar. His name became synonymous with 'traitor.'*
Dutch: (Pub. Einhovensch Dagblad) Circa 1944. Value C

776 *'Hail to you in Victory-wreath.'*
Dutch: (Pub. Einhovensch Dagblad) Circa 1944. Value C

777 *'Race.'*
Dutch: (Pub. Einhovensch Dagblad) Circa 1944. Value C

778 *'Hurra!'*
Danish: (Pub. Stenders Forlag) No. 5006. Artist Ingvar. Value B

779 *'From a young girl's bedroom.' The picture is, of course, of Montgomery.*
Danish: (Pub. Stenders Forlag) No. 5006. Artist Ingvar. Value B

780 *'I Love You!'*
Danish: (Pub. Stenders Forlag) No. 5006. Artist Ingvar. Value B

781 *'How many autographs have you got?' 'Eight Brown and fourteen Smith.'*
Danish: (Pub. Stenders Forlag) No. 5006. Artist Ingvar. Value B.

782 *'Hurra!'*
Danish: (Pub. Stenders Forlag) No. 5006. Artist Ingvar. Value B

783 *'Hurra For Montgomery.'*
Danish: (Pub. Stenders Forlag) No. 5006. Artist Ingvar. Value B

784, 785, 786 & 787 *On V.E. day the American land forces in Europe numbered 61 divisions, containing a total of over three million men. There were almost as many British. A pastime popular that summer amongst the Allied forces was looting. Popular items were watches and binoculars 'liberated' from German soldiers and officers and usually sent home free via the Army postal services. The American military police had a reputation for being effective liberators of desirable items and earned the title 'The Lootwaffe.' These four cards, printed in France, make the benefits of Occupation very clear. Each card Value B*

784

785

786

787

1943

Hitler op het hoogtepunt van zijn macht, laat Mussolini zien, hoe sterk hij is. | Hitler almighty shows Mussolini how powerful he is.

788

1944

In dit jaar kan Hitler zijn krachttoer niet meer volbrengen zonder de steun van Mussolini. | In this year Hitler can't complete his 'stunt' without Mussolini's support.

789

1945

In 1945 is hun vonnis voltrokken en zouden zij gaarne als bedelmuzikanten verder geleefd hebben. | 1945: they have preferred to live as streetmusicians but it's all over now! Their doom being sealed.

790

3 UNIEKE FOTO'S van HITLER EN MUSSOLINI

PRIJS PER SERIE

PRACHTIGE CURIOSITEIT

If you boys want ever to get away from here—help me fix dis motor!

791

Back To HADES—
Son Of HE — —.

792

» PRZECHODNIU POWIEDZ POLSCE ŻEŚMY POLEGLI WIERNI JEJ SŁUŻBIE. «   » PASSER-BY TELL POLAND THAT WE FELL FAITHFUL IN HER SERVICE. «

793

'THREE UNIQUE PICTURES & THE PACKET

The dates on these cards are misleading. The packet in which the cards were sold has the identification number 20,000-7'41, which is in the style of a simple code indicating the number of sets printed (20,000) and the date (July 1941). The paper and printing is of poor quality and there is no origin identification. It is therefore highly likely that the set was produced by an Underground press during the Nazi occupation and the year dates are forecasting what is ahead for the Führer and the Duce.
Complete set Value D

788   1943 'Hitler almighty shows Mussolini how powerful he is.'
Dutch (probably): Photomontage. Value B

789   1944 'In this year Hitler can't complete his stunt without Mussolini's support.' Italy surrendered in 1943 and Mussolini was unable to support himself, let alone Hitler.
Dutch (probably): Photomontage. Value B

790   '1945: they have preferred to live as street musicians but it's all over now! Their doom being sealed.'
Dutch (probably): Photomontage. Value B

791   'Frank Littlefield's Card.' This was probably a local production on an Army training base. The German bending over his truck is saying, 'If you boys want ever to get away from here — help me fix dis motor.'
American: Posted 25 June 1945, three days after the U.S. 10th Army recaptured Okinawa. Value A

792   'Back To HADES — Son of HE--' This card was posted on 2 August 1945 from the Marine Recruit Training Depot at

Paris Island, South Carolina. The 1st Marine Division had landed at Okinawa two months earlier and the sender of the card could well have been anticipating a posting to the Pacific Theatre of Operations. If he did go it would not have been to fight, because four days after posting the card he would have learned of the dropping of the atomic bomb on Hiroshima and then eight days after that of the Japanese surrender.
American: (Pub. Ted Harrington. Denver, Colorado) Artist Len Borkowski. Advertising message on reverse for 'Patriotic Envelopes.' Value A

793 *'Passer-by Tell Poland That We Fell Faithful In Her Service.'* This card, produced after the war's end, shows the Polish cemetery at Monte Cassino with a battered abbey in the background. Sadly, the Poland for which the soldiers, who lie buried there, fell, no longer exists, and the present government refuses to pay towards the upkeep of the cemetery or the memorial.
Polish: Value B

794 *'Brothers In Arms.'* The Polish Government in exile was based in London, hence the Union Jack and the Royal Coat of Arms, but the Provisional Government formed in Poland following Liberation owed more to Russia than to Britain.
Polish (produced in Britain): 1941. Value C

795 *'Strakonice Thanks The Americans.'* Strakonice is a town in Czechoslovakia about 30 miles from the German border and it is pro-bable that the liberating Americans were advance elements of the 12th Corps of General George Patton's 3rd Army. The caption reads:
'The town of Strakonice in Czechoslovakia saved by the American Army from German bestiality on the 6 May 1945.' During the closing days of the War many German S.S. concen-tration camp guards began an orgy of slaughter, and as Patton's armoured columns raced across Germany towards Czechoslovakia they uncovered horrible evidence of mass killings, both in camps like Mauthausen and Gusen near Linz, and of marching columns of prisoners. Strakonice must have been almost at the limit

794

795

796

797

"But, darling, I just *had* to buy it, it was such a bargain."

798

of the American advance and little more than 100 miles to the East were the advancing Russians. This is a remarkable card because it was posted on 17 July 1945 hardly more than two months after Liberation and was therefore produced within that eight week period. It carries Czech adhesive stamps and special cancellations naming 'Generala Pattona.' There can be very few examples of this card in existence.
Czech: (Pub. possibly the town itself) Artist Jarko Dvorak Sumavsky. Value D

796 *'Bundles For Britain.'* This Canadian card was posted on 25 June 1945, when Britain and Europe's needs were no longer men, but food and materials for reconstruction. By mid-August 1945 both Germany and Japan had capitulated and most food controls in North America were abolish-ed. However, the require-ments of devastated Europe

799

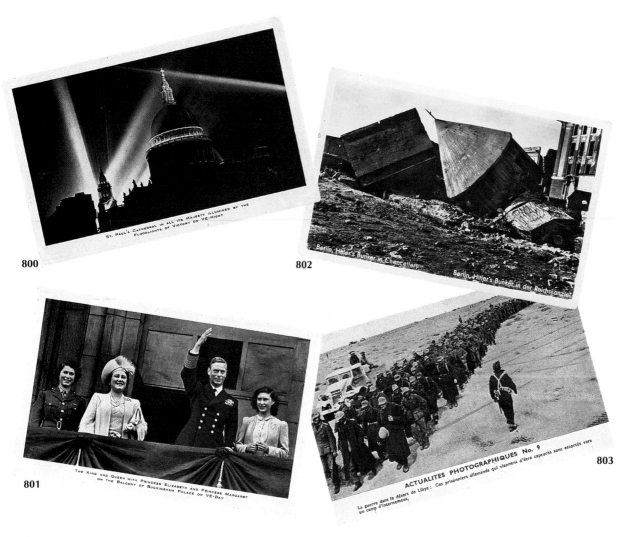

800

ST. PAUL'S CATHEDRAL IN ALL ITS MAJESTY ILLUMINED BY THE FLOODLIGHTS OF VICTORY ON VE-NIGHT

802

Berlin, Hitler's Bunker in Chancellery.

Berlin, Hitler's Bunker in der Reichskanzlei

801

THE KING AND QUEEN WITH PRINCESS ELIZABETH AND PRINCESS MARGARET ON THE BALCONY OF BUCKINGHAM PALACE ON VE-DAY

803

ACTUALITES PHOTOGRAPHIQUES No. 9

La guerre dans le désert de Libye : Ces prisonniers allemands qui viennent d'être capturés sont escortés vers un camp d'internement.

804

Brandenburger Gate

805

The Reichstag

had not been fully anticipated, and in supplying vast quantities of foodstuffs the Americans brought on themselves a serious food crisis.
Canadian: (Pub. Photogelatine Engraving Co. Ottawa) Artist Wilf Long. Value B

DEMOBILISATION

797 '*Meredith We're Out.*' The elation at being 'out' and the thought of saying as the caption puts it: '*Kiss me Searg (or famous last words)*' made the transformation to civilian life a memorable occasion. Going home for those who had been prisoners of war was an even greater emotional experience, for both returned and his family. One P.O.W. expressed his feelings in a letter to the editor of a prisoner of war news sheet — 'You will find that we are moody . . . we will not eat as much as we used to . . . we shall be like convalescents from an illness. As we get better . . . we will pass through a very irritable stage . . . try to help us through as much as you can.'
British: Circa 1945. Value B

798 '*War Surplus.*' Although the war in Europe and in Japan ended abruptly in 1945, it was not possible to call to a halt overnight the industrial complexes which produced the myriad items needed to sustain a nation at war. Throughout the conflict the rapidly changing needs of the armed forces had made redundant vast quantities of equipment and official government organizations existed to dispose of these to interested civilian buyers. Surplus war equipment represented large monetary investments and after hostilities ceased the auction of such stores provided urgently needed funds. The larger capital items of war surplus like aeroplanes, tanks and ships were touted around the smaller nations of the world and offered at bargain prices for 'defence' purposes. Many 'Battle of Britain' period aeroplanes, for example, were sold to Spain.
British: (Pub. Tuck) No. 53. Posted 11 July 1947. Value B

799 '*The Montgomery Club, Brussels.*' The welfare of the Armed Forces was recognised as a major factor in maintaining high morale, and N.A.A.F.I. (Navy, Army and Air Force Institute) and the E.F.I. (Expeditionary Forces Institute), who ran the Brussels Montgomery Club, were only two of the many organisations devoted to catering for the off-duty comforts of soldiers, sailors and airmen. However, on the day that this card was sent, morale was at its highest. The message written on the reverse reads: *'V' Day. 7/5/45. 9.0 p.m. This is the restaurant. Everyone going crazy here celebrating.'* Belgian: Value B

800 *'St. Paul's Cathedral On VE-Night.'* Hitler committed suicide on 30 April 1945. Field Marshal Montgomery took the surrender of the German forces in North West Europe on 4 May. The German High Command surrendered at Rheims on 7 May and 8 May 1945 was officially named VE-Day — Victory in Europe Day. Prime Minister's slogan on the reverse reads: *'We must now devote all our strength and resources to the completion of our tasks both at home and abroad.'* British: (Pub. Tuck) 1945. Value A

801 *'The King and Queen on VE-Day.'* As the news of Victory spread, great crowds of people gathered and surged through London heading for the Palace. The streets blackened with their numbers and rang with cheers and hurrahs. The King broadcast a message that went by radio to the Army, the Navy at sea, and all the countries of the Commonwealth. The Royal Family came out onto the balcony above the entrance to the Palace repeatedly and listened to the crowds singing *Long live the King.* Winston Churchill occasionally joined them. British: (Pub. Tuck) 1945. Value B

802 *'Berlin, Hitler's Bunker in The Chancellery.'* The destruction of the Führer's bunker was for, the Russians, the 'ultimate symbolism of the death of Nazi Germany.' This picture shows on the left the toppled 20 ft high, rectangular emergency exit from the bunker and on the right, with a conical top, an unfinished concrete tower. Both these structures were still standing when Berlin was captured and were later demolished and the debris removed by the Russians. Behind them in this picture

can be seen some of the upper floors of the Reich Chancellery. The complex of underground rooms from which Hitler conducted the final months of the war lay beneath the Reich Chancellery protected by six feet of earth and sixteen feet of concrete, the whole arrangement being guarded night and day by S.S. troops. Hitler arrived in Berlin on 16 January 1945 and from 27 January remained almost continuously underground until his suicide on 30 April 1945. German: Value C

803 *'Actualités Photographiques No. 9'* German prisoners being escorted to a prisoner of war camp. French: Circa 1942. Value B

804 *'Brandenburger Gate.'* This German card, printed with an English caption, was obviously produced for the Army of occupation market. The Gate now falls in the Eastern or Russian Sector of Berlin. The damaged Quadriga group surmounting the Gate has been restored in an unusual act of East/West co-operation. The Western Allies found the original mould in a barracks store at Spandau and the East Berliners repaired and remounted the statue. German: (Pub. Neuroder Kunstanstalten) 1946. Value B

805 *'The Reichstag.'* A month after Hitler came to power in 1933 a great fire swept through the Reichstag, causing immense damage. The Nazis blamed the Communists for this act of arson and made it an excuse to arrest many extreme Socialists. It has now been proved that the fire was started by Hitler's S.S. The Reichstag was again so badly damaged during the Battle for Berlin that its dome had to be blown up as it threatened to collapse. Today is has been painstakingly rebuilt, but without the dome, and houses not only Berlin's House of Representatives, but also a fine museum. German: (Pub. Neuroder Kunstanstalten) 1946. Value B

ITALIAN FUND RAISING CARDS
806 Italian: (Pub. G. Ricordi & Co. Milan) No. 43 22 February 1946. Value C

PRESTITO DELLA RICOSTRVZIONE

806

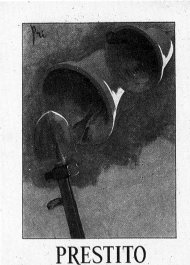

PRESTITO DELLA RICOSTRVZIONE

807

PRESTITO DELLA RICOSTRVZIONE

808

PRESTITO DELLA RICOSTRVZIONE

809

NON PONTE DI SOSPIRI MA DI VITA

PRESTITO DELLA RICOSTRVZIONE

810

IL LAVORO DISCIPLINATO, PAZIENTE, PRECISO, E' FONTE DI PROGRESSO. AFFRATELLA GLI UOMINI. UNISCE I POPOLI.

PRESTITO DELLA RICOSTRVZIONE

811

812

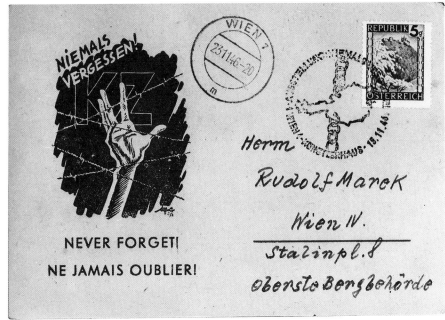

813

815

807   Italian: (Pub. G. Ricordi & Co. Milan) No. 43 22 February 1946. Stamp of Co-operative Bank of Como on reverse. Value C

808   Italian: D.D.L. 42. 22 February 1946. Stamp of Co-operative Bank of Como on reverse. Value C

809   Italian: (Pub. G. Ricordi & Co., Milan) No. 43 Artist Guilio Cisari. 'D.D.L.' 22 February 1946. Value C

810   Quotation from Cardinal Nasalli Rocca de Corneliano, Archbishop of Bologna (translated) reads: 'Not a Bridge of Sighs, but of Life.' Italian: (Pub. G. Ricordi & Co., Milan) No. 43 Artist Guilio Cisari. 'D.D.L.' 22 February 1946. Stamp of Co-operative Bank of Como on reverse. Value C

CAPITULATION AND ARMISTICE

811   The quotation from Cardinal Ernesto Ruffini, **Archbishop of Palermo** (translated) reads: 'Disciplined, patient and precise work is the bridge of progress which unites men and nations.' Italian: (Pub. Calcografia and Cartevalori, Milan) No. 43 'D.D.L.' 22 February 1946. Value C

812   'Salle de la Capitulation.' General Eisenhower, the Supreme Allied Commander, had his headquarters, (SHAEF), in the Modern and Technical College at Reims. It was here that Hitler's successor, Admiral Doenitz, sent his representatives to negotiate the general surrender. Left to right: Yvan Chermaoff, Colonel Zukovitch signing the document, Major-General Suslaparoff behind him, General Spaatz and Marshal Sir J. M. Robb. French: (Pub. H. Debar & Co. Reims) Postmarked 7 July 1945 with the slogan 'Salle de la Reddition: Ceremonie **de la Reddition de la Salle** à la Ville de Reims 7 May 1945.' Value D

813   'Armistice de Berlin.' The Russians demanded their own Surrender Ceremony at Berlin on 9 May 1945. This postcard commemorates the 25th Anniversary of the Signing and bears a First Day of Issue postmark. French: (Pub. G. Parison et B. Regnier) On reverse 'Carte Philatelique.' 8 May 1970. Value B

814

816

820

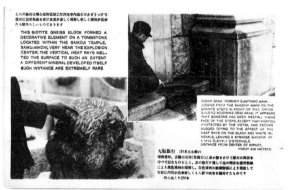

817

818

821

819

822

JOURNÉES NATIONALES DU SOUVENIR

COMPIEGNE

DU 15 AU 18 AOUT 1946

GUY GEORGET

Organisées par :
UNION FRANÇAISE DES ASSOCIATIONS D'ANCIENS COMBATTANTS.
FÉDÉRATION NATIONALE DES PRISONNIERS DE GUERRE
FÉDÉRATION NATIONALE DES DÉPORTÉS ET INTERNÉS RÉSISTANTS ET PATRIOTES
FÉDÉRATION NATIONALE DES DÉPORTÉS DU TRAVAIL

MERCURE-PUBLICITÉ

COMITÉ EXÉCUTIF NATIONAL, 10, RUE LEROUX, PARIS

823

THE CONCENTRATION CAMPS

814 *'Never Forget.'* KZ is the German abbreviation for *Konzentrationslager* — Concentration camp. This card was produced to mark a special 'Never Forget' Exhibition in Vienna on 23 November 1946, shortly after the Nazi war criminals Frick, Jodl, Kaltenbrunner, Keitel, Rosenberg, Sauckel, Seyss-Inquart and Streicher were executed at Nuremberg. *Austrian: 1946. With special Exhibition Postmark. Value D*

815 *'Free. Remember.'* Between April and May 1945 Buchenwald, Dachau, Struthof and all the Nazi concentration camps revealed their terrible secrets. Some of the most hideous crimes were perpetrated by the S.S. Caption on reverse (translated) reads: *'This card is sold for the profit of the Social Work of the Federation of the District of Moselle, of Deportees and Internees, Resistance Members and Patriots.'* French: (Pub. 'Editions ''Le Lorrain.''') Artist E. Burner. 1945. Value D*

HIROSHIMA

This Japanese series is a unique record of the event. It was published in 1946, a year after the explosion. Each card bears an incongruously decorative purple cachet. *'ATOM HIROSHIMA'* on the reverse and the phrase *'This is a real photograph.'*

816 *'Ruins Of Hiroshima Castle Completely Reduced To Ashes and View Of Burnt Down·Area. Japanese: (Pub. Nippon Syasin Kogeisya) Value D*

817 *'Formation Of A Pattern on a Tombstone As A Result Of Vertical Heatwaves and Shadow Of a Man Scorched On To The Osaka Bank.' Japanese: (Pub. Nippon Syasin Kogeisya) Value D*

818 *'Evidences Of The Intense Heat Caused By the Explosion On A Gas Tank and In A Bamboo Grove.' Japanese: (Pub. Nippon Syasin Kogeisya) Value D*

819 *'Fires Broke Out Everywhere 25 Minutes After The Explosion: Viewed From 7-Chome, Ujina-Machi, Hiroshima. K. Kimura By Photography.' Japanese: (Pub. Nippon Syasin Kogeisya) Value D*